1,000
Easy Recipes
SUPER FUN FOOD FOR EVERY DAY

1,000
Easy Recipes

SUPER FUN FOOD FOR EVERY DAY

HYPERION
New York

Food Network Magazine

Editor in Chief Maile Carpenter
Design Director Deirdre Koribanick
Managing Editor Maria Baugh
Food Editor Liz Sgroi
Art Director Ian Doherty
Photo Director Alice Albert
Deputy Photo Editor Kathleen E. Bednarek
Associate Art Director Shira Gordon
Copy Chief Joy Sanchez
Copy Editor Paula Sevenbergen
Recipe Editor Ruth Kaplan
Assistant Editor Erin Phraner
Photo Assistant Casey Oto
Art Assistant Brian Hardiman

Food Network Kitchens

Senior Vice President,
Culinary Production Susan Stockton
Vice President, Test Kitchen
Katherine Alford
Executive Culinary Producer Jill Novatt
Test Kitchen Manager Claudia Sidoti
Recipe Developers Andrea Albin,
Bob Hoebee, Amy Stevenson
Recipe Tester Leah Brickley

Hearst Communications

Editorial Director Ellen Levine
Vice President, Publisher Hearst Books
Jacqueline Deval

Food Network Magazine and the
Food Network Magazine logo are trademarks
of Food Network Magazine, LLC.

Foodnetwork.com/magazine

Library of Congress Cataloging-in-Publication Data
Food Network Magazine's 1,000 Easy Recipes: Super Fun
Food for Every Day / Food Network Magazine. — 1st ed.
p. cm.
Includes Index.
ISBN: 978-1-4013-1074-5
1. Cooking, American. 2. Cookbooks. I. Food Network
(Firm) II. Food Netork Magazine.
TX715.F6845 2012
641.5973—dc23

Hyperion books are available for special promotions and
premiums. For details, contact the HarperCollins Special
Markets Department in the New York office at 212-207-7528,
fax 212-207-7222 or e-mail spsales@harpercollins.com.

FIRST EDITION
10   9   8   7   6   5   4   3   2   1

We try to produce the most beautiful books possible, and
we are also extremely concerned about the impact of our
manufacturing process on the forests of the world and the
environment as a whole. Accordingly, we've made sure
that all of the paper we use has been certified as coming
from forests that are managed, to ensure the protection of
the people and wildlife dependent upon them.

SUSTAINABLE FORESTRY INITIATIVE · Certified Fiber Sourcing · www.sfiprogram.org

THIS LABEL APPLIES TO TEXT STOCK

To our readers.
Thanks for keeping
us cooking!

ACKNOWLEDGMENTS

Every recipe in this book was developed, tested and retested by the tireless team at Food Network Kitchens. Thanks, above all, to the group's incredible leaders, Susan Stockton, senior vice president, culinary production, and Katherine Alford, vice president, test kitchen. Under Susan and Katherine's direction, the chefs in Food Network Kitchens create an endless supply of amazing recipes for *Food Network Magazine,* and we are grateful every day to work with them: Andrea Albin, Bob Hoebee, Claudia Sidoti and Amy Stevenson, along with recipe testers Leah Brickley and Treva Chadwell. Big jobs like this cookbook require big grocery-shopping trips, so we are thankful to Jake Schiffman and Dave Mechlowicz for keeping the kitchens stocked (and for knowing how to get their hands on any ingredient, any time, anywhere). They are truly the world's greatest shoppers.

Enormous thanks to the magazine's food editors, led by Liz Sgroi, for dreaming up this book and for putting more than 1,000 recipes together into such a fun package. Liz, along with Ruth Kaplan and Erin Phraner, created this cookbook for food lovers like themselves, filling it with tips and ideas and making sure each chapter would inspire all of us. Thanks, also, to Laurie Buckle and Megan Steintrager for helping us pull off such an enormous editing feat. Our managing editor, Maria Baugh, as always, kept the entire team on task, and Copy Chief Joy Sanchez and Copy Editor Paula Sevenbergen checked every word until the recipes were perfect. Thanks to Jacqueline Deval, Vice President, Publisher, Hearst Books, who made the book happen, and who introduced us to our great partners at Hyperion, led by President and Publisher Ellen Archer.

We can't say enough to thank the design team behind this book, who brought the same energy to every page that they bring to *Food Network Magazine* month after month. Design Director Deirdre Koribanick and Photo Director Alice Albert, along with Art Director Ian Doherty, former Associate Art Director Shira Gordon, Designer Stephen Wilder, Deputy Photo Editor Kate Bednarek, Photo Assistant Casey Oto, Art Assistant Brian Hardiman and Digital Imaging Specialist Hans Lee, worked their usual magic, putting hundreds and hundreds of recipes and images into a package that is clear, colorful and fun. They surround themselves with other great artists to create the magazine every month, so we're thankful to the talented stylists and photographers they brought to this project.

We are most of all grateful to the strong partnership behind *Food Network Magazine,* and to the leaders of Food Network and Hearst Magazines: Food Network President Brooke Bailey Johnson; General Manager, Scripps Enterprises Sergei Kuharsky; Vice President, Marketing, Partnerships Amanda Melnick; Hearst President David Carey; President, Marketing and Publishing Director Michael Clinton; Executive Vice President and General Manager John P. Loughlin; and especially to our editor and mentor— the woman who started it all, and who keeps us going—Editorial Director Ellen Levine.

Contents

Someone recently asked the head of Food Network Kitchens how she keeps thinking up new recipes. It was a fair question: We sometimes joke around here that one day we'll come to work and realize that we're all tapped out—that we've thought of every grilling tip, photographed every burger, published every pasta recipe, every soup, every sandwich and salad, every cookie and cake, every everything. We're done. Good job, everyone. The world's recipe bank is complete!

Of course, Katherine Alford, who creates recipes for a living, never has these crazy thoughts, so she answered the question without skipping a beat: "Asking us how we keep coming up with recipes is like asking musicians how they keep coming up with new songs. There's always a new way." This book you're holding is proof of that—more than 1,000 recipes' worth. Open to any chapter and you'll see just how many riffs Katherine and her team can do on a single dish. Need a new salad idea? Pick from 57. A dip? Try one of 60. Need breakfast, lunch and dinner? No problem: There are 44 pancakes and waffles, 43 panini, 53 soups, and 91 burgers and dogs. What's truly amazing, beyond the sheer number of recipes these chefs have generated, is how great each individual idea is on its own. For every dish you see on these pages, two or three others didn't make it past the tasting committee in Food Network Kitchens. This is really good stuff.

What I love most about this book, though, is that the recipes are so short and simple. Each one is like a tweet (but so much more useful!). If you're on Twitter, you know that it isn't easy to edit your thoughts down to 140-character sound bites. Trust me, it's even harder to edit a recipe down to 40 or 50 words, but that's the only way we could deliver so many original ideas in one book. I hope you find more than a few recipes that you love in here, and when you do, I hope you'll tweet about it.

Maile

Maile Carpenter
Food Network Magazine
Editor in Chief

Suggested Menus

PIZZA PARTY

Caesar Salad 221

Margherita Pizza 199

Barbecue Chicken Pizza 203

Mocha Mousse 351

SUNDAY BRUNCH

Dutch Baby Pancake 100

Beet-Orange Salad 237

Maple-Walnut Trunks 338

Sparkling Ginger Cider 294

BOOK CLUB SNACKS

Pesto-Tomato Crostini 5

Slow-Cooker Spinach Dip 28

Taleggio and Walnut Crostini 12

Potato Chip Toffee 67

TEX-MEX NIGHT

Smoky Tomato Salsa 28

Margarita Shrimp Nachos 52

Taco Burgers 161

Jalapeño Margaritas 306

SOUTHERN PICNIC

Pulled Pork and
Cheese Panini 196

Balsamic Beans 257

Red Velvet Brownies 325

Cherry Coolers 298

THAI DINNER PARTY

Beef Satay 155

Coconut Chicken
Soup 130

Lychee-Mint
Spritzers 309

Ginger Crackles 331

BIG APPLE FARE

Deli Pastrami
Potato Skins 55

New York Street Dogs 181

Black and Whites 335

Nutella Egg Cream 299

LOBSTER SHACK MEAL

Fish Chowder 142

Lobster Salad Panini 195

Crab Boil Potato Salad 244

Easy Whoopie Pies 340

Suggested Menus

BACON-LOVER'S BRUNCH

Bacon-Pecan Waffles 105

Perfect Bacon 124

Escarole-Bacon Salad 236

White Grape Spritzer 297

SUPER BOWL PARTY

Blue Cheese Dip 15

Buffalo Chicken
Nachos 47

Swiss Sliders 162

Bar-Snack Blondies 326

MOVIE NIGHT

Pizza Dip 27

Perfect Popcorn 74

Movie-Concession
Cookies 339

Godfather 318

ITALIAN SUPPER

Pesto-Parmesan
Crostini 3

Vegetable
Pappardelle 211

Broccoli Rabe with
Cherry Peppers 268

Neapolitan Ice Cream
Sandwiches 343

DINER SPECIAL

Classic Skillet
Cheeseburgers 158

Tangy Mashed
Potatoes 279

Classic Chocolate-
Chip Cookies 329

Caramel–Root Beer
Float 347

OPEN HOUSE SPREAD

Avocado-Feta Dip 23

Onion-Herb Focaccia 208

Lemon Volcanoes 340

Sage Limeade 293

AUTUMN DINNER PARTY

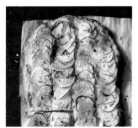

Potato-Rosemary
Pizza 200

Warm Spinach-
Mushroom Salad 225

Vanilla Poached
Pears 355

Peppered Whiskey 318

FARMERS' MARKET LUNCH

Bell Pepper–Pasta
Salad 254

Heirloom Tomato
Salad 229

Berry-Guava
Lemonade 290

Berry-Chocolate
Fools 352

Suggested Menus

GREEK GET-TOGETHER

Rosemary Lamb
Kebabs 155

Baby Bell Peppers with
Feta and Mint 267

Lemon Orzo 265

Fig Pinwheels 329

BISTRO SUPPER

Aïoli 19

French Onion Soup 141

Bistro Bacon Salad 222

Stuffed Crêpes 358

ASIAN COOKOUT

Teriyaki Snack Mix 72

Hoisin Burgers 175

Carrot-Sesame
Potato Salad 247

Peach-Ginger
Iced Tea 289

AFTERNOON TEA

Salmon-Cucumber Tea
Sandwiches 31

Chicken Salad Tea
Sandwiches 32

Honey-Lemon Tea 302

Walnut-Lavender
Shortbread 330

KIDS' SLEEPOVER

Pizza Nachos 48

Juicy Lucys 174

Yogurtwiches 358

Classic Lemonade 299

FONDUE PARTY

Hot Vegetable Chips 64

Cheese Fondue 16

Watercress with Oranges 236

Red-Wine Punch 317

EASY BARBECUE

Steakhouse Kebabs 146

Barbecued Corn 271

Grilled Vegetable Potato Salad 248

Watermelon-Coconut Coolers 319

VEGETARIAN NIGHT

Black Bean Hummus 28

Veggie Burgers 173

Tomato–Bell Pepper Salad 236

Nutty Chocolate Cookies 336

Suggested Menus

POOL PARTY

Mango Salsa 28

Southern Dogs 182

Lime Cookies 341

Frozen Strawberry
Margaritas 305

MOTHER-DAUGHTER LUNCH

Ham and Brie Crostini 9

Cucumber-Butter
Tea Sandwiches 39

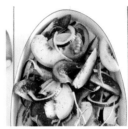

Tomato-Peach Salad 230

Mint Limeade 299

FAMILY PICNIC

BLT Club Tea
Sandwiches 36

Bacon-Ranch
Potato Salad 240

Fudgy Brownies 323

Blackberry
Lemonade 298

FRIDAY-NIGHT COCKTAILS

Chocolate Apricots 358

Honey-Spice Peanuts 68

Rosemary Gin
and Tonic 313

Pineapple Margaritas 306

COZY WINTER SUPPER

Roast Beef–Caramelized Onion Panini 187

Pasta-Cheddar Soup 138

Oat-Walnut Thins 335

Hot Dulce de Leche 302

BABY SHOWER

Crab Salad Tea Sandwiches 35

Spring Frittata 114

Niçoise Potato Salad 243

Lemon Shortbread 326

HEALTHY DINNER

California Burgers 176

Broccoli and Peppers 283

Mushroom Barley 261

Peanut Butter Mousse 348

GOURMET HAPPY HOUR

Fennel-Raisin Crostini 3

Salmon-Mushroom Potato Skins 61

Pine-Nut Cheese Crisps 71

Mint Martini 314

Appetizers & Snacks

Crostini

How to make crostini:
1. Slice a baguette into ¼-inch-thick rounds. Brush each slice with olive oil or melted butter.
2. Place the rounds on baking sheets and bake at 350° until crisp and lightly golden, about 15 minutes.

≪ GOAT CHEESE AND BEET
Spread **toast** with **goat cheese;** top with chopped canned **beets, orange** segments and **fresh mint.**

≪ PESTO-PARMESAN
Spread **toast** with **pesto;** top with shaved **parmesan.**

≪ APPLE BUTTER–BLUE CHEESE
Spread **toast** with **apple butter;** top with crumbled **blue cheese** and chopped **fresh sage.**

≪ EGG SALAD AND ASPARAGUS
Halve **asparagus tips** lengthwise; steam until crisp-tender and season with **salt.** Spread **egg salad** on **toast;** top with an asparagus tip. Sprinkle with **fresh thyme** and **pepper.**

≪ FENNEL-RAISIN
Sauté thinly sliced **fennel** and **golden raisins** in **olive oil** until soft; spoon onto **toast.** Top with fennel fronds.

≪ BACON, GRAPE AND MASCARPONE
Spread **toast** with **mascarpone;** top with crumbled cooked **bacon** and chopped **grapes.**

BUTTER AND PICKLE
Spread **toast** with **butter**; top with thinly sliced **bread-and-butter pickles.**

MANCHEGO AND CHORIZO
Brush **toast** with **olive oil.** Top with a thin slice of **manchego** and sliced **dried chorizo.**

RED PEPPER AND RICOTTA
Spread **toast** with **ricotta**; top with chopped **roasted red peppers.** Season with **salt** and **pepper.**

GARLIC-TOMATO
Rub **toast** with a **garlic clove**; top with sliced **plum tomatoes** and sprinkle with **sea salt.**

RADISH AND SEA SALT
Spread **toast** with **butter**; top with thinly sliced **radishes** and sprinkle with **sea salt.**

ITALIAN TUNA SALAD
Toss canned **tuna** with **lemon juice** and **zest, olive oil,** chopped **parsley** and **salt**; spread on **toast.**

PEAR AND GORGONZOLA
Spread **toast** with **gorgonzola**; top with sliced **pears.**

TRY THIS

Set up a crostini bar: Put out a platter of toast and different toppings so guests can mix and match.

BARBECUE CHICKEN
Chop **rotisserie chicken** and toss with **barbecue sauce**; spoon onto **toast** and top with chopped **dill pickles.**

APPLE AND CHEDDAR
Top **toast** with thinly sliced **apples** and grated **cheddar**; broil until melted.

PESTO-BACON
Spread **toast** with **pesto**; top with crumbled cooked **bacon** and chopped **tomatoes.**

AVOCADO-BACON
Spread **toast** with mashed **avocado**; top with crumbled cooked **bacon** and **sprouts.**

RICOTTA–OLIVE OIL
Spread **toast** with **ricotta**; drizzle with **olive oil** and season with **salt** and **pepper.**

WASABI-CRAB
Spread **wasabi mayonnaise** on **toast.** Top with **crabmeat.**

PEPPER JELLY
Spread **toast** with **cream cheese**; top with **hot pepper jelly.**

« **PESTO-TOMATO** Spread **toast** with **pesto.** Top with chopped **sun-dried tomatoes.**

Crostini

RICOTTA AND HONEY
Spread **toast** with **ricotta**; drizzle with **honey** and sprinkle with **pepper**.

SPICY BEAN AND CHEESE
Combine **refried beans** with canned chopped **green chiles**; spread on **toast**. Top with shredded **pepper jack** and broil until melted.

HAM AND APPLE
Sauté sliced **apples** in **butter** until soft; spoon onto **toast** and top with sliced **ham**.

CHIPOTLE-TURKEY
Combine **cream cheese** and chopped **chipotles in adobo sauce**; spread on **toast**. Top with thinly sliced **smoked turkey**.

TURKEY AND CRANBERRY
Spread **toast** with **cranberry sauce**; top with thinly sliced roast **turkey**. Season with **sea salt** and **pepper**.

HORSERADISH–ROAST BEEF
Combine equal parts **sour cream** and **cream cheese** with some **horseradish**; spread on **toast**. Top with thinly sliced **roast beef**.

MIX IT UP

Try toasting bread rounds on the grill.

SPINACH, BACON AND EGG
Wilt **baby spinach** and toss with crumbled cooked **bacon**; spoon onto **toast**. Top with chopped hard-boiled **eggs**.

CAESAR
Toss finely chopped **romaine** with **Caesar dressing** and grated **parmesan**; spoon onto **toast**. Top each with an **anchovy**.

HUMMUS-TAPENADE
Spread **toast** with **hummus**; top with **olive tapenade**.

PROSCIUTTO AND GRAPE
Top **toast** with chopped **grapes** and wrap with **prosciutto**.

TOMATO-BASIL
Top **toast** with grated **tomato**; sprinkle with **sea salt** and chopped **fresh basil**.

ROASTED GARLIC–TOMATO
Cut off the top of 2 heads **garlic**. Drizzle with **olive oil**, wrap in foil and roast at 400°, 45 minutes. Squeeze out the garlic and mash. Fry **sage** in olive oil. Spread **butter** on **toast**. Top with the roasted garlic, sliced **sun-dried tomatoes**, the fried sage and **salt**.

ASPARAGUS-RICOTTA Spread **ricotta** on **toast**; top with thinly sliced **asparagus**. Season with **salt** and **pepper** and drizzle with **olive oil**.

PROSCIUTTO-MELON
Spread **toast** with **mascarpone**; top with thinly sliced **cantaloupe** and **prosciutto**.

TURKEY-MOZZARELLA
Spread **toast** with a thin layer of **orange marmalade**; top with thinly sliced **smoked turkey** and **smoked mozzarella**.

WASABI-TUNA
Toss finely chopped **sushi-grade tuna** with **sesame oil**. Spread **wasabi mayonnaise** on **toast**; top with the tuna.

SMOKED SALMON
Whip **cream cheese** with chopped **fresh dill**; spread on **toast**. Top with thinly sliced **smoked salmon**.

ASPARAGUS-PROSCIUTTO
Cut **asparagus** spears into pieces; toss with **olive oil**, **salt** and **pepper** on a baking sheet. Roast at 450° until slightly crisp, about 7 minutes. Spread on **toast** with **butter**. Top with **prosciutto** and the roasted asparagus.

TIP

Toast the bread and prepare the toppings in advance, then assemble when guests arrive.

BRIE, APPLE AND ONION
Sauté thinly sliced **onions** in **butter** until caramelized. Spread **toast** with **brie**; top with thinly sliced **apple** and the caramelized onions.

GORGONZOLA-PROSCIUTTO
Spread **toast** with **fig jam**; top with crumbled **gorgonzola** and **prosciutto**.

SPICY SHRIMP
Toss ½ pound peeled **shrimp** with 1 tablespoon each chopped **chives** and **parsley**, 1 teaspoon each **red pepper flakes** and **lemon zest**, ½ teaspoon **paprika**, a drizzle of **olive oil** and a pinch of **cayenne pepper**. Grill 2 to 3 minutes per side. Spread **marinara sauce** on **toast**. Top with the shrimp and drizzle with olive oil.

MUSHROOM-PARMESAN
Sauté finely chopped **mushrooms** in **butter** and season with **salt** and **fresh thyme**; spread the mushroom mixture on **toast** and top with shaved **parmesan**.

≪ **HAM AND BRIE** Spread **toast** with **brie**; top with thinly sliced **ham** and a dollop of **whole-grain mustard**.

Crostini

FIG AND HONEY
Top **toast** with sliced **figs.** Drizzle with **honey** and top with **sea salt.**

NUTELLA-ORANGE
Spread **toast** with **Nutella;** top with **orange marmalade.**

PEANUT BUTTER–BANANA
Spread **toast** with creamy **peanut butter;** top with sliced **bananas** and drizzle with **honey.**

FLUFFERNUTTER
Whip creamy **peanut butter** and **marshmallow cream;** spread the peanut butter mixture on **toast.** Top with shaved **chocolate.**

TIRAMISU
Whip **mascarpone** and **confectioners' sugar.** Brush **toast** with **espresso** and spread with the sweetened mascarpone; top with shaved **chocolate** and **cocoa powder.**

APPLE PIE
Melt 2 tablespoons **butter** in a skillet; add 1 diced **apple,** 1 tablespoon **brown sugar** and ¼ teaspoon **apple pie spice** and cook until the apple is soft. Spread **caramel sauce** on **toast** and top with the cooked apple. Top with a dollop of **whipped cream.**

Serve these sweet crostini for dessert or with a cheese plate.

ORANGE-CREAM

Segment a **blood orange** over a bowl; reserve the juice. Toss the segments with 1 tablespoon **superfine sugar.** Simmer the juice and 1 tablespoon superfine sugar until syrupy. Spread **whipped cream** on **toast;** top with the orange segments and shaved **chocolate.** Drizzle with the orange syrup.

ALMOND–PINE NUT
Spread softened **almond paste** on **toast.** Press toasted **pine nuts** into the paste, then brush with melted **butter;** dust with **confectioners' sugar.**

BLUEBERRY-ALMOND
Spread **butter** on **toast.** Top with **blueberry preserves** and fresh **blueberries.** Sprinkle with toasted **sliced almonds.**

ANISE-LEMON
Simmer ¼ cup water, some thin strips of **lemon zest,** ½ teaspoon **anise seeds** and 2 tablespoons **sugar** in a saucepan until syrupy. Spread **lemon curd** on **toast.** Top with the candied lemon zest and anise seeds.

FIG AND WALNUT
Spread **toast** with **fig jam;** top with **goat cheese** and chopped **walnuts.**

TALEGGIO AND WALNUT
Spread **toast** with **taleggio;** top with
chopped **candied walnuts or pecans.**

SHRIMP AND AVOCADO
Mash **avocado** with **salt** and **lime juice;**
spread on **toast.** Top with cooked **shrimp.**

ZUCCHINI–RICOTTA SALATA
Shave a small **zucchini** into long ribbons
with a vegetable peeler. Toss with **lemon
juice, olive oil** and a big pinch of **salt.** Rub
toast with a smashed **garlic clove.** Top
with the zucchini, crumbled **ricotta salata**
and **pepper.**

LEMON-RASPBERRY
Whip **cream cheese** with **lemon zest**
until smooth; spread on **toast** and top
with **fresh raspberries.**

BANANA-HAZELNUT

Toss 2 sliced **bananas** with 1 tablespoon melted **butter;** spread on a baking sheet. Sprinkle with **sugar** and bake at 425˚ until golden, about 10 minutes. Spread **hazelnut butter** on **toast.** Top with the roasted bananas, **whipped cream** and chopped **hazelnuts.**

BALSAMIC BERRY

Toss 1 cup sliced **strawberries,** 2 tablespoons **superfine sugar** and 1 tablespoon **balsamic vinegar;** set aside 30 minutes. Mix ½ cup **mascarpone,** ¼ cup **confectioners' sugar** and a dash of **vanilla.** Spread the mascarpone on **toast.** Top with the berries and their juice.

PEACH-AMARETTI

Spread **butter** on **toast.** Top with **peach preserves** and sprinkle with crushed **amaretti cookies.**

PISTACHIO CANNOLI

Beat ½ cup **ricotta,** ¼ cup **confectioners' sugar** and a dash of **vanilla** until smooth; spread on **toast.** Top with chopped **pistachios** and shaved **chocolate.** Dust with confectioners' sugar.

Dips

BLUE CHEESE DIP
Puree 1½ cups **sour cream**, ¾ cup **mayonnaise** and ½ pound **blue cheese**. Add **Worcestershire sauce**, chopped **chives**, **celery salt** and **pepper** to taste.

PIMIENTO-CHEESE DIP
Mix ½ pound each grated **cheddar** and **pepper jack**, ¼ cup each **mayonnaise** and **sour cream** and 2 tablespoons diced **pimientos**. Season with **hot sauce, onion powder** and **garlic powder**.

HOT CHORIZO DIP
Sauté 3 tablespoons minced **onion** and ¼ pound sliced **dried chorizo** in **olive oil** until the chorizo is browned. Add 1 diced **jalapeño**, 2 tablespoons **flour**, ⅓ cup **beer**, ¼ pound each grated **muenster** and **cheddar** and a handful of chopped **cilantro;** cook until the cheese melts, then transfer to a baking dish and broil until bubbly.

HOT CRAB DIP
Mix 8 ounces each **crabmeat** and **cream cheese**, ¼ cup **heavy cream**, ½ cup each grated **parmesan** and **muenster**, a splash of **lemon juice**, 1 minced **garlic clove** and a pinch of **pepper** in a baking dish. Add ½ cup mixed chopped **basil, parsley** and **chives**. Bake at 375°, 30 minutes.

FRUIT DIP
Mix 1 cup **low-fat sour cream** and 2 tablespoons each **brown sugar** and **lime juice;** sprinkle with **cinnamon sugar.** Thread **fruit** onto skewers; serve with the dip.

SALSA VERDE
Puree 1 cup each **parsley**
and **basil,** 3 chopped **scallions,**
2 tablespoons **capers,**
1 tablespoon **red wine vinegar,**
2 **anchovies,** 2 **garlic cloves**
and ⅓ cup **olive oil.** Season with
salt; thin with water as needed.

SEVEN-LAYER DIP
Layer **salsa, guacamole,
refried beans, sour cream,**
shredded **cheddar,** crushed
tortilla chips and shredded
lettuce in a large baking dish.

OLIVE TAPENADE
Pulse 1 cup **black olives,**
3 **anchovies,** 2 tablespoons
each **olive oil** and **capers,**
1 tablespoon each **lemon
juice** and **parsley,** 1 teaspoon
fresh thyme and 1 **garlic clove**
in a food processor.

HERB MAYONNAISE
Blanch 1 cup each **fresh parsley**
and **basil** in boiling water,
30 seconds. Puree with ¼ cup
mayonnaise, 1 tablespoon **sour
cream,** 2 tablespoons **mango
chutney** and ½ teaspoon **salt.**
Add a splash of **lime juice.**

CLASSIC SALSA
Mix 4 diced **tomatoes,** 1 minced
red onion, 1 minced **garlic
clove,** 1 to 2 minced **jalapeños**
and a handful of chopped
cilantro. Season with **salt.**

GOAT CHEESE DIP
Sauté 1 minced **garlic clove** in
¼ cup **olive oil.** Puree ½ cup
jarred piquillo peppers,
1 teaspoon chopped **rosemary,**
11 ounces **goat cheese,** half
of the garlic oil, and **salt**
and **pepper;** drizzle with the
remaining garlic oil.

WHITE-BEAN DIP
Fry 10 **sage leaves,** 4 chopped
garlic cloves and a pinch of
red pepper flakes in ¼ cup
olive oil. Add 1 can **cannellini
beans** and ⅓ cup water; warm
through, then puree. Add a
splash of **lemon juice** and
a pinch of **salt.**

BAKED RICOTTA
Mix 1 cup **ricotta,** 1 teaspoon
each chopped **sage** and
lemon zest, and **salt** and
pepper. Bake in an oiled
ramekin at 300°, 20 minutes.

TIP

Use your leftover dip as a sandwich spread or serve on baked potatoes.

CHEESE FONDUE Rub a small pot with **garlic;** add 1 cup **white wine** and simmer. Whisk in 1 tablespoon **cornstarch** mixed with a splash of **cognac,** then ¼ pound each shredded **gruyère** and **emmentaler;** add **salt, pepper** and **nutmeg.** Serve hot with **apples** and **bread.**

AÏOLI

Whisk 2 minced **garlic cloves** with 2 pasteurized **egg yolks**. Slowly whisk in 1½ cups **olive oil**. Add **lemon juice, salt** and **pepper** to taste; thin with water.

EGGPLANT CAVIAR

Roast 1 **eggplant** at 400° until tender, 45 minutes; peel and chop. Mix with 2 tablespoons each **olive oil** and chopped **parsley**, the juice of 1 **lemon**, 1 chopped **garlic clove**, and **salt** and **pepper**.

OLIVE AÏOLI

Whisk 2 minced **garlic cloves** with 2 pasteurized **egg yolks**. Slowly whisk in 1½ cups **olive oil**. Add 3 tablespoons **olive tapenade**, some **lemon juice, salt** and **pepper**; thin with water.

BAGNA CAUDA

Melt 1 stick **butter** in a saucepan with ½ cup **olive oil**. Add 5 chopped **garlic cloves** and 8 chopped **anchovies**; mash.

ORANGE-SAFFRON AÏOLI

Whisk 2 minced **garlic cloves** with 2 pasteurized **egg yolks**. Slowly whisk in 1½ cups **olive oil**. Add **orange juice, salt** and **pepper** to taste. Steep ½ teaspoon **saffron** in 2 tablespoons **Pernod**, 5 minutes. Add to the aïoli; thin with water.

TRY THIS

Serve dip in an edible bowl, like a hollowed-out bread loaf or bell pepper.

REFRIED-BEAN DIP

Sauté ½ chopped **onion**, 2 chopped **garlic cloves** and 2 teaspoons **ground cumin** in **olive oil**. Add 2 cans **pinto beans** and **salt**; mash, gradually adding **chicken broth** until creamy.

TROPICAL SALSA

Mix 1½ cups each diced **mango** and **pineapple**, 1 minced **red onion**, 1 to 2 minced seeded **jalapeños**, 1 teaspoon grated **ginger** and a handful of chopped **cilantro**. Add a splash of **rum** and a pinch of **allspice**. Season with **salt**.

GREEN GODDESS DIP

Puree 4 **anchovies**, 1 **garlic clove** and 2 tablespoons each chopped **basil, chives, tarragon, parsley** and **dill**. Mix with 1 cup each **sour cream** and **mayonnaise**. Add **salt, pepper** and **lemon juice** to taste.

TOMATO TAPENADE

Pulse 2 cups **oil-packed sun-dried tomatoes**, 3 **anchovies**, 2 tablespoons each **olive oil** and **capers**, 1 tablespoon each **white wine vinegar** and **parsley**, 1 tablespoon chopped **basil** and 1 **garlic clove** in a food processor until chunky. Thin with water.

CAPONATA

Roast 1 **eggplant** at 400° until tender, 45 minutes; peel and chop. Mix with 2 tablespoons each **olive oil** and chopped **parsley,** the juice of 1 **lemon,** 1 chopped **garlic clove,** and **salt** and **pepper.** Sauté ½ cup each chopped **celery, red bell pepper, tomato** and **red onion** in olive oil, then stir in 2 tablespoons **sherry vinegar** and 2 teaspoons **sugar;** add to the eggplant mixture. Stir in 2 teaspoons **capers.**

ROMESCO DIP

Puree ½ cup toasted **almonds,** 2 **roasted red peppers,** 2 chopped seeded **tomatoes,** 1 **garlic clove,** 1 slice **toast** and 1 teaspoon **smoked paprika.** Add 2 tablespoons **sherry vinegar** and ¼ cup **olive oil;** puree.

TAHINI DIP

Puree ½ cup **tahini** (sesame paste), the juice of 2 **lemons,** 2 teaspoons **ground cumin** and 1 minced **garlic clove.** Drizzle in ½ cup hot water; puree until smooth.

TIP

Find tahini for hummus in jars or cans in the ethnic foods aisle. Once opened, store in the fridge for about 6 months.

QUICK AVOCADO HUMMUS

Puree 2 **avocados** with half a **jalapeño** until smooth. Mix with a 7-ounce tub of **hummus,** a pinch of **salt** and some **lemon juice.**

EDAMAME HUMMUS

Puree ¼ cup **tahini** (sesame paste), the juice of 1 **lemon,** 1 teaspoon **ground cumin** and ½ minced **garlic clove.** Drizzle in ¼ cup hot water; puree until smooth. Add a 16-ounce bag thawed frozen shelled **edamame** and ⅓ cup **olive oil;** puree, adding water until smooth.

TZATZIKI

Mix 1 grated peeled **cucumber,** 2 cups **Greek yogurt,** 1 small minced **garlic clove** and 1 tablespoon each chopped **mint, dill** and **white wine vinegar.**

GREEN CHUTNEY

Puree 1 inch **ginger,** 3 chopped **scallions,** 1 cup each **fresh cilantro** and **mint,** ½ cup **plain yogurt,** some **lime juice,** 1 chopped **jalapeño** and **salt;** thin with water.

WARM HUMMUS Simmer 2¾ cups salted water. Whisk in ¾ cup **chickpea flour** (available at health-food stores) to make a paste; cook 2 minutes. Puree with ¼ cup **tahini** (sesame paste), 3 tablespoons **olive oil** and the zest and juice of 1 **lemon.** Toast ¼ teaspoon each **cumin** and **fennel seeds** in a skillet; add some **red pepper flakes** and 2 tablespoons olive oil and cook 30 seconds. Drizzle on the hummus; top with **parsley.**

BASIC GUACAMOLE

Mash 3 **avocados** with ½ cup minced **red onion** and 1 to 2 minced **jalapeños.** Stir in 1 diced **tomato,** ½ cup chopped **cilantro** and a splash of **lime juice.** Season with **salt.**

TOMATILLO GUACAMOLE

Cook 4 husked and rinsed **tomatillos** in boiling water, 5 minutes. Puree ½ cup chopped **cilantro,** ½ cup chopped **white onion,** 1 chopped **jalapeño** and a splash of the tomatillo cooking water in a blender. Drain the tomatillos, add to the blender and pulse. Add 2 chopped **avocados** and **salt** to taste; pulse.

SPICY PAPAYA GUACAMOLE

Toss 1 diced small **papaya** and the juice of 1 **lime** in a bowl. Mash ½ chopped seeded **habanero pepper** and ½ teaspoon **kosher salt** into a paste with the flat side of a knife, then add ½ cup **cilantro** and mince. Add the pepper-cilantro paste, 2 diced **avocados** and ½ diced **red onion** to the bowl; stir to combine and season with salt.

TIP

To keep avocado dips from browning, press plastic wrap directly on the surface.

SOUTHWEST GUACAMOLE

Brush 1 ear of **corn** with **vegetable oil;** sprinkle with **chili powder, ground coriander** and **salt.** Broil the corn, 2 **plum tomatoes** and 1 bunch **scallions,** 5 to 7 minutes. Chop the scallions and tomatoes; mash with 3 diced **avocados,** 2 minced **jalapeños,** ¼ cup chopped **cilantro** and the juice of 1 **lime.** Cut the corn off the cob and add to the avocado mixture. Add more chili powder, coriander and salt.

ASIAN GUACAMOLE

Mash 3 chopped **avocados** with 1 bunch chopped **scallions** and 1 to 2 minced **jalapeños.** Stir in 1 diced **tomato,** 1 teaspoon grated **ginger,** 1 cup diced peeled **cucumber,** ½ cup chopped **cilantro** and a splash each of **lime juice, sesame oil** and **soy sauce.** Season with **salt.**

SALSAMOLE

Mix ½ cup **salsa,** 2 mashed **avocados,** 2 tablespoons each **lime juice** and chopped **cilantro,** and **salt** to taste.

« AVOCADO-FETA DIP Cook ½ diced **red onion** and 1 diced seeded **jalapeño** in **olive oil,** 6 minutes. Puree with 1 diced **avocado,** 1 cup **fresh cilantro,** ¾ cup crumbled **feta,** ¼ cup **lemon juice,** 3 tablespoons **vegetable oil,** and **salt** to taste.

WASABI DIP

Mix 2 tablespoons each **wasabi powder** and water; set aside 20 minutes. Mash with 8 ounces each **cream cheese** and **ricotta** and 3 tablespoons each **mirin** (rice wine) and **rice vinegar.**

SPINACH-WALNUT DIP

Puree 2 cups **spinach** and 1 **garlic clove.** Mix with ¾ cup **Greek yogurt,** ¼ cup finely chopped **walnuts,** 1 teaspoon each chopped **tarragon, dill** and **cilantro,** and ½ teaspoon **red pepper flakes.** Season with **salt.**

SPICY RANCH DIP

Whisk ¼ cup each **sour cream** and minced **red onion,** ⅓ cup **buttermilk,** ½ cup **mayonnaise,** 1 minced **garlic clove** and 1 tablespoon each chopped **chives, parsley** and **chipotles in adobo sauce;** add **salt.**

CHARRED-TOMATO SALSA

Broil 2 **tomatoes** until charred; cool and core. Pulse in a food processor with 1 minced **jalapeño,** 1 **scallion,** 1 **garlic clove** and 1 tablespoon **fresh mint;** add **salt.**

MIX IT UP

For lighter dips, use plain Greek yogurt in place of sour cream.

TOMATO CHUTNEY

Toast 1 teaspoon each **coriander, fennel** and **cumin seeds** in **vegetable oil.** Add 2 pounds chopped **tomatoes,** 2 tablespoons each **tomato paste** and grated **ginger,** and a pinch each of **curry powder, cayenne pepper, sugar** and **salt.** Sauté until thick.

QUESO DIP

Sauté 3 tablespoons minced **onion** in **olive oil.** Add 1 can chopped **green chiles,** 2 tablespoons **flour,** ⅓ cup **beer,** ¼ pound each grated **muenster** and **cheddar** and a handful of chopped **cilantro;** cook until the cheese melts, then transfer to a baking dish and broil until bubbly.

CLAM DIP

Puree 2 cans **clams** with 8 ounces **cream cheese,** a handful of **parsley,** ½ cup each **cottage cheese** and **mayonnaise,** ½ chopped **onion,** 2 tablespoons **clam juice** and ½ teaspoon **celery salt.** Add the zest and juice of 1 **lemon,** and **salt** and **pepper.**

ROASTED GARLIC–BACON DIP

Cut the tops off 2 heads **garlic,** drizzle with **olive oil,** wrap in foil and roast at 400° until tender, 45 minutes. Cool, then squeeze out the garlic; mix with 1½ cups **sour cream,** ¾ cup **mayonnaise** and some chopped **chives** and **scallions.** Add **Worcestershire sauce, salt** and **pepper;** stir in 6 slices chopped cooked **bacon.**

»

PIZZA DIP

Simmer 2 cups **tomato sauce** in a small ovenproof skillet. Top with 1 cup **ricotta;** warm through. Sprinkle with diced **mozzarella** and **pepperoni,** then bake at 350° until bubbling. Top with **fresh basil** and **olive oil.**

PEANUT DIP

Scoop out the cream from a can of **coconut milk.** Mix with 1 cup coconut milk, ⅓ cup **peanut butter,** 2 tablespoons **red curry paste,** 2 tablespoons **brown sugar** and 1 tablespoon each **soy sauce** and **lemon juice.**

FRIED-CHICKPEA HUMMUS

Puree ½ cup **tahini** (sesame paste), the juice of 2 **lemons,** 2 teaspoons **ground cumin,** 1 minced **garlic clove,** ½ cup hot water and ½ can **chickpeas.** Microwave until warm. Fry the other ½ can chickpeas in **olive oil** with **salt** and **pepper.** Top the hummus with the fried chickpeas, **red pepper flakes** and **parsley.**

TOMATILLO SALSA

Broil 20 **tomatillos,** 1 sliced **onion** and 4 unpeeled **garlic cloves** until charred. Peel the garlic; puree with the tomatillos, onion, 1 **chipotle in adobo sauce,** 2 tablespoons **fresh cilantro,** and some **sugar** and **salt.**

MIX IT UP

Instead of chips, try dipping naan bread, pita wedges, breadsticks or rice crackers.

SPICY RAITA

Mix 1 grated peeled **cucumber,** 2 cups **Greek yogurt,** 1 small minced **garlic clove,** 1 diced **jalapeño,** 1 diced **tomato,** ½ teaspoon **ground cumin** and 1 tablespoon each chopped **cilantro** and **mint.**

HORSERADISH DIP

Mix 1 pound grated **cheddar,** 1 grated **apple** and ¼ cup each **mayonnaise, sour cream, horseradish** and **beer.** Add 1 teaspoon each **dijon mustard** and **Worcestershire sauce.** Add a pinch each of **onion powder** and **garlic powder.**

ONION DIP

Sauté 1 each chopped **yellow and red onion** in a skillet with **olive oil** over low heat until caramelized, 30 minutes; cool. Mix with 1½ cups **sour cream,** ¾ cup **mayonnaise** and some chopped **chives** and **scallions.** Add **Worcestershire sauce, salt** and **pepper** to taste.

SWEET-POTATO DIP

Puree a can of **white beans** and 2 peeled roasted **sweet potatoes** with ¼ cup **olive oil,** ½ cup grated **parmesan,** and **salt** and **pepper.**

SLOW-COOKER SPINACH DIP

Mix 1 cup grated **smoked mozzarella,**
½ cup grated **parmesan,** 8 ounces **cream
cheese,** 1 minced **garlic clove,** 1 box
thawed frozen **spinach** (drained), 1 jar
artichoke hearts, and **salt** and **pepper** in
a slow cooker. Cover; cook on high, 2 hours.

SMOKY TOMATO SALSA

Broil 5 **plum tomatoes** and 1 sliced **red
onion,** about 6 minutes. Pulse in a food
processor with 1 **chipotle in adobo sauce**
plus 1 teaspoon sauce from the can,
2 tablespoons chopped **cilantro** and
1 teaspoon **cider vinegar.**

BLACK BEAN HUMMUS

Puree a can of **black beans** with 1 **garlic
clove,** 2 tablespoons each **lemon juice**
and **tahini** (sesame paste), and 1 teaspoon
ground cumin; add water if needed.
Season with **salt.**

MANGO SALSA

Toss 1 cup each diced **mango** and **black
beans** with ¼ cup diced **red onion.** Add
2 tablespoons each chopped **pickled
jalapeños** and liquid from the jar, chopped
cilantro and **lime juice.** Season with **salt.**

CHUNKY GUACAMOLE
Pile ¼ cup chopped **onion,**
¾ cup torn **cilantro,** 1 to 3 chopped
serrano chiles and a big pinch of
kosher salt on a cutting board.
Chop, then mash into a paste with
the flat side of the knife. Transfer to
a bowl and add 3 diced **avocados;**
mash with a wooden spoon until
combined but still chunky. Stir in
1 diced **tomato.** Season with salt.

DEVILED EGG DIP
Puree 8 hard-boiled **eggs** with
¼ cup **mayonnaise,** 1 chopped
pickle, 1 tablespoon **yellow
mustard,** a dash of **hot sauce,**
and **paprika, salt** and **pepper**
to taste. Top with **chives.**

Tea Sandwiches

SALMON-CUCUMBER
Spread softened **cream cheese** on **white bread.** Sandwich with **smoked salmon** and sliced **cucumber.** Trim the crusts and cut into pieces.

SHRIMP SALAD
Mix 1 cup chopped cooked **shrimp** with 3 tablespoons **mayonnaise,** 1 teaspoon each grated **lemon zest** and **lemon juice,** and 1 teaspoon each chopped **chives, parsley** and **capers.** Sandwich **white bread** with the shrimp salad and **Bibb lettuce.** Trim the crusts and cut into pieces.

PEA AND CARROT
Puree ½ cup thawed **frozen peas** with 1 tablespoon each **olive oil** and water; season with **salt** and **pepper.** Cut **whole-grain toast** into squares; spread with the peas and top with shaved **carrot.** Drizzle with **lemon juice** and olive oil and top with grated **parmesan,** salt and pepper.

ASPARAGUS-EGG
Mix 3 tablespoons softened **butter** with 1 tablespoon chopped **fresh herbs.** Spread on **pumpernickel bread;** cut into strips. Slice cooked **asparagus** tips in half lengthwise; lay on the bread and drizzle with **lemon juice** and **olive oil.** Top with chopped hard-boiled **egg, salt** and **pepper.**

STEAK AU POIVRE
Mix 4 tablespoons each softened **butter** and chopped **fresh herbs.** Spread on **baguette rounds.** Top with thinly sliced cooked **steak** and crushed **peppercorns.**

TOMATO-CHEDDAR
Spread **mayonnaise** on **white bread.** Sandwich with sliced **tomato, aged cheddar** and **watercress.** Trim the crusts and cut into pieces.

WATERCRESS-HERB
Mix 4 tablespoons softened **butter,** ½ teaspoon grated **lemon zest** and 1 tablespoon chopped **fresh herbs.** Spread on **white bread** and sandwich with **watercress.** Trim the crusts and cut into pieces.

PESTO CHICKEN
Mix 2 teaspoons **pesto** with 2 tablespoons **olive oil;** brush on thin **baguette rounds.** Top with sliced cooked **chicken** and halved **grape tomatoes.** Drizzle with more pesto oil.

ROAST BEEF–HORSERADISH
Spread **horseradish cream** on **rye cocktail bread.** Sandwich with sliced **cucumber, roast beef** and **watercress;** season with **salt** and **pepper.**

TIP

Use thin bread slices for tea sandwiches so the bread won't overwhelm the filling.

CHICKEN SALAD
Whisk ¼ cup **mayonnaise,** 2 tablespoons each chopped **shallot** and **tarragon,** 2 teaspoons **dijon mustard,** and **salt** and **pepper;** stir in 1 cup shredded **rotisserie chicken.** Sandwich toasted **white bread** with the chicken salad, **watercress** and sliced **cornichons.** Trim the crusts; cut into pieces. Top with cornichons.

RADISH-ANCHOVY
Mix 3 tablespoons softened **butter** with 4 minced **anchovies.** Spread on **white bread** and sandwich with thinly sliced **radishes.** Trim the crusts and cut into pieces.

PEANUT BUTTER–BACON
Spread **peanut butter** on **white bread.** Top with chopped cooked **bacon,** sliced **banana** and then bread spread with **mayonnaise.** Trim the crusts; cut into pieces.

RICOTTA-ORANGE
Cut **whole-wheat bread** into squares. Sandwich with **ricotta** and **orange marmalade.**

CAMEMBERT-FIG
Toast **brioche** slices and cut into pieces. Spread with **camembert.** Top with sliced **fresh figs** and **candied walnuts.**

HAM, BRIE AND APPLE
Spread softened **butter** and
dijon mustard inside a split
baguette. Fill with sliced **ham,
brie** and **green apple**. Cut
into pieces.

 CRAB SALAD
Mix 1 cup **crabmeat** with
3 tablespoons **mayonnaise,**
1 teaspoon each grated **lemon
zest** and **lemon juice,** and
1 teaspoon each chopped **chives,
parsley** and **capers**. Sandwich
white bread with the crab
salad, sliced **avocado** and **Bibb
lettuce**. Trim the crusts and cut
into pieces.

SALMON SALAD
Combine 1 cup flaked cooked
salmon, 3 tablespoons each
mayonnaise, chopped **chives**
and **dill,** and 1 teaspoon each
dijon mustard and **lemon
juice.** Layer the salmon
salad and sliced **radishes** on
pumpernickel bread. Trim the
crusts and cut into pieces.

BRESAOLA-ARTICHOKE
Mix 4 tablespoons softened
butter and ¼ cup chopped
jarred artichoke hearts; season
with **salt** and **pepper**. Spread
on **baguette rounds**. Top with
sliced **bresaola** and drizzle with
olive oil.

TIP

Cover
sandwiches
with a slightly
damp paper
towel until
serving time
so they don't
dry out.

COUNTRY PÂTÉ
Spread **dijon mustard** on
white bread. Layer **country
pâté** and chopped **cornichons**
on top. Cover with buttered
bread. Trim the crusts and
cut into pieces.

EGGPLANT-YOGURT
Fill **mini pita halves** with
chopped grilled **eggplant** and
diced **cucumber**. Add a dollop
of **Greek yogurt** mixed with
chopped **mint.**

CREAM CHEESE AND JELLY
Sandwich softened **cream
cheese** and **raspberry jelly**
between slices of **whole-wheat
bread.** Trim the crusts and cut
into pieces.

PROSCIUTTO-PEAR
Spread softened **butter** and
fig jam inside a split
baguette. Fill with **prosciutto,**
sliced **pears** and **Bibb lettuce;**
season with **salt** and **pepper**.
Cut into pieces.

CALIFORNIA CHICKEN
Cut **whole-wheat toast**
into pieces. Spread with
green goddess dressing.
Sandwich with sliced **smoked
chicken,** sliced **avocado,** diced
tomato and **sprouts;** season
with **salt** and **pepper.**

Tea Sandwiches

ANCHOVY–LEMON BUTTER
Mix 1 stick softened **butter** with
1 tablespoon grated **lemon zest.** Spread on
white bread. Sandwich with **anchovies,**
sliced **tomato** and **Bibb lettuce.** Trim the
crusts and cut into pieces.

GRILLED SHRIMP–HAM
Puree ¼ cup **jarred piquillo peppers**
with 3 tablespoons **mayonnaise.** Spread
on **white bread.** Sandwich with grilled
shrimp and sliced **serrano ham.** Trim the
crusts and cut into pieces.

MANCHEGO-QUINCE
Trim **white toast** crusts and cut the bread
into pieces. Top with sliced **manchego,**
quince paste and sliced **almonds.**

SMOKED TURKEY–APPLE
Spread the inside of a split **baguette** with
softened **butter** and **apple jelly.** Fill
with sliced **smoked turkey, cheddar** and
apple; season with **salt** and **pepper.**

TUNA SALAD
Combine 12 ounces drained canned
tuna, 2 tablespoons each minced **red**
onion and chopped **niçoise olives,**
and ¼ cup **olive oil.** Drizzle the inside
of **mini potato rolls** with olive oil;
fill with the tuna salad and chopped
hard-boiled **egg.**

LIVERWURST-ONION
Spread **dijon mustard** on **pumpernickel**
cocktail bread. Sandwich with sliced
liverwurst and **red onion.**

PÂTÉ–SOUR CHERRY
Spread **sour cherry preserves** on
sliced **brioche.** Sandwich with **duck**
or goose liver pâté. Trim the crusts;
cut into pieces.

BLUE CHEESE–GRAPE
Spread soft **blue cheese** on
pumpernickel cocktail bread. Top
with thinly sliced **red grapes.**

CHOCOLATE-RASPBERRY
Sandwich **Nutella** and **seedless**
raspberry jam between **white bread.**
Trim the crusts and cut into pieces.

MEATLOAF-TOMATO
Spread **mayonnaise** on **potato bread.**
Sandwich with sliced **meatloaf** and
tomato jam. Trim the crusts and cut
into pieces. Top with more tomato jam.

CHEDDAR-PICKLE
Spread **mayonnaise** on **white bread.**
Sandwich with sliced **pickles** and
aged cheddar. Trim the crusts and
cut into pieces, then press the edges in
chopped **parsley.**

BLT CLUB Mix ⅓ cup each **mayonnaise** and finely chopped cooked **bacon;** season with
pepper. Spread on toasted **white bread.** Make double-decker sandwiches with deli-sliced
turkey, sliced **cherry tomatoes** and **baby greens.** Trim the crusts and cut into pieces.

CURRIED EGG SALAD
Mix 3 chopped hard-boiled **eggs,**
3 tablespoons each chopped
celery, red onion and **cilantro,**
2 teaspoons each **dijon mustard**
and **lime juice,** ¼ cup
mayonnaise and a pinch of
curry powder. Cut **white
bread** into pieces; spread with
mango chutney. Sandwich
with the egg salad.

 CUCUMBER-BUTTER
Mix 4 tablespoons softened
butter, ½ teaspoon grated
lemon zest and 1 tablespoon
chopped **fresh herbs.** Spread
on **white bread** and sandwich
with sliced **cucumber.** Trim the
crusts and cut into pieces.

SWEET ONION
Spread softened **butter** on
white bread. Top with thinly
sliced **sweet onion** and season
with **salt;** top with bread spread
with **mayonnaise.** Trim the
crusts and cut into pieces; press
the edges in chopped **parsley.**

ROASTED VEGETABLE
Spread **goat cheese** inside the
bottom half of a split **baguette**
and **sun-dried tomato pesto**
inside the top half. Fill with
roasted **eggplant** and **zucchini**
slices and **roasted red pepper**
strips. Cut into pieces.

TRY THIS

Use cookie
cutters to
make fun
sandwich
shapes: Cut
out circles,
stars or
flowers.

PIMIENTO CHEESE
Mix 2 ounces softened **cream
cheese,** ½ cup each shredded
cheddar and **jack cheese,**
¼ cup **mayonnaise,** and **salt**
and **pepper** to taste; stir in ¼ cup
chopped **pimientos.** Sandwich
on **white bread.** Trim the crusts
and cut into pieces.

PEA-PROSCIUTTO
Puree ½ cup thawed frozen **peas**
with 1 tablespoon each **olive
oil** and water; season with **salt**
and **pepper.** Spread inside
split **focaccia** and fill with
prosciutto and shaved
parmesan. Cut into squares.

SMOKED TROUT
Mix 4 tablespoons softened
butter with 1 teaspoon
grated **lemon zest.** Spread
on **pumpernickel bread.**
Sandwich with flaked **smoked
trout** and sliced **cucumber** and
onion. Trim the crusts and cut
into pieces.

CAPRESE
Layer sliced **mozzarella,
tomatoes** and **fresh basil** on
split **focaccia.** Add **salt, pepper**
and chopped **jarred artichoke
hearts;** drizzle with **olive oil.**
Wrap the sandwich in plastic;
put a heavy skillet on top for
30 minutes. Unwrap and slice.

OLIVE-FOCACCIA

Mix 1 cup chopped **kalamata olives** and 3 tablespoons chopped **parsley.** Drizzle the inside of split **focaccia** with **olive oil;** fill with the olive mixture and sliced **provolone.** Cut into squares.

MORTADELLA-ARUGULA

Spread softened **butter** on **white bread;** sandwich with sliced **mortadella,** then **arugula or watercress** and another layer of mortadella. Trim the crusts and cut into pieces.

HAM-CORNBREAD

Mix 6 tablespoons softened **butter,** 2 teaspoons chopped **scallion** and 1 teaspoon **honey.** Spread on split **mini corn muffins** and fill with sliced **ham** and **pickled jalapeños.**

STRAWBERRY–CREAM CHEESE

Spread softened **cream cheese** on **date-nut or raisin-nut bread** and sandwich with thinly sliced **strawberries.** Cut into pieces.

TALEGGIO-PEAR

Spread softened **butter** inside a split **baguette**; spread one side with **fig jam** and the other with **taleggio.** Fill with thinly sliced **pear.** Season with **salt** and **pepper.** Cut into pieces.

TOFU-CUCUMBER

Spread **wasabi mayonnaise** on **white bread**; sandwich with sliced **baked tofu** and thinly sliced **cucumber.** Trim the crusts and cut into pieces. Press the edges in **sesame seeds,** if desired.

HERB BUTTER–RADISH

Mix 4 tablespoons softened **butter,** ½ teaspoon **lemon zest** and 1 tablespoon chopped **fresh herbs**; spread on **white bread.** Sandwich with sliced **radishes.** Trim the crusts and cut into pieces.

TOMATO-AVOCADO

Spread **mayonnaise** on **pumpernickel bread**; sandwich with sliced **tomatoes** and **avocado** and season with **salt** and **pepper.** Trim the crusts and cut into pieces.

Nachos & Potato Skins

How to make nachos:
1. Spread 8 cups chips on a rimmed baking sheet or in a shallow baking dish. Add toppings.
2. Bake at 475˚ in the upper third of the oven until the cheese melts, about 7 minutes.

BASIC NACHOS
Sprinkle **tortilla chips** with 3 cups shredded **cheddar.** Bake, then top with **salsa** and **pickled jalapeños.**

SPICY CORN NACHOS
Cook 4 cups **corn** in a skillet with a pinch each of **ground cumin** and **cayenne pepper.** Stir in ½ cup **mayonnaise** and some **lime juice.** Spread on **tortilla chips** and bake. Top with **avocado.**

CAJUN NACHOS

Top **tortilla chips** with 3 cups shredded **cheddar,** 1 pound cooked diced **andouille sausage** and 1 cup each diced **green bell pepper, celery** and **onion.** Bake, then top with **salsa** and **pickled jalapeños.**

BACON AND EGG NACHOS

Top **tortilla chips** with 1 can **refried beans,** 1 pound crumbled cooked **bacon** and 3 cups shredded **cheddar;** crack 4 **eggs** on top. Bake until the whites are set, 10 minutes. Top with sliced **scallions** and **salsa.**

SKILLET NACHOS

Heat 1 cup each diced **dried chorizo** and **refried beans** in a cast-iron skillet. Top with **tortilla chips** and shredded **cheddar** and cover to melt. Top with **salsa, pickled jalapeños** and **sour cream.**

SHRIMP NACHOS

Top **tortilla chips** with 1½ cups each shredded **white cheddar** and **muenster.** Bake, then top with sautéed **shrimp,** diced **onion, avocado** and **cilantro.**

TIP

Grate cheese yourself if you have time—it melts better than pre-shredded.

DOUBLE-DECKER NACHOS

Top **tortilla chips** with 1 can **refried beans** and 3 cups shredded **cheddar;** add another layer of chips, another can of beans and 3 more cups cheddar. Bake, then top with warm **jarred nacho cheese sauce, salsa** and **pickled jalapeños.**

BARBECUE CHICKEN NACHOS

Bring 1½ cups **barbecue sauce** and ½ cup water to a simmer. Add 4 cups shredded cooked **chicken;** heat through. Top **tortilla chips** with the chicken and 3 cups shredded **cheddar.** Bake, then top with chopped **scallions.**

SUPER-CHEESY NACHOS

Top **cheese-flavored tortilla chips** with 1 cup each shredded **cheddar, pepper jack** and **mozzarella.** Bake, then top with warm **salsa con queso.**

FRANK AND BEAN NACHOS

Brown 4 sliced **hot dogs** in a skillet; add 1 can **baked beans** and bring to a simmer. Spoon onto **tortilla chips** and top with 3 cups shredded **cheddar.** Bake; top with **scallions.**

JERK PORK NACHOS Rub 1 pound **pork tenderloin** with ¼ cup **jerk seasoning;** grill until cooked through, then chop. Top **tortilla chips** with the pork, 1 cup diced **pineapple** and 3 cups shredded **pepper jack.** Bake; top with sliced **jalapeños, cilantro** and **lime juice.**

BARBECUE PORK NACHOS

Bring 1½ cups **barbecue sauce** and ½ cup water to a simmer. Add 4 cups shredded cooked **pork;** heat through. Top **tortilla chips** with the pork and 3 cups shredded **pepper jack.** Bake, then top with sliced **pickles** and diced **red onions.**

DUCK CONFIT NACHOS

Brown 2 **confit duck legs** in a skillet until crisp; shred the meat. Top toasted slices of **baguette** with 1 cup **sauerkraut,** the duck and 1½ cups shredded **emmentaler.** Bake, then top with chopped **parsley** and **cornichons.**

FOUR-BEAN NACHOS

Top **black bean chips** with 1 cup each **refried beans** and **white beans** and 3 cups shredded **pepper jack.** Bake; top with **bean salsa** and **sour cream.**

CHILI–CORN CHIP NACHOS

Top **corn chips** with 2 cups **chili** and 3 cups shredded **cheddar.** Bake, then top with **pickled jalapeños** and **sour cream.**

TRY THIS

Look for Mexican crema in the dairy aisle or at a Latin market. It's thinner than sour cream and perfect for drizzling on nachos.

CHIMICHURRI NACHOS

Puree ½ cup each **fresh parsley, cilantro** and **olive oil,** 1 **garlic clove** and some **hot sauce.** Rub 1 pound **skirt steak** with half of the sauce; grill and slice. Top **lime-flavored tortilla chips** with 1½ cups each shredded **mozzarella** and crumbled **cotija cheese.** Bake; top with the steak and remaining sauce.

BREAKFAST NACHOS

Top **tortilla chips** with 1 can **refried beans** and 3 cups shredded **cheddar;** bake. Scramble 6 **eggs,** adding ¼ cup each **salsa** and **pickled jalapeños.** Top the nachos with the eggs and some torn **cilantro.**

WILD MUSHROOM NACHOS

Cook 5 cups wild **mushrooms** in **butter.** Add 1 chopped **garlic clove,** 1 tablespoon each chopped **chives** and **parsley,** ¼ cup each **white wine** and **heavy cream,** and **salt** and **pepper;** simmer until thickened. Spoon onto **multigrain chips** and sprinkle with shredded **gruyère,** then bake.

BUFFALO CHICKEN NACHOS Bring 1½ cups **wing sauce** and ½ cup water to a simmer. Add 4 cups shredded cooked **chicken;** heat through. Strain the chicken (reserving the sauce) and spread on **ranch-flavored tortilla chips.** Sprinkle with 3 cups shredded **cheddar.** Bake, then top with **blue cheese,** chopped **celery** and the reserved wing sauce.

VEGGIE FAJITA NACHOS

Top **tortilla chips** with sautéed sliced **bell pepper, zucchini, mushrooms, red onion** and **corn,** and 3 cups shredded **jack cheese.** Bake; top with **salsa verde** and **sour cream.**

CHEESY SQUASH NACHOS

Roast 4 cups diced **butternut squash** at 425°, 15 to 20 minutes. Top **tortilla chips** with the squash, 3 cups shredded **queso blanco** and ¼ cup **pumpkin seeds.** Bake; top with **sour cream** and **cilantro.**

CHORIZO-BEAN NACHOS

Top **tortilla chips** with 1 can **refried beans,** 3 cups shredded **manchego** and 1 pound cooked crumbled **chorizo.** Bake, then top with **pickled jalapeños, salsa** and **sour cream.**

CHEESESTEAK NACHOS

Top **cheese-flavored tortilla chips** with 2 cups each sliced **roast beef** and caramelized **onions,** and 3 cups **jarred nacho cheese sauce.** Bake, then top with **hot sauce** and **pickled Italian peppers.**

MIX IT UP

Think beyond tortilla chips for nachos: Try crackers, toasted baguette rounds—even tater tots!

PLANTAIN NACHOS

Top **plantain chips** with 2 cups diced **dried chorizo** and 1½ cups each shredded **mozzarella** and **queso blanco.** Bake; top with **salsa, avocado, sour cream, cilantro** and **lime juice.**

COBB SALAD NACHOS

Top **tortilla chips** with 2 cups shredded cooked **chicken** and ½ cup crumbled cooked **bacon;** bake 2 minutes. Top with chopped **lettuce, tomato, scallions, avocado, blue cheese** and **ranch dressing.**

FRIED-CHICKEN NACHOS

Heat 2 cups **chicken gravy** with a small can of chopped **green chiles.** Top **tortilla chips** with 3 cups each chopped **fried chicken** and shredded **cheddar.** Bake, then top with the gravy and **scallions.**

CRAB AND CORN NACHOS

Mix 8 ounces **crabmeat,** ¾ cup **corn,** ¼ cup **mayonnaise,** 2 tablespoons minced **chives** and 1 teaspoon **mustard.** Spoon into **tortilla scoops** and top with shredded **jack cheese;** bake.

PIZZA NACHOS Thinly slice half of a **baguette,** brush the slices with **olive oil** and bake until crisp, about 7 minutes. Top with 2 cups **tomato sauce,** 3 cups shredded **mozzarella** and ½ cup shredded **parmesan.** Bake, then sprinkle with chopped **basil.**

SAUSAGE-PEPPER NACHOS

Sauté 4 sliced **Italian sausages,** 1 sliced **onion** and 1 sliced **bell pepper** in a skillet with **olive oil.** Thinly slice half of a **baguette,** brush the slices with olive oil and bake until crisp, 7 minutes. Top with 2 cups **tomato sauce,** 3 cups shredded **mozzarella** and ½ cup shredded **parmesan.** Bake, then top with the sausage mixture and chopped **basil.**

PRETZEL NACHOS

Heat 2 boxes frozen **soft pretzel nuggets** as the label directs. Top with 3 cups shredded **cheddar.** Bake, then top with **pickled jalapeños, scallions** and **mustard.**

CHICKEN MOLE NACHOS

Bring 1½ cups prepared **mole sauce** and ½ cup water to a simmer. Add 4 cups shredded cooked **chicken;** heat through. Top **tortilla chips** with the chicken and 1½ cups each shredded **mozzarella** and crumbled **cotija cheese.** Bake, then top with **sour cream** and **pumpkin seeds.**

TRY THIS

Make individual nachos: Use cup-shaped chips, or spread out large chips and top each separately.

CHILE NACHOS

Top **tortilla chips** with 3 cups shredded **pepper jack** and ½ cup each **pickled jalapeños** and canned chopped **green chiles.** Bake; top with **fresh jalapeños, salsa** and **sour cream.**

MEXICAN TUNA NACHOS

Mix 1 can **tuna** with ¼ cup chopped **Spanish olives.** Top **tortilla chips** with the tuna and 3 cups shredded **cheddar.** Bake; top with **cilantro.**

FAJITA NACHOS

Rub 1 pound **skirt steak** with **ground cumin, cayenne pepper, lime juice** and **olive oil.** Grill with sliced **peppers** and **onions.** Slice the steak; spoon the steak and vegetables over **tortilla chips.** Top with **salsa** and **sour cream.** (Do not bake.)

TATER TOT NACHOS

Cook one 2-pound bag frozen **tater tots** as the label directs. Top with 3 cups shredded **cheddar.** Bake, then top with **salsa, pickled jalapeños, sour cream, red onions** and **cilantro.**

THAI BEEF NACHOS Mix sliced **roast beef** with shredded **carrot,** sliced **red onion** and chopped **mint** and **cilantro;** toss with **lime juice** to taste, a dash of **fish sauce** and a pinch of **sugar.** Spoon into **tortilla scoops;** top with shredded **mozzarella,** then bake 2 minutes. Top with **peanut sauce** and sliced **jalapeños.**

NAAN-CHOS
Cook 1 sliced **onion** and
¼ teaspoon **curry powder** in
vegetable oil; add 1 can drained
chickpeas, ½ cup frozen **peas,**
and **salt;** mash. Spoon over
toasted **naan** triangles. Add 1 cup
shredded **mozzarella** and bake
2 minutes. Top with **plain yogurt,
mango chutney** and **cilantro.**

CHEESEBURGER NACHOS
Top **ridged potato chips** with
¼ pound cooked **ground beef**
and 2 cups shredded **cheddar.**
Bake, then top with sliced **red
onion,** sliced **pickles,** shredded
lettuce and **ketchup.**

BROCCOLI-CHEESE NACHOS
Mix 2 cups shredded **cheddar,**
1 cup **mayonnaise,** 2 chopped
scallions and 2 chopped
jalapeños. Top **potato chips**
with cooked **broccoli** and the
cheese mixture; bake.

BAGEL NACHOS
Top **bagel chips** with **whipped
cream cheese** and chopped
scallions. Bake, then top with
**smoked salmon, tomato, red
onion, dill** and **capers.**

TIP

Avoid deep
baking
dishes for
nachos:
You want
each chip
to get some
toppings.

SWEET FRIED NACHOS
Cut **flour tortillas** into triangles.
Fry in 350° **vegetable oil** until
golden, 2 minutes. Drain on paper
towels; sprinkle with **sugar** and
drizzle with **honey.** (Do not bake.)

MINI WAFFLE NACHOS
Top 1 box toasted frozen **mini
waffles** with 2 cups shredded
cheddar and 8 ounces diced
Canadian bacon. Bake, then
drizzle with **maple syrup.**

NUTELLA-BANANA NACHOS
Drizzle **pretzel crisps** with
½ cup warm **Nutella** and top
with 2 sliced **bananas,** ¼ cup
chopped **peanuts** and **whipped
cream.** (Do not bake.)

APPLE PIE NACHOS
Sauté 3 cubed peeled **apples** in
butter. Top **cinnamon-sugar
pita chips** with the apples,
warm **caramel sauce, ice
cream, whipped cream** and
cinnamon. (Do not bake.)

S'MORES NACHOS
Top **graham crackers** with
marshmallow cream. Bake,
then drizzle with **hot fudge.**

MARGARITA SHRIMP NACHOS Marinate ½ pound **shrimp** in **margarita mix** with a dash of
cayenne pepper; grill. Top **lime-flavored tortilla chips** with 1½ cups each shredded **cheddar**
and **muenster.** Bake; top with the shrimp, **onion, avocado, cilantro** and **lime juice.**

How to make potato skins:
1. Pierce 4 russet potatoes with a fork. Bake on the oven rack at 350° until tender, 1 hour. Let cool, then quarter lengthwise and scoop out the flesh.
2. Brush both sides with melted butter and season with salt and pepper. Bake, skin-side up, at 450° until crisp, about 15 minutes. Add toppings. (For cheesy skins, sprinkle the flesh side with 1 cup grated cheddar and bake an extra 5 minutes before topping.)

DELI PASTRAMI SKINS
Top **cheesy potato skins** with deli-sliced **pastrami.** Drizzle with **Russian dressing** and top with sliced **dill pickle.**

LOADED TACO SKINS
Top **potato skins** with shredded cooked **chicken** mixed with **taco seasoning.** Top with **queso blanco, salsa, pickled jalapeños,** chopped **tomato,** shredded **lettuce,** chopped **cilantro** and **sour cream.**

CHICAGO SKINS
Top **potato skins** with **sweet pickle relish, dill pickle spears, pickled peppers, yellow mustard,** chopped **onion** and **tomato, celery salt** and **poppy seeds.**

MAC AND CHEESE SKINS
Top **potato skins** with prepared **mac and cheese,** then bake 5 more minutes.

TIP

Don't wrap potatoes in foil before baking: The steam will make the skin soft.

HOT WING SKINS
Top **potato skins** with **blue cheese dressing, hot sauce** and diced **celery** and **carrots.**

SLAW SKINS
Top **potato skins** with **coleslaw** and crumbled cooked **bacon.**

OLD BAY SKINS
Top **potato skins** with melted **butter, Old Bay Seasoning,** grated **parmesan** and chopped **chives.**

CHEESY HAM SKINS
Top **cheesy potato skins** with sautéed **green bell pepper, onion** and **ham, paprika** and chopped **parsley.**

BARBECUE SKINS
Top **cheesy potato skins** with **pulled pork, barbecue sauce** and sliced **scallions.**

DEVILED CRAB SKINS
Top **potato skins** with **crab salad, cayenne pepper** and **paprika;** bake 5 more minutes.

TEX-MEX SKINS
Top **potato skins** with **canned refried beans,** cooked crumbled **chorizo,** shredded **jack cheese, hot sauce** and **pickled jalapeños;** bake 5 more minutes.

CALZONE SKINS
Top **potato skins** with **ricotta** mixed with grated **parmesan** and chopped **basil, tomato sauce** and shredded **mozzarella;** bake 5 more minutes.

MAPLE-BACON SKINS
Top **cheesy potato skins** with **apple butter,** cooked **bacon** and **maple syrup.**

CHEESESTEAK SKINS
Top **potato skins** with sautéed **onions** and **roast beef, Worcestershire sauce** and **jarred nacho cheese sauce;** bake 5 more minutes.

TEXAS CHILI SKINS
Top **potato skins** with warm **beef chili,** grated **cheddar,** chopped **onion, sour cream** and **hot sauce.**

TRY THIS

Don't toss all the extra potato you scoop out: Mash it with milk and butter for another meal.

CHEESEBURGER SKINS »
Top **cheesy potato skins** with grilled **mini burgers, lettuce, tomato, ketchup** and **pickles.**

CORNED BEEF SKINS
Top **potato skins** with deli-sliced **corned beef,** shredded **Swiss cheese,** grated **horseradish** and **spicy mustard;** bake 5 more minutes.

MOJO SHRIMP SKINS
Top **potato skins** with **shrimp** sautéed with **rum** and bottled **mojo sauce.**

KIELBASA-KRAUT SKINS
Top **potato skins** with sautéed **onions,** sliced **kielbasa, sauerkraut** and grated **Swiss cheese;** bake 5 more minutes.

CHEESY ARTICHOKE SKINS
Top **potato skins** with **jarred artichoke hearts** pureed with **goat cheese, garlic, fresh herbs** and **olive oil;** bake 5 more minutes.

MUFFULETTA SKINS »
Top **potato skins** with assorted sliced **Italian deli meat, provolone, olive salad** and sliced **pepperoncini.**

GUACAMOLE SKINS
Top **potato skins** with **guacamole, sprouts** and diced **red onion**.

BEER AND BRAT SKINS
Top **potato skins** with **beer cheese spread,** sliced grilled **bratwurst** and **brown mustard**.

GEORGIA PEACH SKINS
Mix **peach preserves** with **yellow mustard** and cubed **ham**. Spread on **cheesy potato skins**. Top with **canned fried onions**.

CUBAN SKINS
Top **potato skins** with **mayonnaise,** sliced **ham** and **Swiss cheese;** bake 5 more minutes. Top with **mustard** and sliced **pickles**.

CILANTRO-LIME SKINS
Mix **sour cream,** some grated **lime zest** and **lime juice,** chopped **cilantro,** and **salt** and **pepper**. Spoon onto **potato skins** and top with **fresh salsa**.

FRIED PORK SKINS
Mix **mayonnaise** with **dijon mustard** and **hot sauce**. Spread on **potato skins** and top with sliced **fried pork or chicken cutlets,** chopped **tomato** and diced **red onion**.

TIP

Russets make the best potato skins— they're low in moisture and high in starch.

SMOKED SALMON SKINS
Mix 6 ounces softened **cream cheese** with 1 tablespoon each minced **red onion** and **capers,** and 4 ounces chopped **smoked salmon**. Spread on **potato skins**.

POUTINE SKINS
Heat ¼ cup each **butter,** minced **onion** and **flour** in a saucepan, stirring, until the onion is soft. Slowly whisk in 2 cups **chicken broth** and 1 teaspoon **Worcestershire sauce;** simmer to thicken. Top **potato skins** with **cheddar cheese curds or grated mozzarella,** then the hot gravy.

PIZZA SKINS
Top **potato skins** with **tomato sauce,** shredded **mozzarella** and **parmesan,** sliced **pepperoni** and a pinch of **dried oregano;** bake 5 more minutes.

BREAKFAST SKINS
Top **cheesy potato skins** with **scrambled eggs** and crumbled cooked **bacon**.

TAPENADE SKINS
Top **potato skins** with **olive tapenade** and sliced **cherry tomatoes**. Sprinkle with chopped **parsley** and **chives**.

CONEY DOG SKINS

Top **potato skins** with sliced cooked **hot dogs,** warm **chili,** diced **onion, yellow mustard** and shredded **cheddar.**

SOUTHWESTERN SKINS

Top **cheesy potato skins** with **fresh salsa, pickled jalapeños,** chopped **scallions** and **cilantro,** and **sour cream.**

SAUSAGE-PEPPER SKINS

Top **potato skins** with sautéed **onions, green bell peppers** and **Italian sausage;** add **mozzarella** and bake 5 more minutes.

SALMON-MUSHROOM SKINS
Top **potato skins** with flaked grilled **salmon**, sautéed **wild mushrooms**, and chopped **parsley** and **chives**.

COUNTRY HAM SKINS
Top **cheesy potato skins** with deli **ham salad**, chopped **parsley** and minced **pickles**.

FIVE-WAY CHILI SKINS
Top **potato skins** with warm **chili**, canned **kidney beans**, chopped **onion**, shredded **cheddar** and crushed **oyster crackers**.

Chips & Party Mixes

SPICY POTATO CHIPS
Spread **potato chips** on a baking sheet; warm in a 350°
oven until oily, about 5 minutes. Sprinkle with **chili powder,
paprika, mustard powder, salt** and **cayenne pepper.**

SESAME POTATO CHIPS
Preheat 2 baking sheets in a 425° oven. Thinly slice 2 **russet
potatoes** (use a mandoline if you have one). Toss with **olive
oil** and **salt.** Spread on the hot baking sheets, sprinkle with
sesame seeds and bake until golden, about 10 minutes.

ROSEMARY POTATO CHIPS
Slice 1½ pounds **russet potatoes** ¼ inch thick. Toss with
2 teaspoons chopped **rosemary,** 1 grated **garlic clove,**
3 tablespoons **olive oil,** ¾ teaspoon **salt** and a pinch of
cayenne pepper. Spread on a baking sheet; roast at
500° until golden, 20 minutes. Flip and cook until crisp,
8 more minutes. Season with salt.

DRIED APPLE CHIPS
Cut an **apple** in half and cut out the seeds and core. Cut into ¼-inch-thick slices. Lay on an oiled baking sheet and bake at 200° until dry, 2 to 3 hours.

GARLIC BAGEL CHIPS
Melt 3 tablespoons **butter** with 2 chopped **garlic cloves** in a saucepan. Slice stale **plain bagels** crosswise into thin rounds. Brush the tops with the garlic butter. Bake at 325°, 10 minutes; flip, brush with more garlic butter, sprinkle with grated **parmesan** and bake until crisp, 10 more minutes.

SWEET BAGEL CHIPS
Slice stale **cinnamon-raisin bagels** crosswise into thin rounds. Brush the tops with melted **butter** and sprinkle with **cinnamon sugar.** Bake at 325°, 10 minutes; flip, brush with more butter, sprinkle with more cinnamon sugar and bake until crisp, 10 more minutes.

TRY THIS

Design your own chips: Heat store-bought potato chips in a 350° oven for 5 minutes, then toss with your choice of spices.

BANANA CHIPS
Slice a **banana** into ⅛-inch-thick rounds and lay on an oiled baking sheet. Bake at 200° until golden, 2 to 3 hours. Let harden.

PANCETTA CHIPS
Sandwich thinly sliced **pancetta** between 2 baking sheets. Bake at 350°, 25 minutes. Blot with paper towels.

CURRY POTATO CHIPS
Preheat 2 baking sheets in a 425° oven. Thinly slice 2 **russet potatoes** (use a mandoline if you have one). Toss with **olive oil, salt** and **curry powder.** Spread on the hot baking sheets and bake until golden, 10 minutes.

KALE CHIPS
Tear the leaves from 1 bunch **kale.** Toss with 2 tablespoons **olive oil,** 2 sliced **garlic cloves,** ½ teaspoon **salt,** and **pepper** to taste on a baking sheet. Roast in a 425° oven until crisp, about 15 minutes, stirring halfway through. Squeeze some **lemon juice** on top.

HOT VEGETABLE CHIPS Mix 1½ tablespoons **paprika** and ½ teaspoon each **cayenne pepper** and **black pepper** in a bowl. Spread 12 cups **vegetable chips** on 2 baking sheets. Warm in a 350° oven until oily, about 5 minutes. Sprinkle the chips with the spice mixture and bake 2 more minutes. Let cool.

CHEESY CHEX MIX

Toss 3 cups **Chex cereal,** 2 cups **mini pretzels** and 1 cup **cheese crackers** with ¾ cup grated **parmesan,** ½ stick melted **butter** and a pinch of **garlic powder.** Spread on a baking sheet and bake at 325°, 15 minutes, stirring occasionally.

EDIBLE PARTY-MIX BOWL

Whip 2 tablespoons water and 2 **egg whites** until stiff. Toss with 8 cups prepared **snack mix.** Coat a 3-quart ovenproof bowl with **cooking spray;** add the snack mix. Crumple a sheet of foil and mold into a bowl shape one-third the size of the 3-quart bowl. Coat the foil bowl with cooking spray and press into the snack mix, forming the mix into a bowl shape. Bake at 325° (with the foil in place), 30 minutes. Cool 5 minutes, then remove the foil and cool 30 more minutes. Invert the edible bowl onto a plate and let cool completely.

MIX IT UP

Combine sweet and salty: Toss mini pretzels with caramel corn, or cheese crackers with M&Ms.

SMOKY PRETZEL MIX

Melt ½ stick **butter** with 3 tablespoons **brown sugar,** 1 teaspoon **smoked paprika** and ¼ teaspoon **cayenne pepper.** Toss with 3 cups **mini pretzels** and 2 cups **mixed nuts.** Spread on a baking sheet and bake at 325°, stirring, 20 minutes.

BACON-PEANUT BRITTLE

Boil 2 cups **sugar** and 1 cup water, without stirring, until a candy thermometer registers 340°, 8 to 10 minutes. Add 1 cup **peanuts,** 5 slices crumbled cooked **bacon,** 1 tablespoon **butter** and a pinch each of **cayenne pepper** and **cinnamon.** Spread on an oiled baking sheet; let harden.

CRUNCHY CHICKPEAS

Sauté 1 drained can **chickpeas** in an ovenproof skillet with 2 tablespoons **olive oil** and 1 teaspoon each **ground cumin** and **smoked paprika,** 2 minutes. Season with **salt,** then transfer to a 425° oven; bake 20 minutes.

POTATO CHIP TOFFEE Line a baking sheet with foil and butter the foil. Cook 2 sticks **butter,** 1 cup **sugar,** 2 teaspoons **vanilla** and 2 tablespoons **cider vinegar** in a large saucepan over medium-high heat, stirring, until a candy thermometer registers 320°, about 10 minutes. Remove from the heat; stir in 4 cups **thick-cut potato chips,** then immediately spoon onto the baking sheet and spread in a thin layer. Press 1 more cup chips on top of the toffee and let cool. Drizzle with melted **chocolate.** Set aside to harden, about 20 minutes, then break into pieces.

MICROWAVE POPCORN

Place ¼ cup **popcorn kernels** in a brown paper lunch bag. Fold the top over a few times, then microwave for about 2 minutes, or until the popping subsides.

SWEET-AND-SPICY POPCORN

Toss a batch of hot **popcorn** with **chili powder** and **brown sugar.**

ITALIAN POPCORN

Toss a batch of hot **popcorn** with **dried oregano, dried basil** and grated **parmesan.**

ASIAN POPCORN

Toss a batch of hot **popcorn** with **wasabi powder, sugar** and **sea salt.**

CARAMEL POPCORN

Boil ½ cup **honey,** 1 tablespoon **molasses,** ½ stick **butter,** 1 teaspoon **vanilla** and ½ teaspoon **salt** in a saucepan. Toss with 10 cups **popcorn.** Spread on a rimmed baking sheet and bake at 300˚ until crisp, 10 to 15 minutes, stirring often. Cool completely.

TRY THIS

Host a movie night and give guests brown lunch bags filled with different kinds of spiced popcorn.

CHEESY BACON POPCORN

Fry 3 strips **bacon** until crisp. Drizzle 4 cups hot **popcorn** with 1 tablespoon of the drippings. Crumble the bacon; toss with the popcorn and ¼ cup each grated **parmesan** and **cheddar.**

COCONUT POPCORN BALLS

Bring ¼ cup **light corn syrup,** 2 tablespoons **butter,** 1 cup **confectioners' sugar,** 1 cup **mini marshmallows** and 1 tablespoon water to a boil in a large pot, stirring. Add a dash each of **almond extract** and **salt,** then stir in 12 cups **popcorn** until coated. Butter your hands; shape the popcorn into balls. Roll in toasted **coconut.**

NUTTY POPCORN BALLS

Bring ¼ cup **honey,** ¼ cup **almond butter,** 2 tablespoons **butter,** ½ cup **confectioners' sugar** and 1 tablespoon water to a boil in a large pot, stirring. Stir in 12 cups **popcorn** and 1 cup **salted nuts** until coated. Butter your hands; shape the popcorn into balls. Roll in **sesame seeds.**

HONEY-SPICE PEANUTS Heat 2 tablespoons **peanut oil** in a skillet over medium heat. Add 2 tablespoons **honey,** ¾ cup **peanuts,** 4 sliced **scallions** and ½ teaspoon each **red pepper flakes** and **five-spice powder.** Cook, stirring, until glazed, about 10 minutes. Stir in 1 teaspoon **balsamic vinegar** and cook 1 minute. Transfer to a foil-lined baking sheet; season with **salt** and let cool.

»

SPICED MIXED NUTS

Mix 1¼ teaspoons **cayenne pepper,** 1 teaspoon **cinnamon,** 1 teaspoon **ginger,** 1 teaspoon **mustard powder,** ½ cup **sugar** and ½ teaspoon **salt** in a small bowl. Whisk 1 **egg white** in a large bowl until frothy. Toss in 4 cups **mixed nuts,** then add the spice mixture and toss. Spread on a parchment-lined baking sheet; bake at 250°, 45 minutes. Let cool.

SWEET NUT CLUSTERS

Whisk 1 **egg white** with 1 tablespoon water in a large bowl until frothy. In a small bowl, mix ⅔ cup **sugar,** 1½ teaspoons **salt,** 1 teaspoon **pumpkin pie or chai spice blend** and ¼ teaspoon **cayenne pepper.** Toss 3 cups **mixed nuts** in the egg white mixture, then stir in the sugar-spice mixture and 2 dashes **Worcestershire sauce.** Spoon the nuts in clusters on a parchment-lined baking sheet; bake at 275° until golden, 30 to 35 minutes. Let cool.

TRY THIS

Make a potluck party mix: Ask friends to bring an ingredient (chips, nuts, pretzels, etc.), then mix them all together!

SUPER-SPICY MIXED NUTS

Mix 1¼ teaspoons **cayenne pepper,** 1 teaspoon **cinnamon,** 1 teaspoon **ginger,** 1 teaspoon **mustard powder,** 2 teaspoons **chipotle chile powder,** ½ cup **sugar** and ½ teaspoon **salt** in a small bowl. Whisk 1 **egg white** in a large bowl until frothy. Toss in 4 cups **mixed nuts,** then add the spice mixture and toss. Spread on a parchment-lined baking sheet; bake at 250° until dry, 45 minutes. Let cool. Meanwhile, fry 4 thinly sliced **serrano peppers** in **vegetable oil** until crisp; season with salt and sprinkle on the nuts.

BACON NUTS

Beat 1 **egg white** until frothy. Toss with 2 cups **mixed nuts,** 2 teaspoons **Cajun seasoning,** 2 tablespoons **brown sugar** and 4 slices crumbled cooked **bacon.** Spread on a parchment-lined baking sheet and bake at 325° until golden, about 10 minutes.

PINE-NUT CHEESE CRISPS Shred 1 pound cold **asiago cheese.** Place 6 tablespoon-size mounds of cheese about 1 inch apart on a parchment-lined baking sheet. Sprinkle with chopped **pine nuts** and **sage.** Bake at 425° until golden, 8 to 10 minutes. Remove each crisp with a spatula and drape around a rolling pin to cool slightly; cool completely on a rack.

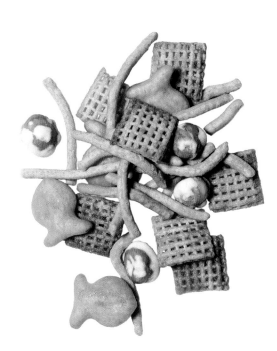

HONEY-NUT POPCORN

Melt ⅓ cup **butter** with 1 tablespoon **honey** and a pinch of **salt.** Toss with 12 cups **popcorn** and 1 cup **pecans.** Spread on a parchment-lined baking sheet and bake 15 minutes at 325°, tossing occasionally. Let cool.

TERIYAKI SNACK MIX

Toss 4 cups **Chex cereal,** 1½ cups **goldfish crackers,** ⅓ cup **teriyaki sauce** and 4 tablespoons melted **butter** in a roasting pan. Bake at 250°, 1 hour, stirring a few times. Spread on paper towels to cool, then toss with **wasabi peas** and **chow mein noodles.**

PRETZEL MELTS

Slice **cheddar** into thin 1-inch squares. Sandwich between **mini pretzels.** Arrange on a parchment-lined baking sheet and bake at 425˚ until the cheese melts, about 10 minutes. Let cool on the baking sheet.

CHOCOLATE CHOW MEIN

Melt ¼ cup each **peanut butter, chocolate chips** and **butter** in the microwave. Put 3 cups each **chow mein noodles** and **Chex cereal** and ½ cup each chopped **peanuts** and **raisins** in a resealable plastic bag; add the chocolate mixture and shake to coat. Add 2 cups **confectioners' sugar** and shake again.

Perfect
POPCORN

Heat $\frac{1}{3}$ cup vegetable oil (movie theaters use coconut oil) until very hot but not smoking (400° to 460°) in a 5-to-6-quart heavy pot with a lid. Add a few kernels—when they pop, add 1 cup kernels in a single layer and put the lid on, leaving it slightly ajar. Shake the pan during popping to keep the kernels from burning. When the popping slows, remove the pot from the heat until the popping stops. Toss the hot popcorn with fine salt.

COUNTING CALORIES?

- 1 cup air-popped corn **31**
- 1 cup oil-popped corn **55**
- 1 cup oil-popped corn with
  2 teaspoons melted butter **122**
- ½ bag "light butter"
  microwave popcorn **180**
- small movie-theater popcorn
  without butter **400**
- small movie-theater popcorn
  with butter **630**
- large movie-theater popcorn
  without butter **1,160**
- large movie-theater popcorn
  with butter **1,640**

GOLDEN RULES

- **STORE** kernels in an airtight container in a cool, dark place, but not in the fridge, where they'll dry out. They need moisture to pop.

- **COVER** the pot loosely during popping; if the lid is tight, the steam inside the pot will moisten the popcorn—and wet popcorn is no fun.

- **SALT** the corn after it's popped; if you salt the kernels or oil beforehand, the popcorn won't turn out as light and fluffy.

HOW TO MAKE
Theater-Style Butter

Movie theaters use butter-flavored oil, which has a lower water content than butter so it makes popcorn less soggy. Real clarified butter has the same effect.

To clarify butter: Microwave 2 sticks in a microwave-safe glass measuring cup until melted. Let sit for a few minutes; the butter will separate into 3 layers. Carefully skim off the top layer of foam, then slowly pour the butter into a heatproof container, leaving the bottom layer of milk solids behind. Use about 3 tablespoons hot clarified butter for 10 cups popcorn.

Breakfast&
Brunch

Smoothies

How to make smoothies:
Combine the ingredients in a blender and blend until smooth. Each recipe serves 2 to 4 but can be doubled or halved as needed.

BLUEBERRY-BANANA
Blend 1 **banana,** 1 cup **blueberries,** ½ cup **unsweetened coconut milk,** 1 tablespoon each **honey** and **lime juice,** ¼ teaspoon **almond extract** and 1 cup ice.

CREAMSICLE
Blend ¾ cup frozen **orange or orange-tangerine concentrate** with ½ cup cold water and 1 cup each **vanilla frozen yogurt** and ice.

RASPBERRY-ORANGE
Blend 1 cup each **orange juice** and **raspberries,** ½ cup **plain yogurt,** 1 cup ice, and **sugar** to taste.

BANANA
Blend 2 **bananas,** ½ cup each **vanilla yogurt** and **milk,** 2 teaspoons **honey,** a pinch of **cinnamon** and 1 cup ice.

TRIPLE BERRY
Blend 1½ cups mixed **blackberries, strawberries** and **raspberries** with 1 cup each **milk** and ice. Add **sugar** to taste.

CARROT-APPLE
Blend 1 cup each **carrot juice** and **apple juice** with 1½ cups ice.

APPLE-GINGER
Blend 1 chopped peeled **apple,** a ½-inch piece peeled **ginger,** the juice of 2 **limes,** ¼ cup **honey,** 1 cup water and 2 cups ice.

GRAPEFRUIT
Peel and seed 2 **grapefruits;** blend with 3 to 4 tablespoons **sugar** and 1 cup ice. Sprinkle with **cinnamon.**

POMEGRANATE-CHERRY
Blend 1 cup frozen pitted **cherries,** ¾ cup **pomegranate juice,** ½ cup **plain yogurt,** 1 tablespoon **honey,** 1 teaspoon **lemon juice,** a pinch each of **salt** and **cinnamon,** and 2 cups ice.

POMEGRANATE-RASPBERRY
Blend 1 cup **pomegranate juice,** ½ cup each **vanilla yogurt** and frozen **raspberries,** and 1 cup ice. Sweeten with **honey.**

SOY-BERRY
Blend 4 ounces **silken tofu,** 2 cups frozen **raspberries or strawberries,** ½ cup **orange juice,** 1 cup **soy milk** and a little **honey.**

TIP

Peel, slice and freeze fruit before it goes bad and save it for smoothies.

CANDIED SWEET POTATO
Blend 1 peeled baked **sweet potato,** 1 tablespoon **brown sugar,** ½ cup **vanilla yogurt,** ½ cup **orange juice** and 1½ cups ice. Top with **cinnamon.**

APPLE-SPINACH
Blend 2 cups **spinach,** 1 chopped peeled **apple,** ½ cup **silken tofu,** ¼ cup each **soy milk** and **orange juice,** 1 tablespoon each **wheat germ, honey** and **lemon juice,** and 1 cup ice.

CUCUMBER-KALE
Blend 1¼ cups **vegetable juice,** ½ peeled and chopped **cucumber,** 3 **kale leaves** and the juice of ½ **lemon.**

TOMATO-VEGGIE
Blend 1¼ cups **tomato juice,** ¼ cup **carrot juice,** ½ peeled and chopped **cucumber,** ½ chopped **celery stalk,** ¼ cup each **fresh parsley** and **spinach,** and ½ cup ice.

PEACH-GINGER
Blend 2 cups frozen sliced **peaches,** 1½ cups **buttermilk,** 3 tablespoons **brown sugar** and 1 tablespoon grated **fresh ginger.**

PINEAPPLE-MANGO Blend 1 cup each chopped **pineapple** and **mango** with 1 cup **coconut water,** a dash of **allspice** and 1 cup ice. Top with toasted **coconut.**

≫

CANTALOUPE-LIME
Blend 2 cups chopped
cantaloupe, the juice of
½ **lime,** 3 tablespoons **sugar,**
½ cup water and 1 cup ice.

POMEGRANATE-BLUEBERRY
Blend 1 cup **blueberries,**
¾ cup each **beet juice** and
pomegranate juice, 1 cup ice,
and **honey** to taste.

PINEAPPLE-COCONUT
Freeze 2 cups **coconut water**
in 1 or 2 ice-cube trays. Blend
2 cups each chopped **pineapple**
and coconut ice cubes with
1½ tablespoons **lime juice,**
1 tablespoon **honey** and ½ cup
coconut water.

HONEYDEW-ALMOND
Blend 2 cups chopped
honeydew melon, 1 cup
each **almond milk** and ice,
and **honey** to taste.

GRAPE
Blend 2 cups **seedless red
grapes** with 1 cup **concord
grape juice** and 1½ cups ice.

LEMON–POPPY SEED
Blend 2 teaspoons **poppy seeds,**
the grated zest and juice of
½ **lemon,** 1 cup **plain yogurt,**
⅓ cup **sugar** and ½ cup each
milk and ice.

TIP

Start the
blender
on low
speed
and then
slowly
increase
to high.

CHAI
Blend 1½ cups **chai tea
concentrate** with 1 cup each
milk and ice. Sprinkle with
cinnamon or chai spice blend.

CHERRY-VANILLA
Blend 1½ cups frozen pitted
cherries, 1¼ cups **milk,**
3 tablespoons **sugar,** ½ teaspoon
vanilla extract, ¼ teaspoon
almond extract, a pinch of
salt and 1 cup ice.

TANGERINE-HONEY
Peel and seed 4 **tangerines,** then
blend with the juice of 2 **limes,**
¼ cup **honey** and 1 cup ice.

PEACH-MANGO-BANANA
Blend 1 cup each chopped
peaches and **mango,** 1 cup
each **plain yogurt** and ice,
½ **banana,** and **sugar** to taste.

APRICOT-ALMOND
Blend 1½ cups **apricot nectar**
with ½ cup **vanilla yogurt,**
2 tablespoons **almond butter**
and 1 cup ice.

BANANA-PB&J
Blend 1 frozen **banana** with
1 cup **soy milk,** ¼ cup
each **creamy peanut
butter** and **wheat germ,**
and 2 tablespoons **seedless
strawberry jelly.**

MEXICAN COFFEE

Blend ½ cup chilled **espresso or strong coffee** with ½ cup **milk or almond milk,** 3½ tablespoons **brown sugar,** ¼ teaspoon **cinnamon,** ⅛ teaspoon **almond extract** and 1½ cups ice.

PEANUT BUTTER–APPLE

Blend 1 chopped peeled **apple,** 3 tablespoons **creamy peanut butter,** 2 tablespoons **flaxseed,** 1½ cups each **soy milk** and ice, and **honey** to taste.

GREEN TEA–ALMOND

Blend 1½ cups chilled strong **green tea** with ⅓ cup **almonds,** ¼ cup **honey** and 1 cup ice.

STRAWBERRY-MAPLE

Blend 2 cups **strawberries,** 1½ cups **milk,** ¼ cup each **maple syrup** and **wheat germ,** a dash of **cinnamon** and 1½ cups ice.

BANANA-DATE

Blend 2 **bananas,** ¾ cup chopped pitted **dates,** the juice of 1 **lime** and 1½ cups each **soy milk** and ice.

TRY THIS

Turn what's left in the blender into pops: Pour into a pop mold and freeze until firm.

BLUEBERRY-PEAR

Blend 1½ cups frozen **blueberries,** 1 chopped **pear,** 1½ cups each **maple or plain yogurt** and ice, and **sugar** to taste.

PEANUT BUTTER MALT

Blend 1 **banana,** 1 cup **vanilla yogurt,** ½ cup **creamy peanut butter,** ⅓ cup **milk,** 2 tablespoons **malted milk powder,** ½ teaspoon **cocoa powder,** a pinch of **salt** and 2 cups ice.

SPICED PUMPKIN

Blend ½ cup each canned **pumpkin puree** and **silken tofu,** 3½ tablespoons **brown sugar,** 1 cup **milk,** ½ teaspoon **pumpkin pie spice,** a pinch of **salt** and 1 cup ice.

HIBISCUS-ORANGE

Make hibiscus syrup: Bring 1 cup water to a boil; add 1 cup **sugar** and 6 **hibiscus tea bags.** Cover, remove from the heat and let steep 1 hour. Blend 3 peeled, seeded **oranges,** the juice of 1 **lime** and 1 cup ice. Add 3 tablespoons hibiscus syrup to each smoothie.

MOCHA Blend ½ cup chilled **espresso or strong coffee,** ¼ cup **sweetened condensed milk** and 1½ cups ice. Top with shaved **chocolate** and **chocolate syrup.**

ORANGE FLOWER–ALMOND

Blend ½ cup **blanched almonds,** 3 tablespoons **sugar,** 1 cup **milk** and ½ teaspoon **orange flower water.** Add 1 cup ice and blend.

CREAMY PINEAPPLE

Blend 2 cups chopped **pineapple,** ½ cup low-fat **cottage cheese,** ¼ cup **milk,** 2 cups ice, 2 teaspoons **honey,** ¼ teaspoon **vanilla** and a pinch each of **salt** and **nutmeg.**

PEACH-MANGO TEA

Blend 2 cups frozen **peaches,** 2 cups chilled strong **mango-passionfruit tea,** the juice of 1 **lime** and 1 cup ice. Add **honey** to taste.

MANGO-AÇAI

Blend two 4-ounce packages frozen **açai berry puree,** 1 cup chopped **mango,** ½ cup **orange juice** and 2 cups ice.

GRANOLA-STRAWBERRY

Blend 1 chopped **banana,** 1 cup **strawberries,** ½ cup each **milk** and **vanilla yogurt,** 1 cup ice, 2 teaspoons **honey** and a pinch of **cinnamon.** Add ¼ cup **granola** and blend.

TRY THIS

Add a handful of oats to your smoothie: It'll give the drink a creamy texture and will make it more filling.

WATERMELON

Freeze 3 cups cubed **seedless watermelon** until firm. Blend with 1 cup cubed fresh seedless watermelon, the juice of 1 **lime,** ¼ cup **sugar** and 1 cup water.

LYCHEE-LIME

Drain one 20-ounce can **lychees in syrup.** Blend the lychees with ½ cup of the syrup, 2 cups ice, 1 tablespoon **lime juice** and a pinch of **salt.**

KIWI-STRAWBERRY

Blend 1 cup **strawberries,** 2 **kiwis,** 2 tablespoons **sugar** and 2 cups ice.

MINT-JALAPEÑO

Blend ⅓ cup **fresh mint,** 1 seeded **jalapeño,** 2½ tablespoons **honey,** a pinch of **salt** and 2 cups each **plain yogurt** and ice. Top with **cilantro.**

CUCUMBER-DILL

Blend 2 peeled, seeded and chopped **cucumbers,** 1 cup **buttermilk,** 2 tablespoons **fresh dill,** 1½ cups ice, 2 teaspoons **honey** and a pinch of **salt.**

STRAWBERRY SHORTCAKE Blend 2 cups **strawberries,** 1 cup crumbled **pound cake,** 1½ cups each **milk** and ice, and **sugar** to taste. Top with **whipped cream** and more berries.

BERRY-BANANA

Blend 1 cup **vanilla yogurt,**
1 cup frozen **strawberries,** 1 frozen
banana and ¼ cup **orange juice.**

CUCUMBER

Peel, seed and chop 2 **cucumbers.**
Blend with the juice of 1 **lime,**
½ cup water, 1 cup ice and
3 to 4 tablespoons **sugar.**

CREAMY MELON
Puree ½ chopped **cantaloupe** with
1 pint **vanilla frozen yogurt** and
½ cup **milk.**

BERRY-VANILLA
Blend 1 pint **blackberries** with
½ cup **raspberries**, 1 cup **vanilla
yogurt** and 1 tablespoon **honey.**

Pancakes, Waffles & French Toast

BASIC PANCAKES

Whisk 1½ cups **flour,** 3 tablespoons **sugar,** 1 tablespoon **baking powder** and ½ teaspoon **salt.** Whisk 1¼ cups **milk,** ½ stick melted **butter,** 2 **eggs** and a little **vanilla,** then whisk into the flour mixture. Cook by ¼ cupfuls in a hot buttered skillet until bubbly, then flip and cook until golden.

BANANA-SPICE PANCAKES

Whisk 1½ cups **flour,** 3 tablespoons **sugar,** 1 teaspoon **baking powder** and ½ teaspoon each **baking soda** and **salt.** Whisk ¾ cup **sour cream,** ¾ cup **milk,** ½ stick melted **butter,** 2 **eggs,** a dash of **cinnamon** and a little **vanilla,** then whisk into the flour mixture. Cook by ¼ cupfuls in a hot buttered skillet until bubbly, then top with sliced **bananas,** flip and cook until golden.

RED VELVET PANCAKES

Whisk 1 cup **flour,** ½ cup **cocoa powder,** ½ cup **confectioners' sugar,** 1 teaspoon **baking powder** and ½ teaspoon each **baking soda** and **salt.** Whisk 1¼ cups **buttermilk,** 2 **eggs** and a little **vanilla,** then whisk into the flour mixture. Add **red food coloring.** Cook by ¼ cupfuls in a hot buttered skillet until bubbly; flip and cook until golden.

BOURBON-BACON PANCAKES

Whisk 1¼ cups **all-purpose flour,** ¼ cup **rye flour,** 3 tablespoons **sugar,** 1 teaspoon **baking powder** and ½ teaspoon each **baking soda** and **salt.** Whisk 1¼ cups **buttermilk,** ½ stick melted **butter,** 2 **eggs,** 1 tablespoon **bourbon** and a little **vanilla,** then whisk into the flour mixture. Cook by ¼ cupfuls in a hot buttered skillet until bubbly, then flip and cook until golden. Heat ½ cup **maple syrup** with 1 tablespoon bourbon and some crumbled cooked **bacon;** drizzle on the pancakes.

BLUEBERRY PANCAKES

Whisk 1½ cups **flour** with 3 tablespoons **sugar,** 1 tablespoon **baking powder** and ½ teaspoon **salt.** Whisk 1¼ cups **milk,** ½ stick melted **butter,** 2 **eggs** and a little **vanilla,** then whisk into the flour mixture. Cook by ¼ cupfuls in a hot buttered skillet until bubbly, then sprinkle with **blueberries,** flip and cook until golden. Top with more blueberries.

TIP

It's fine if a few lumps remain in pancake batter. Overmixing can make the cakes tough.

LEMON-BERRY PANCAKES

Whisk 1½ cups **flour** with 3 tablespoons **sugar,** 1 tablespoon **baking powder** and ½ teaspoon **salt.** Whisk ½ cup **milk,** 1 cup **cottage cheese,** ½ stick melted **butter,** 2 **eggs,** 2 teaspoons grated **lemon zest,** and a little **vanilla,** then whisk into the flour mixture. Cook by ¼ cupfuls in a hot buttered skillet until bubbly, then flip and cook until golden. Top with sliced **strawberries** and **honey.**

MINI LEMON PANCAKES

Whisk 1½ cups **flour** with 3 tablespoons **sugar,** 1 teaspoon **baking powder** and ½ teaspoon each **baking soda** and **salt.** Whisk ¾ cup **sour cream,** ⅔ cup **milk,** 2 **eggs,** the zest and juice of 1 **lemon** and a little **vanilla,** then whisk into the flour mixture. Cook mini cakes by 2 tablespoonfuls in a hot buttered skillet until bubbly, then flip and cook until golden. Serve with **lemon curd** and **whipped cream.**

BERRY-TOPPED PANCAKES Toss 3 cups **mixed berries** with 2 tablespoons **sugar** and 1 tablespoon **lemon juice;** set aside. Meanwhile, whisk 1½ cups **flour,** 3 tablespoons **sugar,** 1 tablespoon **baking powder** and ½ teaspoon **salt.** Whisk 1¼ cups **milk,** ½ stick melted **butter,** 2 **eggs** and a little **vanilla,** then whisk into the flour mixture. Cook by ¼ cupfuls in a hot buttered skillet until bubbly, then flip and cook until golden. Top the pancakes with the berries and juices.

COCOA-BANANA PANCAKES

Whisk 1 cup plus 3 tablespoons **flour,** ⅓ cup **cocoa powder,** ⅔ cup **sugar,** 1 tablespoon **baking powder** and ½ teaspoon **salt.** Whisk 1¼ cups **milk,** ½ stick melted **butter,** 2 **eggs** and a little **vanilla,** then whisk into the flour mixture. Stir in 2 mashed **bananas** and ½ cup **mini chocolate chips.** Cook by ¼ cupfuls in a hot buttered skillet until bubbly; flip and cook until golden.

PEACH CORN CAKES

Whisk ¾ cup **flour,** ¾ cup **cornmeal,** 3 tablespoons **sugar,** 1 teaspoon **baking powder** and ½ teaspoon each **baking soda** and **salt.** Whisk 1¼ cups **buttermilk,** 2 **eggs** and a little **vanilla,** then whisk into the flour mixture. Stir 1 cup chopped **peaches** into the batter. Cook by ¼ cupfuls in a hot buttered skillet until bubbly, then flip and cook until golden. Top with more chopped peaches warmed in **maple syrup.**

TIP

Avoid pressing pancakes as they cook: They'll turn out dense, not fluffy.

BUTTERMILK PANCAKES

Whisk 1½ cups **flour** with 3 tablespoons **sugar,** 1 teaspoon **baking powder** and ½ teaspoon each **baking soda** and **salt.** Whisk 1¼ cups **buttermilk,** ½ stick melted **butter,** 2 **eggs** and a little **vanilla,** then whisk into the flour mixture. Cook by ¼ cupfuls in a hot buttered skillet until bubbly, then flip and cook until golden.

RHUBARB PANCAKES

Simmer 1 cup chopped **rhubarb** with ½ cup **sugar** until soft. Cool, then drain; reserve the syrup. Whisk 1½ cups **flour,** 3 tablespoons sugar, 1 teaspoon **baking powder** and ½ teaspoon each **baking soda** and **salt.** Whisk 1¼ cups **buttermilk,** ½ stick melted **butter,** 2 **eggs** and a little **vanilla,** then whisk into the flour mixture. Stir in half of the rhubarb. Cook by ¼ cupfuls in a hot buttered skillet until bubbly, then flip and cook until golden. Top with **strawberries** and the remaining rhubarb and syrup.

RUM-RAISIN PANCAKE SUNDAES Whisk 1½ cups **flour,** 3 tablespoons **sugar,** 1 teaspoon **baking powder** and ½ teaspoon each **baking soda** and **salt.** Whisk 1¼ cups **buttermilk,** ½ stick melted **butter,** 2 **eggs** and a little **vanilla,** then whisk into the flour mixture; stir in ⅓ cup plumped **raisins.** Cook by ¼ cupfuls in a hot buttered skillet until bubbly, then flip and cook until golden. Heat ¼ cup **maple syrup** with 1 tablespoon **rum** and ¼ cup raisins. Top the pancakes with **ice cream** and the rum-raisin syrup.

PANCAKES WITH STRAWBERRY SAUCE Mix 1½ cups sliced **strawberries** and 2 tablespoons each **strawberry jam** and warm water. Whisk 1½ cups **flour,** 3 tablespoons **sugar,** 1 tablespoon **baking powder** and ½ teaspoon **salt.** Whisk 1¼ cups **milk,** ½ stick melted **butter,** 2 **eggs** and a little **vanilla,** then whisk into the flour mixture. Cook by ¼ cupfuls in a hot buttered skillet until bubbly, then flip and cook until golden. Top with the strawberry sauce.

OAT PANCAKES

Whisk ¾ cup **flour,** ½ cup ground **oats,** ¼ cup **wheat germ,** 3 tablespoons **sugar,** 1 tablespoon **baking powder** and ½ teaspoon **salt.** Whisk 1¼ cups **milk,** ½ stick melted **butter,** 2 **eggs** and a little **vanilla,** then whisk into the flour mixture until just combined. Cook by ¼ cupfuls in a hot buttered skillet until bubbly, then flip and cook until golden.

CHOCOLATE-CHIP PANCAKES

Whisk 1½ cups **flour,** 3 tablespoons **sugar,** 1 tablespoon **baking powder** and ½ teaspoon **salt.** Whisk 1¼ cups **milk,** ½ stick melted **butter,** 2 **eggs** and a little **vanilla,** then whisk into the flour mixture. Cook by ¼ cupfuls in a hot buttered skillet until bubbly. Sprinkle with **chocolate chips;** flip and cook until golden.

CLASSIC CORN CAKES

Whisk 1 cup **cornmeal,** ½ cup **flour,** 3 tablespoons **sugar,** 1 tablespoon **baking powder** and ½ teaspoon **salt.** Whisk 1¼ cups **milk,** ½ stick melted **butter,** 2 **eggs** and a little **vanilla,** then whisk into the flour mixture. Cook by ¼ cupfuls in a hot buttered skillet until bubbly, then flip and cook until golden. Top with **honey.**

BACON-APPLE PANCAKES

Whisk 1½ cups **flour,** 3 tablespoons **sugar,** 1 tablespoon **baking powder** and ½ teaspoon **salt.** Whisk 1¼ cups **milk,** ½ stick melted **butter,** 2 **eggs** and a little **vanilla,** then whisk into the flour mixture. Stir ¼ cup crumbled cooked **bacon** and ½ grated **apple** into the batter. Cook by ¼ cupfuls in a hot buttered skillet until bubbly, then flip and cook until golden.

YOGURT PANCAKES

Whisk 1½ cups **flour,** 3 tablespoons **sugar,** 1 teaspoon **baking powder** and ½ teaspoon each **baking soda** and **salt.** Whisk 1¼ cups **yogurt,** ½ stick melted **butter,** 2 **eggs** and a little **vanilla,** then whisk into the flour mixture. Cook by ¼ cupfuls in a hot buttered skillet until bubbly, then flip and cook until golden.

BLUE CORN CAKES

Whisk 1 cup **blue cornmeal,** ½ cup **flour,** 3 tablespoons **sugar,** 1 tablespoon **baking powder** and ½ teaspoon **salt.** Whisk 1¼ cups **milk,** ½ stick melted **butter,** 2 **eggs** and a little **vanilla,** then whisk into the flour mixture. Cook by ¼ cupfuls in a hot buttered skillet until bubbly, then flip and cook until golden.

BLINTZES Make the crêpes: Mix 3 **eggs,** 1¾ cups **milk,** 1 cup **flour,** 5 tablespoons melted **butter** and a pinch of **salt** in a blender. Pour a thin film of batter into a small hot buttered nonstick pan; cook until set, then flip and cook 30 more seconds. Repeat. Make the filling: Mix 1½ pounds **farmer cheese,** 2 eggs, 3 tablespoons **confectioners' sugar** and some **lemon zest** and **cinnamon.** Spoon the filling onto the crêpes and fold each into a packet. Cook in a hot buttered skillet until crisp; top with **jam.**

BASIC CRÊPES WITH BERRIES

Mix 3 **eggs,** 1¾ cups **milk,** 1 cup **flour,** 5 tablespoons melted **butter** and a pinch of **salt** in a blender. Pour a thin film of batter into a small hot buttered nonstick pan; cook until set, then flip and cook 30 more seconds. Repeat. Top with berries.

CRÊPES SUZETTE

Mix 3 **eggs,** 1¾ cups **milk,** 1 cup **flour,** 5 tablespoons melted **butter** and a pinch of **salt** in a blender. Pour a thin film of batter into a small hot buttered nonstick pan; cook until set, then flip and cook 30 more seconds. For the sauce, melt 1 stick butter in a skillet. Stir in 6 tablespoons **orange liqueur** and tilt to ignite. When the flame dies, add the crêpes, 1 tablespoon **sugar** and 1 strip each **orange peel** and **lemon peel.** Warm through.

SWEDISH PANCAKES

Mix 3 **eggs,** 2 cups **milk,** 1½ cups **flour,** 6 tablespoons melted **butter,** 1 tablespoon **sugar** and a pinch of **salt** in a blender. Pour a thin film of batter into a small hot buttered nonstick pan; cook until set, then flip and cook 30 more seconds. Repeat. Serve with **lingonberry jam.**

SOUR CREAM SILVER DOLLARS

Whisk 1½ cups **flour,** 3 tablespoons **sugar** and ½ teaspoon each **baking soda** and **salt.** Whisk ¾ cup **sour cream,** ¼ cup **milk,** 2 **eggs** and a little **vanilla,** then whisk into the flour mixture. Cook by tablespoonfuls in a hot buttered skillet until bubbly, then flip and cook until golden.

SHORTCUT MUESLI PANCAKES

Prepare a boxed **pancake mix,** substituting ½ cup finely ground **muesli** for ½ cup of the mix. Add 2 extra tablespoons **milk** or water. Cook as directed. Top with **yogurt.**

SHORTCUT APPLE PANCAKES

Prepare a boxed **pancake mix.** Add ¼ cup **applesauce** and ¼ teaspoon **cinnamon** to 2 cups batter and cook as directed.

SHORTCUT CRANBERRY PANCAKES

Prepare a boxed **pancake mix.** Add ¼ cup **sugar,** 1 teaspoon grated **orange zest** and ½ cup chopped fresh **cranberries** to 2 cups batter; cook as directed. Cook ¾ cup cranberries in a saucepan with 1 cup **maple syrup.** Spoon over the pancakes.

DUTCH BABY PANCAKE

Mix 4 **eggs,** 1 cup **milk,** ⅔ cup **flour,** ½ stick melted **butter,** 3 tablespoons **sugar** and a little **vanilla** in a blender. Melt some butter in a cast-iron skillet. Add 1 sliced **pear,** then the batter; bake at 375°, 35 minutes. Dust with **confectioners' sugar.**

PISTACHIO WAFFLES
Whisk 1¾ cups **flour**, 4 teaspoons **baking powder**, 2 tablespoons **sugar**
and 1 teaspoon **salt.** Whisk in 2 **eggs,** 1½ cups **milk,** 6 tablespoons melted **shortening** and
4 tablespoons melted **butter;** stir in ⅓ cup chopped **pistachios** and 2 tablespoons **orange
zest.** Cook in a waffle iron until crisp. Top with **honey,** pistachios and orange zest.

CLASSIC WAFFLES Whisk 2 cups **flour,** 4 teaspoons **baking powder,** 2 tablespoons **sugar** and 1 teaspoon **salt.** Whisk in 2 **eggs,** 1½ cups **milk,** 5 tablespoons melted **shortening** and 4 tablespoons melted **butter.** Cook in a waffle iron until crisp.

SPICED WAFFLES

Whisk 2 cups **flour,** 4 teaspoons **baking powder,** ¼ cup **sugar,** ¾ teaspoon **pumpkin-pie spice** and 1 teaspoon **salt.** Whisk in 2 **eggs,** 1½ cups **milk,** 5 tablespoons melted **shortening** and 4 tablespoons melted **butter.** Cook in a waffle iron until crisp.

CHICKEN AND WAFFLES

Whisk 2 cups **flour,** 4 teaspoons **baking powder,** 2 tablespoons **sugar** and 1 teaspoon **salt.** Whisk in 2 **eggs,** 1½ cups **milk,** 5 tablespoons melted **shortening** and 4 tablespoons melted **butter.** Cook in a waffle iron until crisp. Top with butter, **maple syrup, fried chicken** and **hot sauce.**

ALMOND WAFFLES

Whisk 1¾ cups **flour,** 4 teaspoons **baking powder,** 2 tablespoons **sugar** and 1 teaspoon **salt.** Whisk in 2 **eggs,** 1½ cups **milk,** 6 tablespoons melted **shortening,** 4 tablespoons melted **butter** and a little **vanilla;** stir in ½ cup sliced **almonds.** Cook in a waffle iron until crisp.

TIP

Chop fruit and nuts into extra-small pieces before you add them to the batter.

MORNING GLORY WAFFLES

Whisk 1¾ cups **flour,** 4 teaspoons **baking powder,** 2 tablespoons **sugar,** 1 teaspoon **salt** and a pinch of **cinnamon.** Whisk in 2 **eggs,** 1½ cups **milk,** 6 tablespoons melted **shortening** and 4 tablespoons melted **butter.** Add ¼ cup each shredded **carrot** and **apple** and a sprinkle each of **currants,** chopped **walnuts** and **coconut.** Cook in a waffle iron until crisp.

WAFFLE FRENCH TOAST

Whisk 4 **eggs** with 2 cups **milk.** Soak thick slices of **white bread** in the mixture, 5 minutes, then cook in a waffle iron until crisp.

HAM AND SWISS WAFFLES

Whisk 1½ cups **flour** with 4 teaspoons **baking powder,** 2 tablespoons **sugar** and 1 teaspoon **salt.** Whisk in 2 **eggs,** 1½ cups **milk,** 6 tablespoons melted **shortening** and 4 tablespoons melted **butter.** Mix in ½ cup each diced **ham** and grated **gruyère;** season with **pepper.** Cook in a waffle iron until crisp.

WILD RICE WAFFLES

Whisk 1 cup **all-purpose flour**, ¾ cup **whole-wheat flour**, 4 teaspoons **baking powder**, 2 tablespoons **sugar** and 1 teaspoon **salt**. Whisk in 2 **eggs**, 1½ cups **milk**, 5 tablespoons melted **shortening** and 4 tablespoons melted **butter**; stir in ½ cup cooked **wild rice**. Cook in a waffle iron until crisp.

BELGIAN WAFFLES

Dissolve 1 packet **yeast** in 3 cups warm **milk**. Whisk in 2 sticks melted **butter**, ½ cup **sugar**, 3 **egg yolks**, 2 teaspoons **vanilla**, 1 teaspoon **salt** and 4 cups **flour**. Cover and let rise 1½ hours. Stir the batter. Beat 3 **egg whites** until stiff, then fold into the batter. Cook in a waffle iron until crisp.

WAFFLES WITH FIGS

Dissolve 1 packet **yeast** in 3 cups warm **milk**. Whisk in 2 sticks melted **butter**, ½ cup **sugar**, 3 **egg yolks**, 2 teaspoons **vanilla**, 1 teaspoon **salt** and 4 cups **flour**. Cover and let rise 1½ hours. Stir the batter. Beat 3 **egg whites** until stiff, then fold into the batter. Cook in a waffle iron until crisp. Top the waffles with **yogurt, fresh figs** and **honey.**

GERMAN CHOCOLATE WAFFLES

Dissolve 1 packet **yeast** in 3 cups warm **milk**. Whisk in 2 sticks melted **butter**, 1 cup **sugar**, 3 **egg yolks**, 2 teaspoons **vanilla**, 1 teaspoon **salt** and 3⅓ cups **flour**; add ⅔ cup **cocoa powder** and ¼ cup melted **coconut oil**. Cover and let rise 1½ hours. Stir the batter. Beat 3 **egg whites** until stiff, then fold into the batter. Cook in a waffle iron until crisp.

APRICOT-HONEY WAFFLES

Simmer 1 cup chopped **dried apricots** with 1 tablespoon **apricot jam**, ½ cup water and 1 teaspoon **honey** in a saucepan until plump. Whisk 2 cups **flour**, 4 teaspoons **baking powder**, 2 tablespoons **sugar** and 1 teaspoon **salt**. Whisk in 2 **eggs**, 1½ cups **milk**, 5 tablespoons melted **shortening** and 4 tablespoons melted **butter**. Cook in a waffle iron until crisp. Top with the apricots.

QUICK LEMON-POPPY WAFFLES

Prepare a boxed **waffle mix.** Add 2 tablespoons **sugar** and 2 teaspoons each grated **lemon zest, lemon juice** and **poppy seeds** to 2 cups batter; cook in a waffle iron until crisp.

BACON-PECAN WAFFLES Make the candied bacon: Sprinkle 12 strips **bacon** with **brown sugar** and bake at 400° until crisp; let cool, then chop. Make the waffles: Whisk 1¾ cups **flour**, 4 teaspoons **baking powder**, 2 tablespoons **granulated sugar** and 1 teaspoon **salt**. Whisk in 2 **eggs**, 1½ cups **milk**, 6 tablespoons melted **shortening** and 4 tablespoons melted **butter**; stir in 1 cup of the candied bacon and ½ cup chopped **pecans**. Cook in a waffle iron until crisp. Top with more candied bacon and nuts.

CLASSIC FRENCH TOAST Whisk 4 **eggs,** 1½ cups **milk,** ½ teaspoon **nutmeg,** 1 teaspoon **vanilla,** 1 teaspoon **sugar** and a pinch of **salt** in a bowl. Dip 6 thick slices **white bread** in the egg mixture and cook in a hot buttered skillet until golden. Transfer to a baking sheet and bake at 350° until puffed, 8 to 10 minutes. Top with **butter** and **maple syrup.**

LEMON FRENCH TOAST

Whisk 4 **eggs,** 1½ cups **milk,** ½ teaspoon **ground ginger,** 1 teaspoon **vanilla,** 1 teaspoon **sugar** and a pinch of **salt** in a bowl. Sandwich sliced **brioche** with **lemon curd** and **blueberries.** Press together; dip in the egg mixture. Cook in a hot buttered skillet until golden, then transfer to a baking sheet and bake at 350° until puffed, 8 to 10 minutes. Top with **confectioners' sugar.**

STICKY-BUN FRENCH TOAST

Whisk 4 **eggs,** 1½ cups **milk,** 1 teaspoon **vanilla,** 1 teaspoon **sugar** and a pinch of **salt** in a bowl. Mix ½ cup each chopped **dried figs** and **dried apricots,** ½ cup chopped **pecans,** 2 tablespoons **sugar** and 1 teaspoon **cinnamon.** Dip 8 slices **white bread** in the egg mixture, then sandwich the fruit-nut mixture between the slices. Cook in a hot buttered skillet until golden, then transfer to a baking sheet and bake at 350° until puffed, 8 to 10 minutes.

TIP

Avoid thin sandwich bread for French toast. Instead, cut 1-inch-thick slices from a whole loaf (stale works great).

CHOCOLATE FRENCH TOAST

Whisk 4 **eggs,** 1½ cups **milk,** ½ teaspoon **nutmeg,** 1 teaspoon **vanilla,** 1 teaspoon **sugar** and a pinch of **salt.** Dip 12 thick **baguette slices** in the egg mixture; cook in a hot buttered skillet until golden, then transfer to a baking sheet and bake at 350° until puffed, 8 to 10 minutes. Meanwhile, melt 3 ounces chopped **bittersweet chocolate** in a saucepan with ⅓ cup **maple syrup,** stirring. Drizzle on the French toast. Top with **confectioners' sugar.**

OATMEAL FRENCH TOAST

Whisk 4 **eggs,** 1½ cups **milk,** ½ teaspoon **cinnamon,** 1 teaspoon each **vanilla** and **sugar** and a pinch of **salt** in a bowl. Spread some **instant oatmeal** on a plate. Soak 8 slices **walnut-raisin bread** in the egg mixture, then press in the oatmeal to coat on both sides. Cook in a hot buttered skillet until golden, then transfer to a baking sheet and bake at 350° until puffed, 8 to 10 minutes. Drizzle with **honey.**

Eggs & Bacon

FRIED EGGS

Heat 2 teaspoons **bacon drippings, butter or oil.** Crack in 4 **eggs,** add **salt** and **pepper** and cook until the edges are opaque, 2 minutes. Cover and cook the yolks to desired firmness, 4 to 6 more minutes.

SCALLOPED EGGS

Place 4 to 6 **eggs** in a large saucepan, cover with cold water by 1 inch and bring to a simmer. Cover, remove from the heat and set aside, 8 to 10 minutes. Drain, then peel in a bowl of cold water. Slice and layer in a buttered baking dish with 2 sliced boiled **potatoes.** Season with **salt, pepper** and **nutmeg.** Whisk 6 tablespoons each **milk** and **sour cream** with 1 tablespoon **flour.** Pour over the eggs, top with **breadcrumbs** and bake at 350˚, 25 minutes.

STEAK AND EGGS

Mix ½ stick softened **butter** with a dash of **Worcestershire sauce.** Season 1 pound **flank steak** with **salt** and **pepper;** sear in plain butter. Crack 4 **eggs** into a hot skillet with 2 teaspoons butter. Add salt and pepper; cook until the edges are opaque, 2 minutes. Cover and cook the yolks to desired firmness, 4 to 6 more minutes. Slice the steak and top with the flavored butter and fried eggs.

SPANISH TORTILLA

Simmer 2½ pounds sliced **potatoes** and 1 sliced **onion** in 1½ cups **olive oil** until tender. Drain, then mix with 8 beaten **eggs.** Spread in a nonstick skillet with 2 tablespoons olive oil and cook 15 minutes. Flip and cook 5 more minutes.

POACHED EGGS

Bring a skillet of water with a splash of **white vinegar** to a simmer over medium-low heat. Crack 4 **eggs** into individual cups, slip into the water and poach until the whites set, 3 to 4 minutes. Remove with a slotted spoon.

HARD-BOILED EGGS

Place 4 **eggs** in a large saucepan, cover with cold water by 1 inch and bring to a simmer over medium-high heat. Cover, remove from the heat and set aside, 8 to 10 minutes. Drain, then peel in a bowl of cold water.

MEDIUM-BOILED EGGS

Place 4 **eggs** in a saucepan of boiling water, then cook over low heat, 7 to 8 minutes. Drain and peel in a bowl of cold water.

TIP

Don't actually boil your hard-boiled eggs; cover with cold water and bring to a simmer.

SCOTCH EGGS

Place 4 **eggs** in a saucepan of boiling water, then cook over low heat, 7 to 8 minutes; drain and peel in a bowl of cold water. Pat **bulk sausage** around each egg. Roll in **flour,** dip in beaten eggs, then roll in **panko.** Shallow-fry in **vegetable oil** until crisp.

BASIC DEVILED EGGS

Halve 4 peeled hard-boiled **eggs** lengthwise and scoop out the yolks. Mash the yolks with 1 tablespoon **sweet pickle relish,** 3 tablespoons **mayonnaise,** 1 teaspoon **mustard,** and a pinch each of **cayenne pepper, salt** and **pepper.** Scoop into the whites.

PICKLED EGGS

Place 4 to 6 peeled hard-boiled **eggs** in a large jar, then fill the jar with **pickled beet juice.** Cover and refrigerate up to 1 week.

EGG-MUSHROOM SALAD

Chop 4 peeled hard-boiled **eggs.** Fry 2 cups sliced **mushrooms** and 1 cup chopped **onion** in **olive oil.** Mix with the eggs, 3 tablespoons **sour cream, salt, pepper** and chopped **parsley.**

SOFT-BOILED EGGS
Place 4 **eggs** in a saucepan of boiling water, then cook over low heat, 4 to 5 minutes; drain. Slice off the tops and season the eggs with **salt** and **pepper.** Serve with strips of **buttered toast.**

TEA EGGS

Place 4 **eggs** in a saucepan, cover with cold water by 1 inch and bring to a simmer over medium-high heat. Cover, remove from the heat and set aside, 8 to 10 minutes; drain. Crack the shells but don't peel. Simmer in a saucepan with ½ cup **soy sauce,** 3 cups water, 4 **star anise pods,** 3 **black tea bags** and a strip of **orange zest,** 1 hour. Drain and peel.

EGGS BENEDICT

Make hollandaise: Puree 1 **egg yolk** with ¼ cup **mayonnaise,** 1 teaspoon **lemon juice,** and **cayenne pepper** and **salt** to taste. Pulse in 2 tablespoons melted **butter.** Place the sauce in a bowl set over a pan of simmering water; whisk until thick. Poach the eggs: Bring a skillet of water with a splash of **white vinegar** to a simmer over medium-low heat. Crack 4 **eggs** into individual cups, slip into the water and poach 3 to 4 minutes. Top **English muffins** with fried **Canadian bacon,** the eggs and hollandaise.

TIP

If you drop an egg, sprinkle it with salt and wait 10 minutes—it'll be much easier to clean up.

MATZO BREI

Cook 1 sliced **onion** in a nonstick skillet with 6 tablespoons **butter.** Crumble 2 **matzos** in a colander and rinse with water. Beat 4 **eggs** with the matzo, add to the skillet and scramble until set; season with **salt** and **pepper.**

MIGAS

Sauté 4 thinly sliced **corn tortillas** and ½ cup each sliced **onion** and roasted **poblano peppers** in a skillet with **vegetable oil,** 5 minutes. Add 5 beaten **eggs** and stir until just set. Top with grated **cheddar, salsa** and **cilantro.**

SKILLET SOUFFLÉ

Whisk 2 **egg yolks** with ¼ cup grated **cheddar;** add some chopped **fresh herbs.** Beat 2 **egg whites** with a pinch of **salt** until soft peaks form; fold into the yolks. Melt **butter** in a small ovenproof skillet over medium heat. Add the egg mixture and cook until puffed and golden. Transfer the skillet to a 375° oven and bake 5 minutes.

MEXICAN EGGS BENEDICT Make hollandaise: Puree 1 **egg yolk** with ¼ cup **mayonnaise,** 1 teaspoon **lemon juice,** and **cayenne pepper** and **salt** to taste. Pulse in 2 tablespoons melted **butter.** Whisk the sauce in a bowl set over a pan of simmering water until thick, then stir in chopped **cilantro.** Bring a skillet of water with a splash of **white vinegar** to a simmer over medium-low heat. Crack 4 **eggs** into individual cups, slip into the water and poach 3 to 4 minutes. Top **corn cakes** with **serrano ham,** the eggs and hollandaise.

BASIC OMELET

Beat 2 **eggs** with **salt** and **pepper.** Place a small nonstick skillet over medium-high heat; add ½ tablespoon **butter** and swirl. Add the eggs and stir briefly with a rubber spatula, then let the bottom set but not brown. Fold like a letter.

SPINACH-CHEESE OMELET

Beat 2 **eggs** with **salt** and **pepper.** Place a small nonstick skillet over medium-high heat; add ½ tablespoon **butter** and swirl. Add the eggs and stir briefly with a rubber spatula, then let the bottom set but not brown. Add 3 tablespoons cooked **spinach** and some **goat cheese;** fold like a letter.

SWEET OMELET

Beat 2 **eggs** with **salt.** Place a small nonstick skillet over medium-high heat; add ½ tablespoon **butter** and swirl. Add the eggs and stir briefly with a rubber spatula, then let the bottom set but not brown. Add 1 tablespoon **jam;** fold like a letter. Top with **confectioners' sugar.**

TIP

Have all your omelet fillings ready before you start: It'll cook quickly!

ASPARAGUS OMELET

Beat 2 **eggs** with **salt** and **pepper.** Place a small nonstick skillet over medium-high heat; add ½ tablespoon **butter** and swirl. Add the eggs and stir briefly with a rubber spatula, then let the bottom set but not brown. Add 3 tablespoons chopped cooked **asparagus** and 2 tablespoons shredded **gouda.** Fold like a letter.

BERRY-RICOTTA OMELET

Beat 2 **eggs** with **salt.** Place a small nonstick skillet over medium-high heat; add ½ tablespoon **butter** and swirl. Add the eggs; stir, then let the bottom set but not brown. Add sliced **strawberries;** fold like a letter. Top with **ricotta.**

FAMILY OMELET

Beat 8 **eggs** with 2 tablespoons **milk,** and **salt** and **pepper.** Place a large nonstick skillet over medium-high heat; add 2 tablespoons **butter** and swirl. Add the eggs; stir, then let the bottom set but not brown. Add ½ cup each diced **ham** and **gruyère;** fold like a letter.

SPRING FRITTATA Soak ½ cup stale **bread cubes** in ½ cup **milk;** mix with 8 beaten **eggs.** Add ¾ cup **ricotta,** 1 teaspoon chopped **thyme,** and **salt** and **pepper.** Sauté 1 cup shredded **zucchini** in an ovenproof nonstick skillet with **olive oil.** Add the egg mixture and cook until the bottom sets, then transfer to a 325° oven and bake 25 minutes.

BASIC SCRAMBLE

Whisk 4 **eggs** in a bowl with 1 tablespoon **milk or heavy cream;** season with **salt** and **pepper.** Melt 2 tablespoons **butter** in a small nonstick skillet over medium-high heat; add the eggs and stir until just set.

HEALTHY SCRAMBLE

Cook and crumble 1 slice **turkey bacon.** Brown ¼ cup **corn** in the drippings; add 2 tablespoons **salsa verde.** Whisk 4 **egg whites** in a bowl with **salt** and **pepper.** Heat ½ tablespoon **olive oil** in a small nonstick skillet over medium-high heat. Add the egg whites and stir until loosely set. Add the bacon and corn mixture; continue stirring until the eggs are just set.

CAVIAR SCRAMBLE

Melt 2 tablespoons **butter** in a bowl set over a saucepan of simmering water. Add 4 beaten **eggs** and stir until just set, 8 to 10 minutes. Add 1 to 2 tablespoons **crème fraîche.** Serve in clean eggshells; top with **caviar.**

TIP

Remove scrambled eggs from the heat before they're done—the heat of the skillet will finish cooking them.

SPICY SCRAMBLE

Whisk 4 **eggs** in a bowl with 1 tablespoon **milk or heavy cream;** season with **salt** and **pepper.** Melt 2 tablespoons **butter** in a nonstick skillet over medium-high heat; add the eggs and stir until loosely set. Add ⅔ cup shredded **cheddar,** and diced **jalapeño** to taste; continue stirring until the eggs are just set.

FRENCH SCRAMBLE

Melt 2 tablespoons **butter** in a bowl set over a saucepan of simmering water. Add 4 beaten **eggs** and stir with a rubber spatula until just set, 8 to 10 minutes. Add 1 to 2 tablespoons **crème fraîche** and sprinkle with chopped **chives.**

CREAMY SCRAMBLE

Heat 2 tablespoons butter in a nonstick skillet over medium-high heat. Add 4 beaten **eggs,** 4 tablespoons **cream cheese,** some chopped **parsley or dill,** and **salt** and **pepper.** Whisk until just set.

SCRAMBLED EGGS WITH SMOKED SALMON

Heat 2 tablespoons **butter** in a nonstick skillet over medium-high heat. Add 4 beaten **eggs,** 4 tablespoons **cream cheese,** 1 tablespoon chopped **chives,** and **salt** and **pepper.** Whisk until just set. Serve on toasted **whole-grain bread** with **smoked salmon.**

PASTRAMI SCRAMBLE

Whisk 4 **eggs** in a bowl with
1 tablespoon **milk or heavy cream;**
season with **salt** and **pepper.** Melt
2 tablespoons **butter** in a small nonstick
skillet over medium-high heat; add the
eggs and 4 ounces sliced **pastrami** and
stir until just set. Top with shredded
smoked gouda and **scallions.**

FRIED EGGWICH

Heat ½ teaspoon **bacon drippings,
butter or oil** in a small skillet. Add
1 **egg,** season with **salt** and **pepper**
and cook until the edges are opaque,
2 minutes. Cover and cook 4 to 6 more
minutes. Fry 2 slices **Canadian bacon.**
Serve the egg and bacon on a toasted
English muffin with sliced **tomato**
and **jack cheese.**

FRY-UP

Fry 2 **sausage links,** 2 **sausage patties**
and 4 **bacon** slices in a skillet. Add 1 sliced
tomato, crack in 4 **eggs,** and season with
salt and **pepper.** Cover and cook until the
eggs are set.

QUICK EGG MUFFIN

Beat 1 **egg** with **salt** and **pepper** in
a microwave-safe mug with a fork;
microwave 45 seconds. Serve on an
English muffin with melted **cheddar.**

HUEVOS RANCHEROS

Sauté 1 each diced **jalapeño** and
garlic clove in a skillet with
vegetable oil and a pinch of **ground
cumin.** Add 1 can **crushed tomatoes**
and 1 tablespoon chopped **chipotles in
adobo sauce;** simmer until thick. Add
4 **eggs** and poach until set. Serve with
tortillas and **queso fresco.**

EGGS IN PURGATORY

Fill a small baking dish halfway with hot
marinara sauce. Crack in 6 **eggs** and
bake at 350° until the whites are firm,
10 to 12 minutes. Top with **parmesan.**

NEST EGG WITH MANCHEGO

Cut a round out of a slice of **bread;**
flatten and press back in the hole.
Toast the bread in an ovenproof skillet
with **butter.** Crack an **egg** into the
hole, sprinkle with ½ cup grated
manchego and bake at 375° until set,
2 minutes. Top with **smoked paprika**
and chopped **parsley.**

MOROCCAN EGGS

Toast 1 cup **chickpeas** and some **ground
cumin** and **paprika** in an ovenproof
skillet with **olive oil.** Fill the skillet
halfway with hot **marinara sauce.** Crack
in 6 **eggs** and bake at 350° until the
whites are firm, 10 to 12 minutes.

HASH-BROWN EGGS Fry 1 cup each chopped **onion** and grated **potato** in a cast-iron
skillet with **butter** until crisp. Add ½ cup grated **cheddar** and crack in 2 **eggs;** season with
salt and **pepper.** Bake at 425° until set; top with **fresh salsa.**

NEST EGG
Cut a round out of a slice of **bread;** toast the bread in a
nonstick skillet with **butter.** Crack an **egg** into the hole,
add **salt** and **pepper,** cover and cook until the white sets.

COFFEE-GLAZED BACON WITH FRIED EGGS

Warm ¼ cup **maple syrup,** 3 tablespoons **instant coffee** and a pinch of **pepper** in a saucepan. Remove from the heat; add 8 slices thick **bacon.** Lay on a rack set on a rimmed baking sheet and drizzle with some of the coffee syrup. Bake 20 minutes at 325˚; flip, drizzle with the rest of the syrup and bake 15 more minutes. Serve with fried **eggs** and **toast.**

SWEET BACON

Press both sides of **bacon** slices in **brown sugar;** lay on a rack set on a rimmed baking sheet. Bake at 375°, flipping once, 20 minutes.

SPICY-SWEET BACON

Sprinkle both sides of **bacon** slices with **ancho chile powder,** then press in **brown sugar;** lay on a wire rack set on a rimmed baking sheet. Bake at 375°, flipping once, 20 minutes.

MAPLE-PEPPER BACON

Position wire racks on 2 rimmed baking sheets. Lay 1 pound **bacon** in a single layer on the racks and bake at 375°, 7 minutes. Brush with **maple syrup** and continue baking until caramelized, about 25 minutes, flipping, brushing with syrup and seasoning with **pepper** every 5 minutes. Let cool on the racks 5 minutes.

BACON MUFFINS

Prepare **corn muffin mix** as directed, adding ¼ cup crumbled cooked **bacon** and 2 tablespoons chopped **chives.**

TIP

Start your bacon in a cold pan— the strips won't shrink and curl as much.

BACON GRITS

Simmer 2 cups each **milk** and water with 1 teaspoon **salt** in a saucepan over medium heat. Stir in 1 cup **grits;** simmer until tender, about 35 minutes. Stir in 2 tablespoons **butter** until melted, then stir in 1 cup each grated **cheddar** and crumbled cooked **bacon.** Top with chopped **chives.**

BACON OATMEAL

Stir 2 tablespoons each **maple syrup** and crumbled cooked **bacon** into 2 cups prepared **oatmeal.**

BACON BANANA BREAD

Stir ½ cup crumbled cooked **bacon** into your favorite **banana bread batter** before baking. Serve with **peanut butter.**

BACON POTATO PANCAKES

Cook 2 slices **bacon;** drain and crumble. Shred 2 peeled **russet potatoes;** squeeze dry. Mix with ¼ grated **onion,** the bacon, and **salt** and **pepper.** Cook potato pancakes in the drippings, 8 minutes per side.

BACON QUICHE Cook 6 ounces diced slab **bacon** in a skillet; drain. Cook 2 sliced **leeks** in 3 tablespoons drippings. Spread the leeks, ⅔ cup shredded **gruyère** and the bacon in a prebaked 9-inch **tart or pie crust.** Whisk 2 whole **eggs, 2 egg yolks,** 1 cup **cream,** and **salt** and **pepper;** pour over the cheese. Bake at 375°, 25 minutes.

Perfect BACON

Bring the bacon to room temperature. Lay the strips in a cold skillet, raise the heat to medium and cook, turning, until desired crispness, 5 to 10 minutes. Drain on paper towels. For large batches, lay the strips on a foil-lined baking sheet in a cold oven; set to 400° and bake, 15 to 20 minutes.

You can microwave bacon, but it won't be as crisp: Lay the strips on a plate lined with a double layer of paper towels. Cover with more paper towels and microwave 5 to 7 minutes.

Make Bacon Bits

Many commercial bacon bits are made from soy! To make the real deal, fry 8 slices bacon until extra crisp. Drain on paper towels, then finely chop and spread on a baking sheet. Bake at 350° for 5 minutes. Let cool on clean paper towels until most of the fat is absorbed.

Use the Fat...

Strain warm fat through a paper towel–lined sieve into a storage container; cover with a lid and refrigerate up to 1 week or freeze up to 2 months. Use it in place of oil or butter in sautés or savory baked goods.

...Or Lose It

Don't pour bacon fat down the drain; it may clog your pipes. To safely discard, line a mug or small bowl with foil, pour in the fat and let it solidify. Then just pull out the foil with the fat and discard.

Know Your Bacon

Canadian bacon

This is more like ham than bacon: It's smoked, fully cooked pork loin. Although Canadian bacon is ready to eat, it tastes best warmed before serving.

Pancetta

Sometimes called "Italian bacon," pancetta is salt-cured pork belly like American bacon, but it isn't smoked. It's rolled into spirals, then sliced or diced for cooking.

Slab bacon

This bacon is not presliced, so you can buy as much as you need from a butcher and cut it to any thickness. Remove the outer rind, or skin, before cutting.

Standard bacon

Bacon is made from pork belly. It's cured with salt and then usually cold-smoked, a process that infuses the meat with smoky flavor but doesn't fully cook it.

Main Dishes

Soup

SPICY TORTILLA

Puree 2 seeded, soaked dried **ancho chiles, 1 onion,**
2 **tomatoes** and 2 **garlic cloves;** fry in **olive oil.** Add
6 cups **chicken broth,** 4 torn **corn tortillas,** some shredded
cooked **chicken** and ½ cup **cilantro;** simmer until thick.
Add **salt;** top with crisp tortilla strips, crumbled **cotija
cheese,** sliced **avocado, cilantro** and **lime juice.**

BASIC CHICKEN

Finely chop 1 **onion,** 1 **celery stalk,** 2 **carrots** and
1 tablespoon **fresh thyme;** sauté in a pot with **butter** until
tender. Season with **salt** and **pepper.** Add 6 cups **chicken
broth;** simmer 20 minutes. Add 2 cups shredded cooked
chicken, 3 tablespoons each chopped **dill** and **parsley,**
and some **lemon juice.**

ITALIAN WEDDING

Finely chop 1 **onion,** 1 **celery stalk,** 2 **carrots** and
1 tablespoon **fresh thyme;** sauté in a pot with **butter.** Add
6 cups **chicken broth** and a **parmesan rind;** simmer
20 minutes. Add 1 pound frozen **mini meatballs** and
1 cup **orzo.** Stir in 3 cups torn **escarole** and simmer until
the orzo is tender.

MINESTRONE

Chop 3 **garlic cloves,** 1 **carrot,** 1 **onion,** 1 **celery stalk**
and ¼ head **cabbage;** sauté in **olive oil.** Add 1 can each
white beans and diced **tomatoes,** 4 cups **chicken broth**
and a **parmesan rind;** simmer 20 minutes. Add 1 cup **small
pasta** and simmer until tender. Add **salt** and **pepper.**

CHINESE DUMPLING

Puree 2 **garlic cloves** with a 2-inch piece peeled **ginger;** fry in **vegetable oil** with 1 bunch sliced **scallions.** Add 3 cups each **chicken broth** and water, 1 tablespoon each **soy sauce** and **sherry,** and a pinch of **sugar;** bring to a boil. Add some frozen **dumplings,** sliced **carrots** and **snow peas;** simmer until tender, 4 to 5 minutes. Drizzle with **sesame oil** and **Asian chile sauce.**

CHICKEN DUMPLING

Mix 1 beaten **egg,** 2 tablespoons **butter,** ½ cup **farina cereal** and ½ teaspoon **salt.** Drop small spoonfuls into simmering **chicken broth;** cook for 3 minutes after the dumplings float.

ESCAROLE AND WHITE BEAN

Cook 3 chopped **garlic cloves** and some **red pepper flakes** in **olive oil.** Add 3 cups **chicken broth,** 1 head chopped **escarole** and a **parmesan rind;** simmer 15 minutes. Add 1 can **white beans,** some grated **parmesan** and **salt;** warm through.

TIP

Use low-sodium broth for soup, then add salt to taste.

CLAM CHOWDER

Sauté 4 ounces chopped **bacon;** add 2 tablespoons **butter,** 2 sliced **leeks** and some **fresh thyme.** Add 2 cups each **clam juice** and water, 1½ cups **cream,** a **bay leaf** and 3 diced **potatoes;** season with **cayenne pepper.** Simmer until the potatoes are tender, adding 2 cups **clams** during the last 5 minutes.

PARSNIP-BACON

Sauté ½ sliced **onion** with some **fresh thyme** in **butter** until soft. Add **salt, pepper,** 2 pounds diced **parsnips** and 5 cups **chicken broth.** Simmer until tender, then puree. Top with crumbled cooked **bacon.**

ASIAN CHICKEN

Puree 2 **garlic cloves** with a 2-inch piece peeled **ginger;** fry in **vegetable oil** with 1 bunch sliced **scallions.** Add 3 cups each **chicken broth** and water, 1 tablespoon each **soy sauce** and **sherry,** and a pinch of **sugar;** boil. Add some shredded cooked **chicken,** sliced **carrots** and **snow peas.** Drizzle with **sesame oil.**

COCONUT CHICKEN Sauté 3 **garlic cloves,** 3 tablespoons grated **ginger,** ¼ cup chopped **lemongrass,** 1 teaspoon each **cumin** and **coriander,** and a minced **Thai chile** in **olive oil.** Add 1 sliced raw **chicken breast** and 1 sliced **onion;** cook 5 minutes. Add shredded **bok choy,** 4 cups water, 1 can **coconut milk, cilantro** and 2 tablespoons **fish sauce;** cook 8 minutes.

»

PEAS AND PESTO

Sauté 2 heads **garlic** (smashed and peeled) in **olive oil.** Add 8 cups **chicken broth** and a bundle of **fresh herbs;** simmer 35 minutes, then add 1 cup frozen **peas** and cook 5 more minutes. Season with **salt** and **pepper.** Stir in a spoonful of **pesto** and some grated **parmesan.**

RED LENTIL AND RICE

Cook 3 chopped **garlic cloves,** 1 each chopped **onion** and **carrot,** ½ tablespoon chopped **ginger** and a pinch of **cayenne pepper** in **olive oil.** Add 6 cups water, 1 can **coconut milk,** 1 cup **red lentils** and ½ cup **rice;** simmer 20 minutes. Top with some **lime juice, cilantro** and sliced **scallions.**

CREAM OF BROCCOLI

Sauté 3 cups each sliced **leeks** and cubed **potatoes** in **butter.** Add 1 sliced **garlic clove** and a pinch each of **salt, pepper, dried thyme** and **nutmeg;** cook 5 minutes. Add 5 cups **chicken broth;** boil until the potatoes are tender. Add 3 cups **broccoli** and simmer 5 minutes. Puree the soup, then reheat with 1 cup **cream.**

SPLIT PEA

Simmer ½ pound **split peas** with 1 each chopped **celery stalk, onion** and **carrot,** a **ham hock** and a bundle of **fresh herbs** in 5 cups water until tender. Remove the ham and bone; pull off the meat. Puree the soup; stir in the ham.

VEGETARIAN PEA

Simmer ½ pound **split peas** with 1 each chopped **celery stalk, onion** and **carrot,** and a bundle of **fresh herbs** in 5 cups water until tender. Puree half of the soup, then mix back in. Add 1 cup diced carrot; warm through. Top with **croutons.**

TOMATO-ALPHABET

Boil 3 cups **chicken broth,** 2 cups **tomato juice** and a pinch of dried **oregano.** Add ½ cup **alphabet pasta;** season with **salt** and **pepper.** Cook until the pasta is tender. Stir in some grated **parmesan.**

PAPPA AL POMODORO

Sauté 1 chopped **onion** in **olive oil** until tender; add 3 chopped **garlic cloves,** a pinch of **red pepper flakes,** 1 large can chopped **tomatoes,** 1 cup water and some **fresh basil.** Add 2 cups stale **bread cubes;** simmer 20 minutes.

PESTO-BEAN Sauté 5 sliced **garlic cloves** and a pinch of **red pepper flakes** in a large saucepan with **olive oil.** Add 2 cans **cannellini beans** and 1 cup water; simmer until thick, 8 minutes. Stir in 3 tablespoons **pesto** and 2 tablespoons grated **parmesan.** Add 3 cups **chicken broth** and 1 cup chopped **celery;** cook 15 minutes. Stir in ½ cup each chopped **olives** and **roasted red peppers;** warm through.

CHEDDAR-HORSERADISH

Sauté 2 each diced **carrots** and **leeks** in **butter**. Add some **salt**, **cayenne pepper**, 3 tablespoons **flour** and 2 tablespoons **mustard powder**; cook 2 minutes. Add 1 bottle **beer**, ¼ cup **horseradish**, 3 cups water and a dash of **Worcestershire sauce**; simmer until thick. Whisk in 2 cups **half-and-half** and 1½ cups **cheddar**.

PISTOU

Chop 3 **garlic cloves**, 1 **carrot**, 1 **onion**, 1 **celery stalk** and ¼ head **cabbage**; sauté in **olive oil** with 1 sliced **zucchini** and 2 cups diced **butternut squash**. Add 1 can each **white beans** and diced **tomatoes**, 4 cups **chicken broth** and a **parmesan rind**; simmer 20 minutes. Add 1 cup **small pasta** and simmer until tender. Add **salt** and **pepper**; swirl in some **pesto**.

SWEET POTATO

Sauté 2 chopped **onions**, 4 chopped **garlic cloves**, 3 peeled and cubed **sweet potatoes** and 1 teaspoon **coriander** in **olive oil**. Add 6 cups **chicken broth**; simmer until soft. Puree.

TIP

Freeze cheese rinds in a resealable plastic bag, then add to simmering soup for extra flavor.

WATERCRESS-POTATO

Sauté 3 cups each sliced **leeks** and cubed **potatoes** in **butter**. Add 1 sliced **garlic clove** and a pinch each of **salt, pepper, fresh thyme** and **nutmeg**; cook 5 minutes. Add 5 cups **chicken broth**; boil until the potatoes are tender. Add 2 bunches chopped **watercress** and simmer 3 minutes, then puree. Gently reheat, stirring in 1 cup **cream**.

WHITE BEAN–TORTELLINI

Chop 3 **garlic cloves**, 1 **carrot**, 1 **onion**, 1 **celery stalk** and ¼ head **cabbage**; sauté in **olive oil**. Add 1 can each **white beans** and diced **tomatoes**, 4 cups **chicken broth** and a **parmesan rind**; simmer 20 minutes. Add 1 cup **tortellini** and simmer until tender. Add **salt** and **pepper**.

CURRIED SWEET POTATO

Sauté 2 chopped **onions**, 4 chopped **garlic cloves**, 3 peeled and cubed **sweet potatoes**, 1 tablespoon **curry powder** and 1 teaspoon **coriander** in **butter**. Add 6 cups **chicken broth** and simmer until soft. Puree; top with **chutney**.

SAUSAGE-BEAN Cook 3 chopped **garlic cloves**, some **red pepper flakes** and 4 crumbled **sweet Italian sausages** in **olive oil**. Add 3 cups **chicken broth**, 1 head chopped **escarole** and a **parmesan rind**; simmer 15 minutes. Add 1 can **white beans, parmesan** and **salt**.

BLACK BEAN–HAM

Soak ½ pound **dried black beans** overnight; drain. Sauté 1 each chopped **celery stalk, onion** and **carrot,** and 2 smashed **garlic cloves** in **olive oil.** Add the beans, some **dried thyme,** a **bay leaf,** a **ham hock** and 5 cups water; simmer 40 minutes. Remove the bone; pull off the meat. Puree the soup and stir in the ham.

MEXICAN BEAN

Soak ½ pound **dried black beans** overnight; drain. Sauté 1 each chopped **celery stalk, onion** and **carrot,** and 2 smashed **garlic cloves** in **olive oil.** Add the beans, a **bay leaf,** 1 teaspoon each **chipotle chile powder** and **cumin,** a **ham hock** and 5 cups water; simmer 40 minutes. Remove the bone; pull off the meat. Puree half of the soup, then mix it back in. Stir in the ham and some **lime juice.**

CURRIED CAULIFLOWER

Cook 4 sliced **leeks** with 1 tablespoon **curry powder** in **butter.** Add 1 head chopped **cauliflower** and 1 **garlic clove;** cook 5 minutes. Season with **salt** and **pepper.** Add 5 cups **chicken broth;** boil until soft, then puree. Add 1 cup **cream** and warm through.

THAI SHRIMP

Sauté 3 sliced **garlic cloves,** 3 tablespoons grated **ginger,** ¼ cup chopped **lemongrass,** 1 teaspoon each **cumin** and **coriander,** and a minced **Thai chile** in **vegetable oil.** Add 1 sliced **onion;** cook 5 minutes. Add some shredded **bok choy,** 4 cups water, 1 can **coconut milk, cilantro** and 2 tablespoons **fish sauce;** simmer 3 minutes. Add ½ pound peeled **shrimp;** simmer until opaque.

HOT POTATO-LEEK

Sauté 3 cups each sliced **leeks** and cubed **potatoes** in **butter.** Add 1 sliced **garlic clove** and a pinch each of **salt, pepper, dried thyme** and **nutmeg;** cook 5 minutes. Add 5 cups **chicken broth;** boil until the **potatoes** are tender, then puree. Reheat with 1 cup **cream.**

COLD POTATO-LEEK

Sauté 3 cups each sliced **leeks** and cubed **potatoes** in **butter.** Add 1 sliced **garlic clove** and a pinch each of **salt, pepper, dried thyme** and **nutmeg;** cook 5 minutes. Add 5 cups water; boil until the potatoes are tender, then puree. Strain, then refrigerate until chilled. Stir in 1 cup **half-and-half** and top with chopped **chives.**

≪ BROCCOLI-CHEDDAR Sauté 1 chopped **onion** and 2 chopped **celery stalks** in **olive oil.** Add 2 cups **chicken broth,** 2 cups **cream,** 2 pounds chopped and peeled **potatoes,** a **bay leaf,** 2 cups water, and **salt** and **pepper.** Bring to a boil, then simmer 10 minutes. Remove the bay leaf and puree the soup. Return to a simmer and stir in 2 cups each cooked **broccoli** and shredded **cheddar.** Season with salt and pepper. Top with **croutons.**

Soup

STRACCIATELLA
Beat 2 **eggs** with ⅓ cup grated **parmesan.** Drizzle into 6 cups simmering **chicken broth;** cook 2 minutes.

BUTTERNUT SQUASH
Sauté ½ sliced **onion** with a pinch of **dried thyme** in **butter** until soft. Add **salt, pepper,** 2 pounds diced **butternut squash** and 5 cups **chicken broth.** Simmer until tender, then puree.

BACON-POTATO
Sauté 4 ounces chopped **bacon;** add 2 tablespoons **butter,** 2 sliced **leeks** and 2 teaspoons each chopped **sage** and **thyme.** Add 4 cups **chicken broth,** 1½ cups **cream,** a **bay leaf** and 3 **chopped potatoes.** Simmer until tender.

GARLIC-HERB
Sauté 2 heads **garlic** (smashed and peeled) in **olive oil.** Add 8 cups **chicken broth** and a bundle of **fresh herbs;** simmer 40 minutes. Add **salt** and **pepper.**

TRY THIS

Make croutons or toast to float in soup: Toss bread cubes or rounds with olive oil and salt and bake at 400° until golden.

POTATO-CHEESE
Sauté 4 ounces chopped **bacon;** add 2 tablespoons **butter,** 2 sliced **leeks** and 2 teaspoons each chopped **sage** and **thyme.** Add 4 cups **chicken broth,** 1½ cups **cream,** a **bay leaf** and 3 chopped **potatoes.** Simmer until tender, then stir in 8 ounces grated **sharp cheddar;** top with **chives.**

EGG DROP
Cook 1 tablespoon chopped **ginger** and 3 chopped **scallions** in **sesame oil.** Add 6 cups **chicken broth** and 2 tablespoons each **soy sauce** and **sherry;** bring to a simmer. Slowly pour in 2 beaten **eggs** and cook 2 minutes.

EGG-LEMON
Cook ½ cup **pastina** in 6 cups simmering **chicken broth** with 3 tablespoons **lemon juice.** Beat 2 **eggs,** 2 **egg yolks** and 3 tablespoons lemon juice; whisk in a little hot broth, then stir the mixture into the soup. Cook over low heat until thick.

PASTA-CHEDDAR Mince 3 **shallots,** 1 **carrot** and 1 **celery stalk;** sauté in **butter** until soft, 4 to 5 minutes. Add ¼ cup **flour** and cook, stirring, 2 minutes. Stir in 3¾ cups **chicken broth** and bring to a boil; cook, stirring, until thick, 6 minutes. Remove from the heat. Add 1¼ cups **milk,** 1½ cups shredded **cheddar,** ¼ cup grated **parmesan** and 4 ounces cooked **macaroni;** stir until the cheese is melted. Season with **pepper.** Top with toasted **baguette** slices and **roasted tomatoes.**

»

SPINACH-CHORIZO
Sauté 2 heads **garlic** (smashed and peeled) in **olive oil**. Add 8 cups **chicken broth** and a bundle of **fresh herbs;** simmer 30 minutes, then add ¼ pound sliced **dried chorizo** and simmer 10 more minutes. Add chopped **spinach** and **salt** and **pepper**.

TOMATO-LIME
Sauté 2 heads **garlic** (smashed and peeled) in **olive oil**. Add 8 cups **chicken broth** and a bundle of **fresh herbs;** simmer 40 minutes, adding 3 chopped **plum tomatoes** during the last 3 minutes. Season with **salt** and **pepper**. Stir in **lime juice** and chopped **cilantro**.

CARROT-GINGER
Sauté 2 sliced **shallots** and 3 tablespoons minced **ginger** in **butter;** season with **salt** and **pepper**. Add 1 pound sliced **carrots,** 2 tablespoons uncooked **rice,** 2 cups **chicken broth** and 3 cups water. Simmer until the rice is tender, then puree.

CARROT-DILL
Sauté 2 sliced **shallots** in **butter;** season with **salt** and **pepper**. Add 1 pound sliced **carrots,** 2 tablespoons **rice,** 2 cups **chicken broth** and 3 cups water. Simmer until the rice is tender. Add chopped **dill;** puree.

GARLICKY BROCCOLI RABE
Sauté 2 heads **garlic** (smashed and peeled) in **olive oil**. Add 8 cups **chicken broth** and a bundle of **fresh herbs;** simmer 30 minutes, then add some chopped **broccoli rabe** and **small pasta** and cook 10 more minutes. Season with **salt** and **pepper;** top with grated **parmesan**.

CHICKEN AND RICE
Chop 1 **onion,** 1 **celery stalk,** 2 **carrots** and 1 tablespoon **thyme;** sauté in **butter** until tender. Season with **salt** and **pepper**. Add 6 cups **chicken broth;** simmer 20 minutes. Add 2 cups shredded cooked **chicken,** ⅓ cup mixed chopped **chives, chervil, tarragon** and **parsley,** and some **lemon juice**. Stir in ⅓ cup cooked **rice**.

VEGETABLE GUMBO
Cook 3 tablespoons **flour** in 3 tablespoons **olive oil** until golden, about 3 minutes. Add 1 chopped **onion,** 1 chopped **green bell pepper,** 2 chopped **celery stalks,** 3 tablespoons water, and **salt** and **pepper;** cook until soft, about 8 minutes. Stir in 1 tablespoon **soy sauce** and 1 teaspoon **smoked paprika,** then add 2 cups **vegetable broth**. Bring to a boil and add 1 pound chopped **kale** and 10 ounces frozen **black-eyed peas;** simmer until tender, 15 minutes.

FRENCH ONION Cook 4 sliced **onions** and 2 **thyme sprigs** in **butter** over low heat, covered, 20 minutes. Uncover; cook 1 hour, or until caramelized, stirring occasionally. Add 6 cups **beef broth;** simmer 10 minutes. Add some **cognac, salt** and **pepper**. Sprinkle toasted **baguette** slices with shredded **gruyère;** broil until melted. Float on the soup.

FISH CHOWDER

Sauté 2 ounces chopped **bacon;**
add 2 tablespoons **butter,** 2 sliced
leeks and 2 teaspoons **fresh thyme.**
Add 4 cups **chicken broth,** 1½ cups
half-and-half, a **bay leaf** and
3 chopped **potatoes.** Simmer until
the potatoes are tender, adding
1 pound chopped **whitefish** and
½ pound flaked **smoked trout**
during the last 5 minutes of cooking.
Top with **chives.**

SQUASH AND SAGE

Sauté 2 sliced **shallots** with a pinch
of **dried thyme** in **butter** until
soft. Add **salt, pepper,** 2 pounds
diced **butternut squash,** 3½ cups
chicken broth and 1½ cups **apple
cider;** simmer until tender. Season
with **nutmeg,** then puree. Top with
crème fraîche and fried **sage.**

FRESH TOMATO

Combine ¼ cup **olive oil,** 1 finely chopped **onion,** 1 chopped **garlic clove,** 1 chopped inner **celery stalk,** 2 pounds chopped **tomatoes,** ½ teaspoon **sugar,** and **salt** to taste in a saucepan; cook, stirring, until tender, about 25 minutes. Puree until smooth. Season with salt and **pepper;** thin with water, if necessary.

BEEF BORSCHT

Sauté ½ head chopped **cabbage** and 2 each chopped **celery stalks, leeks, carrots** and **parsnips** in **olive oil.** Add some **fresh thyme,** 1 tablespoon **tomato paste,** a **bay leaf** and 10 cups **beef broth;** simmer 30 minutes. Add 4 diced roasted **beets** and 2 cups shredded cooked **beef;** simmer 15 minutes. Top with **sour cream** and **dill.**

Kebabs

BACON-BEEF
Boil **bacon** strips 5 minutes, then cut into pieces. Skewer cubed **beef tri-tip, onion** and **bell pepper** with **cherry tomatoes** and the bacon; season with **salt** and **pepper**. Grill, basting with a mix of equal parts **barbecue sauce** and **olive oil.**

KOREAN BEEF
Marinate thinly sliced **short ribs** and **scallion** pieces in ⅓ cup each **sugar** and **white wine,** 3 tablespoons **sesame oil,** ½ cup **soy sauce,** 2 crushed **garlic cloves** and 1 grated **Asian pear.** Skewer so the meat lies flat; grill.

HUNGARIAN BEEF
Marinate cubed **beef tri-tip** in ½ cup **olive oil,** 2 smashed **garlic cloves,** a pinch of **salt,** ½ teaspoon **paprika** and 2 teaspoons crushed **caraway seeds.** Skewer with chunks of **onion** and **bell pepper** and grill.

STUFFED PEPPERS

Mix 1 pound **ground beef,** 2 minced **shallots,** 3 minced **garlic cloves,** ½ cup each chopped **parsley** and **olives,** 2 teaspoons each **cumin, dried mint, coriander** and **paprika,** and ½ teaspoon **cinnamon.** Pack into hollowed **baby bell peppers,** skewer and brush with **olive oil.** Grill; season with **salt** and baste with **lemon juice.**

CHILI BEEF

Toss cubed **beef tri-tip** with 3 tablespoons each **brown sugar** and **chili powder,** 1 tablespoon **salt,** and ½ teaspoon each **fresh thyme** and **pepper;** marinate. Skewer and grill, basting with a mix of ¼ cup each **cider vinegar** and **brown sugar,** and 1 teaspoon **chili powder.**

BEEF KEFTA

Mix 1 pound **ground beef,** 2 minced **shallots,** 3 minced **garlic cloves,** ½ cup chopped **parsley,** 2 teaspoons each **cumin, coriander, paprika** and **dried mint,** and ½ teaspoon **cinnamon.** Form into 1-inch balls; skewer and grill.

TIP

Leave a bit of space between kebab ingredients so they cook evenly.

HERBED BEEF

Marinate cubed **beef tri-tip** in ½ cup **olive oil,** 1 smashed **garlic clove,** a pinch each of **salt** and **red pepper flakes,** and torn **herbs.** Skewer and grill.

BASIC LAMB

Toss cubed **lamb leg** with 1 grated **onion,** ⅓ cup **olive oil,** and **salt** and **pepper.** Skewer with **lemon, onion** and **bell pepper** slices; grill.

INDIAN LAMB

Marinate cubed **lamb leg** in 1 cup **plain yogurt,** ½ cup each minced **onion** and **cilantro,** 2 tablespoons **garam masala** and 1¼ teaspoons **salt.** Skewer and grill; top with **chutney.**

LAMB IN GRAPE LEAVES

Mix 1 pound **ground lamb,** 2 minced **shallots,** 3 minced **garlic cloves,** ½ cup chopped **parsley,** 2 teaspoons each **cumin, coriander, paprika** and **dried mint,** and ½ teaspoon **cinnamon.** Wrap the mixture in **grape leaves,** creating cylindrical packages; skewer. Brush with **olive oil** and grill.

STEAKHOUSE Marinate cubed **beef tri-tip** in 3 tablespoons **olive oil** and 1 tablespoon each **soy sauce, Worcestershire sauce,** chopped **parsley** and **thyme;** add **salt** and **pepper.** Skewer with chunks of **onion, mushroom** and boiled **new potato;** grill. »

◀◀ CHICKEN CAESAR Mix 1 pound **ground chicken,** 2 tablespoons **Caesar dressing,** ½ cup **parmesan,** ¼ cup **breadcrumbs** and 1 teaspoon **lemon zest.** Form into ovals, skewer and grill. Serve on **romaine** leaves with grilled **bread** and more dressing.

SESAME PORK

Mix 1 pound **ground pork,** 2 chopped **scallions,** 2 teaspoons each **soy sauce,** grated **garlic** and grated **ginger,** and ½ teaspoon each **sesame oil** and **salt.** Roll into 1-inch balls and roll in **sesame seeds;** skewer and grill.

THAI PORK

Mix 1 pound **ground pork,** 3 tablespoons each chopped **mint, cilantro** and **basil,** 1 minced **shallot,** 1 minced **hot chile pepper** and 2 tablespoons each **fish sauce** and **lime juice.** Form into 2-inch ovals; skewer and grill.

SAUSAGE WITH CHIMICHURRI

Thread fresh **pork sausages** onto skewers; grill. Meanwhile, blend 1 cup each **fresh parsley** and **cilantro,** ¾ cup **olive oil,** 2 **garlic cloves,** 3 tablespoons **lemon juice,** and **salt** and **pepper.** Serve the sausages with the chimichurri sauce.

SAUSAGE WITH SALSA

Thread fresh **pork sausages** onto skewers; grill. Meanwhile, toss 1 each chopped **tomato** and **green bell pepper,** ½ chopped **onion,** 2 tablespoons each **olive oil** and **cilantro,** 1 tablespoon **red wine vinegar,** and **salt** and **pepper.** Serve the sausages with the salsa.

CHICKEN-PEACH

Toss quartered **peaches** with chopped **thyme, vegetable oil** and **salt.** Skewer with cooked **chicken sausage;** grill.

SMOKY CHICKEN

Toss cubed **chicken breast** with 1 cup **barbecue sauce,** some **salt** and 1 minced **chipotle in adobo sauce.** Skewer and grill.

CHICKEN TERIYAKI

Marinate cubed **chicken thighs** in a mix of ¼ cup **teriyaki sauce** and 1 tablespoon **vegetable oil.** Skewer and grill.

CURRIED CHICKEN

Mix ⅔ cup **coconut milk,** 3 tablespoons **creamy peanut butter,** 1 tablespoon each **Thai curry paste** and **lime juice,** and **salt.** Marinate cubed **chicken thighs** in half of the sauce. Skewer with **bell pepper** chunks. Grill, basting with the remaining sauce.

CHICKEN TIKKA

Marinate cubed **chicken thighs** in 1 cup **plain yogurt,** 2 tablespoons **garam masala,** ½ cup chopped **cilantro,** 1½ teaspoons each grated **garlic** and **ginger,** 1 tablespoon **lime juice,** and **salt** and **cayenne pepper.** Skewer and grill.

JERK CHICKEN

Marinate whole **chicken thighs** and **pineapple** chunks in 2 tablespoons **jerk seasoning,** 1 tablespoon **vegetable oil** and 2 teaspoons **lime juice.** Thread the chicken and pineapple on double skewers; grill.

CHICKEN FAJITA

Puree ½ cup **olive oil,** a handful of **cilantro,** 2 seeded **jalapeños,** 2 **garlic cloves** and **salt;** add cubed **chicken breast** and marinate. Skewer with chunks of **onion** and **poblano pepper.** Grill, basting with **lime juice.**

TURKEY MEATBALL

Heat ⅓ cup **cranberry sauce,** 1½ tablespoons each **barbecue sauce** and water, 2 teaspoons **cider vinegar,** and **salt.** Mix 1 pound **ground turkey,** ¼ pound **ground bacon,** and salt. Form into balls, skewer and grill, brushing with the sauce.

TURKEY SANDWICH

Brush a split **baguette** with **dijon mustard;** fill with **smoked turkey** and **brie.** Cut into 2-inch pieces, skewer and grill.

TRY THIS

Add something unexpected to your kebabs: Lemon slices, herbs and olives all taste great grilled.

HOISIN SALMON

Marinate cubed **salmon** in a mix of 3 tablespoons **hoisin sauce** and 1 tablespoon each **soy sauce, rice wine, honey** and **olive oil.** Skewer with **scallion** pieces; grill.

SESAME SHRIMP

Toss large **shrimp** with 1½ tablespoons each **olive oil** and water, 2 teaspoons each **rice vinegar,** toasted **sesame seeds** and **soy sauce,** and ½ teaspoon **sesame oil.** Skewer and grill.

GREEK SHRIMP

Marinate large **shrimp** in **olive oil** and chopped **marjoram, dill** and **garlic.** Skewer with **grape tomatoes** and **lemon** slices. Grill, then top with **feta.**

CHIPOTLE SHRIMP

Mix ¼ cup **barbecue sauce,** the juice of ½ **orange,** 3 tablespoons minced **chipotle in adobo sauce** and **salt.** Reserve a quarter of the sauce; marinate large **shrimp** in the rest. Skewer and grill, basting with the reserved sauce.

CHORIZO-SHRIMP Marinate large **shrimp** and sliced **dried chorizo** in ¼ cup each **olive oil** and minced **roasted red pepper,** 1 tablespoon **cognac** and some minced **parsley** and **garlic.** Wrap the shrimp around the chorizo, skewer and grill.

CHICKEN NIÇOISE Toss cubed **chicken breast** and **pancetta, olives** and **cherry tomatoes** with **olive oil,** chopped **oregano** and **salt.** Skewer and grill.

DILL SALMON
Marinate cubed **wild salmon** in **olive oil** and chopped **dill.** Skewer and grill.

SWORDFISH ROLLS
Sprinkle thin **swordfish** slices with **lemon juice,** chopped **parsley, salt** and **pepper.** Lay thinly sliced **zucchini** on top, roll into a coil and wrap with **sage leaves.** Skewer with sliced **lemon** and **tomato;** brush with **olive oil** and grill.

SMOKY MACKEREL
Skewer 4-inch pieces scored **mackerel fillets.** Brush with **olive oil,** season with **salt** and grill. Sprinkle with **smoked paprika** and serve with **lemon wedges.**

ITALIAN VEGGIE
Marinate **bell pepper** chunks and rounds of **zucchini** and **eggplant** in **olive oil,** chopped **thyme** and **rosemary,** and minced **garlic.** Skewer and grill, basting with **lemon juice.** Season with **salt.**

STUFFED PEPPERS
Cut a slit in **baby bell peppers,** keeping the stem intact. Scrape out the seeds. Season the insides with **salt** and **pepper** and stuff with a cube of **haloumi or feta cheese.** Skewer with **olives** and grill.

CURRIED CAULIFLOWER
Toss **cauliflower florets** with **olive oil, curry powder** and **salt.** Skewer and grill over indirect heat, covered.

HALOUMI
Marinate cubed **haloumi cheese** in ¼ cup **olive oil,** ½ cup chopped **parsley,** 3 minced **garlic cloves,** and 2 teaspoons each **cumin, coriander, paprika** and **dried mint.** Skewer with **scallion** pieces and grill.

PROSCIUTTO-FIG
Wrap halved **fresh figs** in **prosciutto.** Season with **pepper,** skewer and grill.

HOISIN TOFU
Marinate cubed **extra-firm tofu** in a mix of 3 tablespoons **hoisin sauce** and 1 tablespoon each **rice wine, soy sauce, honey** and **olive oil.** Skewer with **scallion** pieces and grill.

VEGGIE SOUVLAKI
Mash 3 **garlic cloves,** 1 tablespoon each **coriander seeds** and **olive oil,** and 1 teaspoon each **cumin, paprika** and **salt** into a paste with the flat side of a knife. Brush the paste on **bell pepper, zucchini** and **eggplant** chunks. Skewer and grill.

CRISPY CHICKEN

Mix ¼ cup **olive oil,** 2 teaspoons
red wine vinegar, 2 tablespoons
chopped **oregano,** 1 tablespoon minced
shallot, 1 teaspoon minced **garlic,**
¼ teaspoon **red pepper flakes** and
1¼ teaspoons **salt.** Toss cubed **chicken
breast** in the marinade, then in 1¼ cups
breadcrumbs. Skewer and grill.

SCALLOP-BACON

Boil **bacon** strips 5 minutes, then
cut into pieces. Toss **scallops** with
1 tablespoon **olive oil,** 1 teaspoon
smoked paprika and **salt.** Skewer
with **lemon** slices and the bacon; grill.

ROSEMARY LAMB

Marinate cubed **lamb leg** in ½ cup **olive oil,** the juice of 1 **lemon,** some **fresh rosemary,** 3 smashed **garlic cloves,** and **salt** and **pepper.** Skewer with **zucchini** and grill.

BEEF SATAY

Marinate thinly sliced **flank steak** in 2 tablespoons each **lime juice** and **fish sauce,** 1 tablespoon each **sugar** and **hot chile sauce,** and 3 tablespoons **cilantro.** Skewer and grill. Top with **peanut sauce** and chopped **peanuts.**

Burgers & Dogs

« CHILE CHEESEBURGERS

Mix 1½ pounds **ground beef chuck** with ¼ cup diced roasted **poblano pepper** and ½ teaspoon **kosher salt.** Form into four ¾-inch-thick patties; make an indentation in the center of each. Heat a cast-iron skillet over medium-high heat; sprinkle the skillet with salt. Cook the burgers 4 to 5 minutes per side. Serve on toasted **buns** with **jarred nacho cheese sauce, guacamole, lettuce** and **pickled jalapeños.**

CLASSIC GRILLED BURGERS

Mix 1½ pounds **ground beef chuck** with ½ teaspoon **kosher salt.** Form into four ¾-inch-thick patties; make an indentation in the center of each. Season with salt; grill on hot oiled grates over high heat, 4 minutes per side. Serve on **buns.**

BLUE CHEESE BURGERS

Mix 1½ pounds **ground beef chuck** with ½ teaspoon **kosher salt.** Form into four ¾-inch-thick patties; make an indentation in the center of each. Heat a cast-iron skillet over medium-high heat; sprinkle the skillet with salt. Cook the burgers 4 to 5 minutes per side. Spread **blue cheese** inside 4 **buns;** melt in the oven. Serve the burgers on the buns.

SWEET ONION BURGERS

Cook 2 sliced **red onions** in **butter** over low heat until caramelized, 35 minutes; add **kosher salt** and **pepper**. Mix 1½ pounds **ground beef chuck** with ½ teaspoon salt. Form into four ¾-inch-thick patties; make an indentation in the center of each. Heat a cast-iron skillet over medium-high heat; sprinkle the skillet with salt. Cook the burgers 4 to 5 minutes per side. Serve on **buns** with the onions.

CHIPOTLE BURGERS

Mix 1½ pounds **ground beef chuck** with ½ teaspoon **kosher salt.** Form into four ¾-inch-thick patties; make an indentation in the center of each. Season with salt and grill on hot oiled grates over high heat, about 4 minutes per side; top with **jack cheese** during the last minute (cover to melt). Mix ¼ cup **mayonnaise,** 1 tablespoon minced **chipotles in adobo sauce** and a splash of **lemon juice.** Serve the burgers on **rolls** with the chipotle mayonnaise and **avocado.**

TIP

Sprinkle a cast-iron skillet with kosher salt before cooking burgers. It will keep the patties from sticking without the need for excess oil.

BBQ BURGERS

Mix 1½ pounds **ground beef chuck** with ½ teaspoon **kosher salt.** Form into four ¾-inch-thick patties; make an indentation in the center of each. Season the patties with salt and grill on hot oiled grates over high heat, about 4 minutes per side; brush with **barbecue sauce** during the last minute of cooking. Serve on grilled **buns** brushed with more barbecue sauce.

PROVENÇAL BURGERS

Brush 4 **bun** tops with beaten **egg whites,** sprinkle with **herbes de Provence** and bake in a 350° oven, 5 minutes. Mix 1½ pounds **ground beef chuck** with ½ teaspoon **kosher salt.** Form into four ¾-inch-thick patties; make an indentation in the center of each. Heat a cast-iron skillet over medium-high heat; sprinkle the skillet with salt. Cook the burgers 4 to 5 minutes per side. Serve on the herbed buns with **olive tapenade, tomato** and **mayonnaise.**

CLASSIC SKILLET CHEESEBURGERS Mix 1½ pounds **ground beef chuck** with ½ teaspoon **kosher salt.** Form into four ¾-inch-thick patties; make an indentation in the center of each. Heat a cast-iron skillet over medium-high heat; sprinkle the skillet with salt. Cook the burgers 4 to 5 minutes per side. Top each with sliced **cheddar** during the last 2 minutes of cooking (cover to melt). Serve on **sesame buns** with **lettuce** and **tomato.**

TRATTORIA BURGERS

Mix 1½ pounds **ground beef chuck** with ½ teaspoon **kosher salt.** Form into four ¾-inch-thick patties and make an indentation in the center of each. Heat a cast-iron skillet over medium-high heat; sprinkle the skillet with salt. Cook the burgers 4 to 5 minutes per side. Serve on **Italian rolls** spread with **gorgonzola.** Top with **arugula, tomato** and fried **pancetta.**

MUSHROOM BURGERS

Cook 1 pound sliced **mushrooms** in **butter** until golden, then add 1 chopped **garlic clove** and 2 tablespoons **Worcestershire sauce** and cook until crisp; add some chopped **parsley.** Mix 1½ pounds **ground beef chuck** with ½ teaspoon **kosher salt.** Form into four ¾-inch-thick patties and make an indentation in the center of each. Heat a cast-iron skillet over medium-high heat; sprinkle the skillet with salt. Cook the burgers 4 to 5 minutes per side. Serve on **buns** and top with the mushrooms.

TIP

Use ground beef chuck for burgers— it's 20% fat, so the patties are super juicy.

BLT BURGERS

Cook 2 **bacon** slices in simmering water, 15 minutes. Drain and cool, then chop and mix with 1 pound **ground beef chuck.** Form into four ¾-inch-thick patties and make an indentation in the center of each. Heat a cast-iron skillet over medium-high heat; sprinkle the skillet with **kosher salt.** Cook the burgers 4 to 5 minutes per side. Serve on **buns** topped with **mayonnaise, lettuce** and **tomato.**

TEXAS CRUNCH BURGERS

Mix 1½ pounds **ground beef chuck** with ½ teaspoon **kosher salt.** Form into four ¾-inch-thick patties and make an indentation in the center of each. Heat a cast-iron skillet over medium-high heat; sprinkle the skillet with salt. Cook the burgers 4 to 5 minutes per side. Spread the inside of 4 **buns** with **refried beans.** Serve the burgers on the buns; top with **jarred nacho cheese sauce,** diced **red onion** and crushed **corn chips.**

TACO BURGERS Mix 1½ pounds **ground beef chuck** with ½ teaspoon **kosher salt.** Form into four ¾-inch-thick patties and make an indentation in the center of each. Sprinkle the patties with salt, **cumin, dried oregano** and **chili powder.** Grill on hot oiled grates over high heat, about 4 minutes per side. Serve on **buns** with **guacamole, salsa, sour cream, tortilla chips, lettuce** and **cheddar.**

STEAMED CHEESEBURGERS

Mix 1½ pounds **ground beef chuck** with ½ teaspoon **kosher salt.** Form into four ¾-inch-thick patties; make an indentation in the center of each. Place the patties in a hot skillet over medium-high heat; add sliced **mushrooms** and **onions** and season with salt. Pour in ¼ cup water, cover and steam 3 minutes. Top the burgers with sliced **cheddar;** steam 1 more minute. Serve on **buns.**

ENGLISH CHEDDAR BURGERS

Combine ½ cup **mayonnaise,** 4 teaspoons **Worcestershire sauce** and 1 teaspoon **mustard.** Mix 1½ pounds **ground beef chuck** with ½ teaspoon **kosher salt.** Form into four ¾-inch-thick patties; make an indentation in the center of each. Heat a cast-iron skillet over medium-high heat; sprinkle the skillet with salt. Cook the burgers 4 to 5 minutes per side; top each with 2 slices **English cheddar** during the last minute (cover to melt). Serve on toasted **English muffins** with the mayonnaise sauce.

TIP

Let burgers rest a minute before eating so the juices redistribute.

BRIE BURGERS

Mix 1½ pounds **ground beef chuck** with ½ teaspoon **kosher salt.** Form into four ¾-inch-thick patties; make an indentation in the center of each. Heat a cast-iron skillet over medium-high heat; sprinkle the skillet with salt. Cook the burgers 4 to 5 minutes per side; top with **brie** during the last minute (cover to melt). Serve on **brioche buns** with **whole-grain mustard, cornichons** and **watercress.**

WESTERN BURGERS

Mix 1½ pounds **ground beef chuck** with ½ teaspoon **kosher salt.** Form into four ¾-inch-thick patties and make an indentation in the center of each. Season the patties with salt. Grill on hot oiled grates over high heat, about 4 minutes per side; during the last minute of cooking, brush with **barbecue sauce** and top with sautéed **onions, pickled jalapeños,** cooked **bacon** and **jack cheese** (cover to melt). Serve on grilled **buns** with **mayonnaise.**

SWISS SLIDERS Mix 1½ pounds **ground beef chuck** with ½ teaspoon **kosher salt.** Form into 12 small patties, making an indentation in the center of each. Heat a cast-iron skillet over medium-high heat; sprinkle the skillet with salt. Cook the burgers 3 minutes per side; top with **Swiss cheese** during the last minute of cooking (cover to melt). Serve on grilled **mini potato buns** with **pickles** and **ketchup.**

BUTTER BURGERS

Mix 1½ pounds **ground beef chuck** with ½ teaspoon **kosher salt.** Form into four ¾-inch-thick patties; make an indentation in the center of each. Heat **butter** in a cast-iron skillet over medium-high heat; sprinkle the skillet with salt. Cook the burgers 4 to 5 minutes per side. Top with more butter and serve on buttered **buns.**

SUPERSIZE BURGERS

Mix ¼ cup each **mayonnaise** and **Thousand Island dressing,** 2 teaspoons each **relish** and minced **onion,** and 1 teaspoon **red wine vinegar.** Mix 1½ pounds **ground beef chuck** with ½ teaspoon **kosher salt.** Form into 8 thin patties. Heat a cast-iron skillet over medium-high heat; sprinkle the skillet with salt. Cook the patties 1 to 2 minutes per side. Spread 4 **bun** bottoms with the sauce; top each with **lettuce, American cheese,** a patty, another bun bottom, sauce, **pickles,** another patty and the bun top.

TRY THIS

Put something crunchy on your burger, like crushed chips or canned fried onions.

DEEP-FRIED BURGERS

Deep-fry four 6-ounce **beef chuck patties** in 360° **canola oil** with **onion** and **pickle** slices until crisp. Drain on paper towels. Serve on **potato buns.**

SMASHED ONION BURGERS

Season 4 thick **onion** slices with **salt** and **pepper;** cook in a hot cast-iron skillet until browned on the bottom. Flip; cover each with a handful of **ground beef chuck.** Flatten with a spatula and brown on both sides. Serve on **buns.**

FRENCH ONION BURGERS

Brush 4 **bun** tops with a beaten **egg white;** sprinkle with **dried thyme** and bake at 350°, 5 minutes. Season 4 thick **onion** slices with **salt** and **pepper;** cook in a hot cast-iron skillet until browned on the bottom. Flip, then cover each with a handful of **ground beef chuck.** Flatten with a spatula and brown on both sides; top each with **gruyère** during the last minute (cover to melt). Serve on the herbed buns.

CHIPOTLE-CORN BURGERS Toss **corn** kernels and sliced **bell pepper** with **lemon juice, olive oil** and **salt.** Mix 1½ pounds **ground beef chuck** with ½ teaspoon **kosher salt.** Form into four ¾-inch-thick patties; make an indentation in the center of each. Sprinkle the patties with **cumin.** Grill on hot oiled grates over high heat, about 4 minutes per side. Mix ¼ cup **mayonnaise,** 1 tablespoon minced **chipotles in adobo sauce,** and lemon juice. Serve on **buns** with the chipotle mayonnaise, corn salsa, **red onion, tomato** and **cilantro.**

BACON-PORK BURGERS Pulse 5 slices **bacon** and 1 minced **garlic clove** in a food processor. Mix with 1 pound **ground pork,** 1 teaspoon **kosher salt** and ¼ teaspoon each **pepper** and **dried sage.** Form into four 1-inch-thick patties. Make an indentation in the center of each. Season the patties with pepper. Grill on hot oiled grates over medium-high heat, 4 to 6 minutes per side. Meanwhile, spread the inside of 4 **potato buns** with **butter** and toast on the grill. Serve the patties on the buns; top with **coleslaw.**

MEATLOAF BURGERS

Mix 1½ pounds **ground meatloaf mix** with ½ teaspoon **kosher salt;** form into 4 balls. Stuff each with a cube of **mozzarella;** shape into a patty. Parcook in a deep skillet of boiling water, 5 minutes. Drain, then wrap each in 2 strips **bacon.** Brush with **ketchup** and bake in a 350° oven, 25 minutes. Serve on **buns.**

BISON BURGERS

Mix 1½ pounds **ground bison** with ½ teaspoon **kosher salt.** Form into four ¾-inch-thick patties; make an indentation in the center of each. Season with salt and grill on hot oiled grates over high heat, 2 to 3 minutes per side. Serve on toasted **buns** with **onion dip.**

COWBOY BISON BURGERS

Cook 2 tablespoons each **flour** and **butter** until browned. Whisk in 1¼ cups **milk,** and **kosher salt** and **pepper;** simmer until thick. Mix 1½ pounds **ground bison** with ½ teaspoon salt. Form into four ¾-inch-thick patties; make an indentation in the center of each. Season with salt. Grill on hot oiled grates over high heat, 2 to 3 minutes per side. Serve on **biscuits;** top with the gravy.

PUERTO RICAN PORK BURGERS

Mix 1½ pounds **ground pork** with ½ teaspoon **kosher salt** and some **cumin.** Form into four ¾-inch-thick patties; make an indentation in the center of each. Season the patties with salt; grill on hot oiled grates over high heat, about 4 minutes per side. Heat equal parts **barbecue sauce, guava paste** and water in a saucepan, whisking until smooth. Brush the burgers with the guava glaze; serve on toasted **buns** with sautéed **onions,** sliced **banana peppers** and sliced **ham.** Drizzle with more guava glaze.

PRETZEL PORK BURGERS

Mix 1½ pounds **ground pork** with ½ teaspoon **kosher salt.** Form into four ¾-inch-thick patties; make an indentation in the center of each. Season the patties with salt; grill on hot oiled grates over high heat, about 4 minutes per side. Mix 2 tablespoons each **apple butter** and **mayonnaise** with 2 teaspoons **spicy mustard.** Top 4 split **pretzel buns** with 2 thick slices **muenster** and broil until melted; top with the pork burgers, apple butter sauce and **pickles.**

LAMB-FETA BURGERS

Mix ½ cup **Greek yogurt** with a dash of **Asian chile oil** and a pinch of **kosher salt**; set aside. Mix 1½ pounds **ground lamb,** ⅓ cup each Greek yogurt and crumbled **feta,** 1 teaspoon each minced **garlic,** finely chopped **mint,** grated **lemon zest** and salt, and a pinch of **red pepper flakes.** Shape into four 1-inch-thick patties. Brush with **canola oil;** grill on hot grates over high heat, 4 to 5 minutes per side. Serve on **flatbread** with the yogurt sauce.

PITA BURGERS

Mix 1½ pounds **ground lamb,** ⅓ cup each **Greek yogurt** and crumbled **feta,** 1 teaspoon each minced **garlic,** finely chopped **mint,** grated **lemon zest** and **kosher salt,** and a pinch of **red pepper flakes.** Shape into four 1-inch-thick patties. Brush with **canola oil;** grill on hot grates over high heat, 4 to 5 minutes per side. Serve in **pitas** with **onion, tomato, cucumber** and **tzatziki.**

TIP

Don't press burgers as they cook— you'll lose flavorful juices!

CLASSIC CHICKEN BURGERS

Mix 1¼ pounds **ground chicken** with ½ cup each grated **onion** and **panko,** 1 minced **garlic clove,** 1 teaspoon chopped **thyme,** and **salt** and **pepper.** Shape into four 1-inch-thick patties and chill. Brush the patties with **canola oil** and grill on hot oiled grates over high heat, 4 to 5 minutes per side. Serve on **sesame buns.**

SALTIMBOCCA BURGERS

Mix 1¼ pounds **ground chicken** with ½ cup each grated **onion** and **panko,** 1 minced **garlic clove,** 1 teaspoon chopped **thyme,** and **salt** and **pepper.** Shape into four 1-inch-thick patties and chill. Brush the patties with **canola oil** and grill on hot oiled grates over high heat, 4 to 5 minutes per side. Top with **fresh sage, fontina** and **prosciutto** during the last minute of cooking (cover to melt). Drizzle with **olive oil** and top with **parsley;** serve on **onion rolls.**

« **TURKEY-MUSHROOM BURGERS** Pulse 1 chopped **portobello mushroom,** 1 tablespoon chopped **shallot** and 3 tablespoons **fresh parsley** in a food processor. Mix with 1¼ pounds **ground turkey,** 2 tablespoons **olive oil,** 1 teaspoon **Worcestershire sauce,** and **salt** and **pepper.** Form into four 1-inch-thick patties and chill. Grill on hot oiled grates over medium heat, 4 to 5 minutes. Give a quarter turn and cook 4 to 5 more minutes. Flip and cook 6 to 7 more minutes, topping with **manchego** during the last 3 minutes (cover to melt). Serve on toasted **English muffins** with **dijon mustard** and **avocado.**

PESTO CHICKEN BURGERS

Mix 1¼ pounds **ground chicken** with ½ cup each grated **onion** and **panko**, 1 minced **garlic clove**, 1 teaspoon chopped **thyme**, and **salt** and **pepper**. Shape into four 1-inch-thick patties and chill. Brush with **canola oil** and grill on hot oiled grates over high heat, 4 to 5 minutes per side. Top with **mozzarella** during the last minute of cooking (cover to melt). Mix equal parts **pesto** and **mayonnaise**; brush on toasted **rolls**. Serve the burgers on the rolls with **tomato** and **arugula**.

TURKEY-APPLE BURGERS

Mix 1 pound **ground turkey**, 1 grated peeled **green apple**, ½ cup minced **scallions**, ¼ cup **panko**, and **salt** and **pepper**. Form into four 1-inch-thick patties and make an indentation in the center of each. Grill on hot oiled grates over high heat, 4 to 5 minutes per side. Serve on toasted **whole-wheat buns**.

TIP

It's time to flip your burgers when the patties pull away from the grill.

THANKSGIVING BURGERS

Mix 1 pound **ground turkey**, 1 grated peeled **green apple**, ½ cup minced **scallions**, ¼ cup **panko**, and **salt** and **pepper**. Form into four 1-inch-thick patties and make an indentation in the center of each. Grill on hot oiled grates over high heat, 4 to 5 minutes per side. Mix ¼ cup each **honey mustard** and **mayonnaise**; brush on toasted **potato buns**. Serve the burgers on the buns with **lettuce, onion** and **canned cranberry sauce**.

TURKEY NIÇOISE BURGERS

Mix 1 pound **ground turkey**, 1 grated peeled **green apple**, ½ cup minced **scallions**, ¼ cup **panko**, and **salt** and **pepper**. Form into four 1-inch-thick patties; make an indentation in the center of each. Grill on hot oiled grates over high heat, 4 to 5 minutes per side. Serve on grilled **multigrain bread**; top with **arugula** tossed with **vinaigrette, goat cheese, olives** and **grape tomatoes**.

LEMONY SALMON BURGERS Pulse ¼ pound **salmon** in a food processor with 2 tablespoons **dijon mustard**, 1 tablespoon **mayonnaise**, 1 tablespoon **lemon juice**, ½ teaspoon **lemon zest** and a pinch of **cayenne pepper**. Transfer to a bowl and mix with 1 pound diced salmon, 2 chopped **scallions**, 2 tablespoons **panko**, and **salt** and **pepper**. Pat into ¾-inch-thick patties on an oiled baking sheet and chill 30 minutes. Press the patties in panko. Heat **olive oil** in a large cast-iron skillet over medium-high heat. Add the patties and cook 3 to 4 minutes per side. Serve on toasted **brioche buns** with **tartar sauce** and **arugula**.

TUNA BURGERS

Dice ¾ pound **tuna.** Puree half of the tuna with 2 tablespoons **olive oil** and 1 tablespoon **soy sauce.** Mix with the remaining tuna. Form into 2 patties. Sear in an oiled cast-iron skillet over medium-high heat, 2 to 3 minutes per side. Serve on **buns;** top with sliced **cucumber** tossed with **sesame seeds, salt** and **sesame oil.**

PESTO SALMON BURGERS

Mix 1 pound flaked cooked **salmon,** 1 cup **panko,** ¼ cup **pesto,** 1 **egg** and 1 tablespoon **lemon zest.** Form into 4 patties; cook in an oiled cast-iron skillet over medium-high heat, 2 to 3 minutes per side. Serve on **buns** with **tartar sauce** mixed with **pesto.**

SCALLOP SLIDERS

Sear **sea scallops** in **butter.** Mix ¼ cup **mayonnaise** and 1 teaspoon **hot chile sauce.** Serve the scallops on **mini buns** with the spicy mayonnaise and **avocado.**

TIP

Homemade veggie burgers are too soft for the grill; cook them on a flat skillet instead.

PORTOBELLO BURGERS

Peel 8 **portobello mushroom caps;** season with **salt.** Top 4 mushroom caps with sliced **muenster;** cover with the remaining mushroom caps and secure with toothpicks. Dip in beaten **eggs,** then dredge in **panko;** fry in hot **vegetable oil** until crisp. Remove the toothpicks. Serve on **buns** with **pickles** and **tomato.**

BEAN BURGERS

Smash 1 can **kidney beans.** Mix with 1 shredded **red onion** (squeezed dry), ⅓ cup chopped **walnuts,** 1 diced **carrot,** ½ cup **breadcrumbs,** 2 chopped **scallions,** 2 tablespoons chopped **parsley** and 1 teaspoon **Worcestershire sauce;** season with **salt** and **pepper.** Form into 4 patties. Press in breadcrumbs. Cook in a skillet with **olive oil** until golden, 2 to 3 minutes per side. Serve on **English muffins** with **mayonnaise, mustard, arugula** and sautéed **mushrooms.**

VEGGIE BURGERS Sauté 1 each chopped **onion** and **celery stalk** with a pinch of **kosher salt** in **olive oil,** 12 to 14 minutes. Add 2 chopped **garlic cloves,** 3 tablespoons **barbecue sauce** and 1 grated **carrot;** cook 2 more minutes. Transfer to a food processor. Add 1½ cups cooked **barley,** 1 cup canned **black beans,** ⅓ cup **breadcrumbs,** ⅓ cup chopped **walnuts,** 2 teaspoons **soy sauce,** 2 **egg whites,** 2 tablespoons chopped **parsley** and ½ teaspoon salt; pulse. Form into 6 patties; chill 2 hours. Cook in an oiled skillet over medium heat, 6 minutes per side. Serve on toasted **buns** topped with barbecue sauce and **onion rings.**

JUICY LUCYS

Mix 1½ pounds **ground beef chuck** with ½ teaspoon **kosher salt.** Shape into 8 thin patties. Top 4 patties with 2 slices **American cheese** each; top with the remaining patties and press to seal. Heat a cast-iron skillet over medium-high heat; sprinkle the skillet with salt. Cook the burgers 4 to 5 minutes per side. Serve on **buns.**

BACON CHEESEBURGERS

Press **bacon** between 2 baking sheets. Bake at 400°, 20 minutes, uncovering after 10 minutes. Mix 1½ pounds **ground beef chuck** with ½ teaspoon **kosher salt.** Form into four ¾-inch-thick patties; make an indentation in the center of each. Heat a cast-iron skillet over medium-high heat; sprinkle the skillet with salt. Cook the burgers 4 to 5 minutes per side; top with **cheddar** during the last minute (cover to melt). Serve on **sesame buns** with the bacon, lettuce and tomato.

HOISIN BURGERS

Brush **bun** tops with a beaten **egg white;** sprinkle with **Japanese rice seasoning.** Bake at 350˚, 5 minutes. Mix 1½ pounds **ground beef chuck** with ½ teaspoon **kosher salt.** Form into four ¾-inch-thick patties; make an indentation in the center of each. Mix 3 tablespoons **hoisin sauce** and 1 tablespoon each **soy sauce, rice wine** and **honey;** brush on the patties and broil 4 minutes per side, brushing with more sauce. Serve on the buns with **mayonnaise** and broiled **scallions.**

HUNTSMAN BURGERS

Mix 1½ pounds **ground beef chuck** with ½ teaspoon **kosher salt.** Form into four ¾-inch-thick patties; make an indentation in the center of each. Heat a cast-iron skillet over medium-high heat; sprinkle the skillet with salt. Cook the burgers 4 to 5 minutes per side; top with **Huntsman cheese** during the last minute (cover to melt). Serve on toasted **English muffins.**

BACON-EGG CHEESEBURGERS
Mix 1½ pounds **ground beef chuck**
with ½ teaspoon **kosher salt.** Form
into four ¾-inch-thick patties; make
an indentation in the center of each.
Heat a cast-iron skillet over medium-
high heat; sprinkle with salt. Cook
the burgers 4 to 5 minutes per side;
top with **cheddar** during the last
minute (cover to melt). Serve on
buns with **bacon** and a fried **egg.**

CALIFORNIA BURGERS
Mix 1¼ pounds **ground chicken,**
½ cup **panko,** 2 teaspoons
Worcestershire sauce, 1 tablespoon
Greek yogurt, and **salt.** Shape
into four 1-inch-thick patties and
chill. Brush with **canola oil** and grill
on hot oiled grates over high heat,
4 to 5 minutes per side. Serve on
whole-grain bread with **sprouts,
cucumber, tomato** and **avocado.**

CREOLE CRAB BURGERS
Mix 1 cup sliced **cabbage,** ¼ cup each sliced **red onion** and chopped **parsley,** 3 tablespoons **mayonnaise** and 1 tablespoon each **Creole mustard, lemon juice** and **honey;** season with **cayenne pepper** and **salt.** Fry your favorite **crab cakes.** Serve on **buns** with the slaw.

SMOKED SALMON BURGERS
Puree 6 ounces **salmon** with 2 **scallions.** Mix with 6 ounces diced salmon, ¼ cup **panko** and 4 ounces chopped **smoked salmon.** Shape into 2 patties. Heat a cast-iron skillet over medium-high heat; sprinkle with **kosher salt.** Cook the patties 4 to 5 minutes per side. Serve on toasted **sesame buns** with **spinach** and **tartar sauce.**

How to cook hot dogs:

- **Grill** on hot oiled grates, turning with tongs, until charred, about 5 minutes.
- **Steam** in a basket set in a pot with a few inches of simmering water, covered, 5 to 7 minutes; add the buns during the last minute.
- **Boil** in a pot of water or beer, 4 to 6 minutes.
- **Fry** in 1 inch of 350° vegetable oil until swollen and crisp, about 2 minutes. (Score the hot dogs lengthwise first.)
- **Sear** in a hot cast-iron skillet with oil or butter, about 5 minutes.

PO'BOY DOGS

Serve grilled **hot dogs** on grilled **buns** with **rémoulade or Creole mustard,** shredded **romaine** and sliced **pickled okra.** Sprinkle with **Creole seasoning.**

LOW-COUNTRY DOGS

Boil 1 cup diced **potatoes** in a pot of water with ¼ cup **Old Bay Seasoning** until tender. Add **hot dogs** and cook 5 minutes, then add 1 cup **corn** kernels and cook 2 more minutes; drain. Separate **mini potato buns** into rows and split open; fill with the hot dogs, potatoes and corn.

CHICAGO DOGS

Serve boiled **hot dogs** on **poppy-seed buns** with **dill pickle** and **cucumber** spears, sliced **tomatoes, sweet pickle relish, pickled peppers,** diced **onion** and **yellow mustard.** Sprinkle with **celery salt.**

TIP

Don't pierce hot dogs before cooking; the dogs will end up dry.

PUPPY DOGS

Serve grilled or boiled **mini hot dogs** on split-top **mini potato rolls.** Top with **ketchup.**

BBQ DOGS

Grill **hot dogs,** brushing with **barbecue sauce.** Serve on toasted **buns** with **coleslaw** and more barbecue sauce.

SAUSAGE-AND-PEPPER DOGS

Halve **hot dogs** lengthwise; sauté in **olive oil** with sliced **bell peppers** and **onions.** Add some chopped **garlic,** a pinch each of **cayenne pepper** and **fennel seeds,** and a splash of water. Serve on toasted **hoagie rolls.**

POUTINE DOGS

Halve **hot dogs** lengthwise and cook in a skillet. Serve on a bed of **french fries,** topped with **cheese curds** and **gravy.**

CHILI-CHEESE DOGS

Serve grilled **hot dogs** on **buns** and top with **beef chili** and shredded **cheddar**.

FRITO DOGS

Serve grilled **hot dogs** on **buns** with **bean chili,** shredded **cheddar, pickled jalapeños** and crushed **Fritos**.

BACON-CHEESE DOGS

Score **hot dogs** lengthwise; stuff each with a stick of **cheddar**. Wrap with **bacon** and grill until crisp. Serve on **buns** with **fried onions**.

BRUSCHETTA DOGS

Toss 2 diced **tomatoes** with 1 chopped **garlic clove,** 1 tablespoon **balsamic vinegar,** 2 tablespoons **olive oil,** some torn **basil** and **salt**. Serve grilled **hot dogs** on toasted **Italian rolls;** top with the tomato mixture and olive oil.

CHIMICHANGA DOGS

Rub **hot dogs** with **chili powder** and wrap each in a **flour tortilla**. Dip in beaten **eggs,** then dredge in **flour** and deep-fry in 350° **vegetable oil** until golden; sprinkle with **cheddar** and bake at 375° until the cheese melts. Top with **salsa, sour cream** and **jalapeños**.

TRY THIS

Set up a condiment bar so guests can choose their own fixings.

CALIFORNIA DOGS

Serve boiled **tofu dogs** on **whole-wheat buns** with diced **avocado** and **cucumber, sprouts** and shredded **carrot**. Drizzle with **green goddess dressing**.

TACO DOGS

Wrap halved grilled **hot dogs,** shredded **cheddar, lettuce, salsa** and **sour cream** in grilled **flour tortillas**.

NEW YORK STREET DOGS

Serve boiled **hot dogs** on **buns** with **sauerkraut** and **spicy brown mustard**.

CORN DOGS

Combine ½ cup each **flour** and **cornmeal,** 1 teaspoon **baking powder** and a pinch each of **sugar, salt** and **mustard powder**. Whisk in ½ cup **milk** and 1 **egg**. Insert sticks into **hot dogs,** dredge in flour, then dip in the batter; deep-fry in 365° **vegetable oil** until golden.

PEKING DOGS

Sprinkle **hot dogs** with **five-spice powder;** grill, brushing with **hoisin or plum sauce**. Serve on toasted **potato buns** with sliced **cucumbers, scallions, cilantro** and more plum sauce.

MEXICAN DOGS

Mix ½ cup **mayonnaise** with ½ finely chopped **chipotle in adobo sauce.** Serve grilled **hot dogs** on grilled **buns** topped with the chipotle mayonnaise, crumbled **cotija cheese** and chopped **avocado.**

PIZZA DOGS

Simmer **hot dogs** in **marinara sauce.** Spoon onto toasted **buns** and sprinkle with grated **mozzarella** and **parmesan,** and **dried oregano;** broil until the cheese melts.

SOUTHERN DOGS

Serve grilled **hot dogs** on **buns** with **pulled pork, coleslaw** and **barbecue sauce.**

BOSTON TERRIERS

Sauté 1 diced **onion** and 4 ounces chopped **bacon.** Add 1 cup **white beans,** ½ cup **ketchup,** ½ cup water and 1 tablespoon each **brown sugar, mustard** and **cider vinegar;** add **hot dogs** and simmer until thick. Serve on toasted **buns.**

SPANISH DOGS

Spread the inside of grilled **buns** with **pimiento cheese spread.** Fill with grilled **hot dogs, serrano ham** and shaved **manchego cheese.**

TRY THIS

Make pigs in a blanket with a twist: Grill cocktail franks and serve on split-top dinner rolls.

HOT DIGGITY DOGS

Serve grilled **hot dogs** on grilled **buns** topped with shredded **pepper jack** and sliced **pickled jalapeños.**

CURRY DOGS

Simmer ¼ cup each **lime juice, brown sugar** and pitted **dates,** ¼ teaspoon each **cumin, chili powder** and **salt,** and a splash of water in a saucepan until thick; puree. Brush **chicken dogs** with **vegetable oil,** sprinkle with **curry powder** and grill. Serve on **buns;** top with the date puree, **curry snack mix,** diced **onion** and **cilantro.**

BACON FRIED DOGS

Score **hot dogs** lengthwise; wrap with **bacon** and fry in 350˚ **vegetable oil** until the bacon is crisp. Serve on **buns.**

CHIMICHURRI DOGS

Puree ½ cup each **fresh parsley** and **cilantro,** and ½ cup **olive oil,** ¼ cup **red wine vinegar,** 2 **garlic cloves,** ½ teaspoon each **red pepper flakes, cumin, dried oregano** and **salt.** Spread **mayonnaise** on split **baguette** pieces and fill with grilled **hot dogs.** Top with chopped **lettuce, tomatoes** and **onions,** and drizzle with the chimichurri sauce.

THAI DOGS

Serve grilled **hot dogs** on **buns;** top with shredded **carrots, cilantro** and **peanut sauce.**

SWEDISH DOGS

Serve grilled **hot dogs** on **buns;** spread with **lingonberry jam,** top with caramelized **onions** and drizzle with **gravy.**

SUNDAY-SUPPER DOGS

Brown 1 pound each **ground pork** and **ground beef** in a large saucepan with **olive oil.** Add 1 small chopped **onion,** a few chopped **garlic cloves,** a pinch of **red pepper flakes,** 1 **bay leaf** and 1 jar **tomato sauce;** fill the sauce jar with water and add to the pan. Add **hot dogs** and simmer until thick, about 1 hour. Serve on **hoagie rolls.**

HAM-AND-CHEESE DOGS

Tightly roll **hot dogs** in sliced **gruyère,** then wrap with sliced **ham.** Dip in beaten **eggs,** then dredge in **flour.** Deep-fry in 350° **vegetable oil** until golden. Slice and serve with **whole-grain mustard** and **cornichons.**

JAPANESE DOGS

Serve grilled **hot dogs** on **buns** with **pickled ginger, Asian snack mix** and **wasabi mayonnaise.**

TIP

Use leftover hot dog buns for panini. The soft, squishy bread is perfect for pressing.

FRENCH POODLES

Serve grilled **hot dogs** on split **baguette** pieces; melt **brie** on top. Add chopped **cornichons** and **dijon mustard.**

KOREAN DOGS

Serve grilled **hot dogs** on **buns** with chopped **kimchi,** diced **red onions** and **Asian mustard.**

GERMAN DOGS

Serve grilled **hot dogs** on grilled **buns** with **sauerkraut,** crushed **pretzels** and **German mustard.**

GREEK DOGS

Spread **tzatziki** on the inside of **buns.** Fill with grilled **hot dogs** and top with diced **kalamata olives** and chopped **cucumber.**

POLYNESIAN DOGS

Brush the inside of grilled **buns** with **hoisin sauce.** Add grilled **hot dogs** and top with chopped **pineapple** and sliced **scallions.** Drizzle with more hoisin sauce.

BLT DOGS

Fry thick strips of **bacon** until crisp, then fry **hot dogs** in the drippings. Serve on toasted **buns** with **mayonnaise, lettuce, tomato** and the bacon.

Panini

> **How to cook panini:**
> - **In a panini press:** Preheat the press. Add your sandwich and cook according to the manufacturer's instructions until golden and crisp, 3 to 5 minutes.
> - **On the stove:** Preheat a skillet with butter or oil over medium-low heat. Add your sandwich, then place a heavy pan on top to weigh it down. Cook until golden and crisp, 3 to 4 minutes per side.

« ROAST BEEF–CARAMELIZED ONION

Spread **dijon mustard** on 2 thick slices of **sourdough bread.** Layer shredded **gruyère,** sliced **roast beef, caramelized onions** and more gruyère between the bread. Press and cook until golden.

PEANUT BUTTER–BANANA

Spread **peanut butter** on a slice of **cinnamon-raisin bread.** Top with sliced **bananas.** Lightly brush another slice of cinnamon-raisin bread with **honey** and set on top. Press and cook until golden.

GRILLED CHEESE

Sandwich shredded **sharp cheddar** and **jack cheese** between thick slices of **white bread.** Cook in a skillet with **butter** until golden (don't press—the bread is soft and there's not a lot of filling).

CANADIAN BACON
Butter a split **English muffin.** Fill with 2 slices sautéed **Canadian bacon** and some sliced **Swiss cheese.** Press and cook until golden.

MUSHROOM-TALEGGIO
Brush the inside of a split crusty **Italian roll** with **olive oil;** season with **salt** and **pepper.** Fill with sautéed sliced **mixed mushrooms** and **onion.** Add sliced **taleggio.** Press and cook until golden.

EGGPLANT-MOZZARELLA
Brush the inside of a split **sub roll or sliced Italian bread** with **olive oil.** Fill with 2 slices each **fresh or smoked mozzarella** and grilled **eggplant,** and a few **basil leaves;** season with **salt** and **pepper.** Press and cook until golden.

BACON-DATE
Brush the inside of a split **French roll** with **olive oil** and spread with soft **goat cheese.** Fill with chopped **dates** and crisp cooked **bacon.** Press and cook until golden.

TIP

If you don't have a panini press, try cooking your sandwich in a waffle iron.

PESTO-TURKEY
Brush the inside of a split **sub roll or sliced Italian bread** with **pesto.** Fill with 3 or 4 slices **roast turkey breast,** 2 slices each **fresh mozzarella** and **tomato,** and a few **basil leaves;** season with **salt** and **pepper.** Press and cook until golden.

SUN-DRIED TOMATO–CHEESE
Brush the inside of a split **ciabatta roll** with **sun-dried tomato pesto.** Fill with a few slices each of **mozzarella, fontina** and **asiago.** Add some **baby spinach.** Press and cook until golden.

APPLE-MANCHEGO
Brush the inside of a split **soft roll** with **olive oil** and **quince paste.** Fill with sliced **apple** and **manchego;** season with **salt.** Press and cook until golden.

MEATLOAF
Layer shredded **sharp cheddar** and **jack cheese,** sliced leftover **meatloaf** and more shredded cheese between 2 slices of **potato bread.** Cook in a skillet with **butter** until golden (do not press). Serve with **ketchup.**

CAPRESE Brush sliced **Italian bread** with **olive oil.** Fill with 2 slices each **fresh mozzarella** and **tomato,** and a few **basil leaves;** season with **salt** and **pepper.** Press and cook until golden.

TUNA MELT

Layer shredded **cheddar, tuna salad** and more shredded cheddar between 2 slices of **rye bread.** Cook in a skillet with **butter** until golden (do not press).

APPLE-CHEDDAR

Spread **apple butter** on a slice of **white bread.** Top with grated **sharp cheddar** and another slice of bread. Cook in a skillet with **butter** until golden (do not press).

CUBAN

Spread the inside of a split **Cuban or other soft sub roll** with **yellow mustard.** Fill with sliced **pickles, ham, roast pork** and **Swiss cheese.** Press and cook until golden. (The traditional method is to use a skillet.)

ITALIAN MELT

Drizzle the inside top half of a split **sub roll** with **olive oil** and **red wine vinegar.** Layer sliced **provolone, salami, ham, turkey, pepperoncini** and more provolone on the roll. Press and cook until golden.

MIX IT UP

Add fruit to your panini: Peaches, apples and pears taste great with cheese.

BREAKFAST BURRITO

Roll up **scrambled eggs,** shredded **pepper jack** and **salsa** in a **flour tortilla.** Press and cook until golden.

CARIBBEAN

Spread the inside top half of a split **soft roll** with **yellow mustard** and drizzle with **hot sauce.** Fill with sliced **queso blanco, ham,** sautéed or fried **plantains,** charred **red onion** and more queso blanco. Press and cook until golden.

STEAK AND CHEESE

Mix equal parts **mayonnaise** and **horseradish.** Stir in some chopped **parsley.** Spread on the inside of a split piece of **baguette.** Fill with thinly sliced cooked **steak** and sliced **gruyère.** Press and cook until golden.

GERMAN

Spread **whole-grain mustard** on 2 slices **pumpernickel bread.** Sandwich thinly sliced **liverwurst** and shredded **muenster** between the bread. Press and cook until golden.

« **THREE-MEAT** Brush the inside of a split **Italian roll** with **olive oil.** Fill with sliced **soppressata, capicola, salami, fontina** and **roasted red peppers.** Press and cook until golden.

BLT GRILLED CHEESE
Thinly slice a **tomato**, pat dry and season with **salt**. Sandwich shredded **sharp cheddar** and **jack cheese,** the tomato, **escarole** and cooked **bacon** between 2 thick slices of **white bread.** Cook in a skillet with **butter** until golden (do not press).

TOMATO-TAPENADE
Thinly slice a **tomato,** pat dry and season with **salt**. Spread 2 slices of **crusty bread** with **olive tapenade.** Fill with grated **fontina,** the tomato and shredded **mozzarella.** Cook in a skillet with **butter** until golden (do not press).

ANCHOVY CAPRESE
Brush the inside of a split **sub roll or sliced Italian bread** with **olive oil.** Fill with 2 slices each **fresh mozzarella** and **tomato,** ½ chopped **anchovy,** a sprinkle of **capers** and a few **basil leaves;** season with **salt** and **pepper.** Press and cook until golden.

MORTADELLA-RICOTTA
Season 2 tablespoons **ricotta** with **salt** and **pepper.** Stir in some chopped **thyme** and **parsley.** Brush 2 slices of crusty **Italian bread** with **olive oil.** Sandwich with the herbed ricotta and sliced **mortadella;** press and cook until golden.

JERK SWORDFISH
Sprinkle 4 ounces **swordfish** with **jerk seasoning;** grill. Spread **mango chutney** and **mayonnaise** on the inside of a split **soft sub roll.** Fill with the fish, sliced **jalapeños** and shredded **pepper jack.** Press and cook until golden.

MORTADELLA-ARTICHOKE
Season 2 tablespoons **ricotta** with **salt** and **pepper.** Stir in some chopped **thyme** and **parsley.** Brush 2 slices of crusty **Italian bread** with **olive oil.** Sandwich with the herbed ricotta, sliced **mortadella** and **jarred artichoke hearts;** press and cook until golden.

MOZZARELLA IN CARROZZA
Sandwich 2 slices **fresh mozzarella** between 2 slices of **white bread.** Beat 1 **egg** with 2 tablespoons **milk** and some **salt** in a bowl. Dredge the sandwich in **flour,** then dip both sides in the egg mixture. Cook in a skillet with **olive oil** until golden (do not press).

GRILLED VEGGIE
Brush the inside of a split **ciabatta roll** with **pesto.** Fill with slices of grilled **eggplant, zucchini, yellow squash** and **roasted red peppers.** Add 2 slices **fresh mozzarella** and a few **basil leaves.** Press and cook until golden.

CHORIZO-PEAR Brush the inside of a split **soft roll** with **olive oil** and **fig jam.** Fill with sliced **pear,** sliced **dried chorizo** and **manchego;** season with **salt.** Press and cook until golden.

SAUSAGE-FETA

Cut a **pocketless pita** in half and brush both halves with **olive tapenade.** Sandwich with sliced cooked **spicy sausage, roasted red peppers** and crumbled **feta.** Press and cook until golden.

SPICY STEAK

Lightly spread **mayonnaise** on the inside of a split **onion roll.** Fill with thinly sliced cooked **steak** and season with **salt;** top with shredded **pepper jack.** Press and cook until golden.

APPLE-BRIE

Spread **dijon mustard** on the inside of a split piece of **baguette.** Fill with sliced **brie** and thinly sliced **green apple.** Press and cook until golden.

REUBEN

Spread **Thousand Island dressing** on 2 slices of **rye bread.** Layer sliced **Swiss cheese, sauerkraut, corned beef** and more cheese between the bread. Press and cook until golden.

TRY THIS

For parties, make a few panini, then cut into squares and serve as small bites.

TOFU REUBEN

Thinly slice **baked tofu** and sear in a skillet with **olive oil** until golden. Spread **Thousand Island dressing** on 2 slices of **rye bread.** Layer sliced **Swiss cheese,** the tofu, **sauerkraut** and more cheese between the bread. Press and cook until golden.

THANKSGIVING

Sandwich sliced **roast turkey, cheddar** and **cranberry sauce** between 2 slices of **potato bread.** Cook in a skillet with **butter** until golden (do not press).

TEX-MEX MELT

Brush the inside of a split **sub roll** with **olive oil.** Fill with sliced **roast beef,** sautéed **peppers** and **onions,** and shredded **pepper jack.** Press and cook until golden.

FLAT BRAT

Butter the inside of a split **hard roll.** Fill with **sauerkraut,** sliced cooked **bratwurst** and shredded **Swiss cheese.** Press and cook until golden.

LOBSTER SALAD Mix 1 cup chopped **lobster meat,** 2 tablespoons each minced **shallot** and melted **butter,** 2 teaspoons chopped **tarragon,** and some **lemon juice** and **salt.** Hollow out a split piece of **baguette;** fill with the lobster salad. Brush the outside with butter. Press and cook until golden.

CHICKEN SALTIMBOCCA
Brush the inside of a split **ciabatta roll** with **pesto.** Fill with sliced grilled **chicken, fontina** and **prosciutto,** and chopped **sage.** Press and cook until golden.

PULLED PORK AND CHEESE
Fill a **soft sesame roll** with **pulled pork,** shredded **cheddar** and charred **red onion.** Press and cook until golden.

HOT DOG, HAM AND CHEESE
Split cooked **hot dogs** in half lengthwise. Layer on a **soft sub roll** with sliced **ham, pickles, yellow mustard** and **Swiss cheese.** Press and cook until golden.

NACHO CUBAN
Spread the inside of a split **Cuban or other soft sub roll** with **yellow mustard.** Fill with chopped **pickled jalapeños,** sliced **ham, roast pork, salsa** and **cheddar.** Press and cook until golden.

Pizza & Pasta

How to make pizza:
1. Place a pizza stone or an inverted baking sheet on the lowest oven rack. Preheat to 500°.
2. Stretch 1 pound dough (store-bought or recipe below) on parchment paper or a floured pizza peel, or press into an oiled pizza pan.
3. Top the dough as desired, then slide the pizza onto the stone or baking sheet. Bake until golden, about 15 minutes.

Basic Pizza Dough
Whisk 3¾ cups **flour** and 1½ teaspoons **salt** in a bowl. Make a well and add 1⅓ cups warm water, 1 tablespoon **sugar** and 1 packet **yeast.** When foamy, mix in 3 tablespoons **olive oil;** knead until smooth, 5 minutes. Transfer to a clean bowl and brush with olive oil; cover and let rise until doubled in size, about 1 hour, 30 minutes. Divide into two 1-pound balls.

◀◀ MARGHERITA PIZZA
Stretch 1 pound **dough** into two thin 9-inch rounds. Top each with ½ cup crushed **San Marzano tomatoes, dried oregano, salt, pepper** and **olive oil;** bake until golden. Sprinkle each with ½ pound diced **mozzarella,** torn **basil** and salt. Bake until the cheese melts, then drizzle with olive oil.

SMOKED MOZZARELLA PIZZA
Stretch 1 pound **dough** into a 15-inch round. Top with **olive oil, salt,** chopped **thyme** and **oregano,** 1 minced **garlic clove** and 6 ounces sliced **smoked mozzarella.** Bake until crisp. Top with ¾ cup **ricotta** and grated **parmesan;** bake until melted.

PUTTANESCA PIZZA
Stretch 1 pound **dough** into two thin 9-inch rounds. Top each with ½ cup crushed **San Marzano tomatoes, dried oregano, salt, pepper** and **olive oil.** Chop 1 **garlic clove,** 6 **anchovies,** 1 tablespoon **capers,** ¼ cup **olives** and some **parsley** and scatter over the pizzas; bake until golden. Sprinkle each with ½ pound diced **mozzarella,** torn **basil** and salt. Bake until the cheese melts, then drizzle with olive oil.

FENNEL-TALEGGIO PIZZA
Stretch 1 pound **dough** into a 15-inch round. Top with **olive oil, salt,** chopped **thyme** and **oregano.** Add 6 ounces sliced **taleggio,** some sautéed chopped **fennel,** 2 tablespoons chopped **hazelnuts** and some grated **pecorino.** Bake until crisp.

To save time, ask to buy a pound of pizza dough from a local pizzeria.

ROASTED PEPPER PIZZA
Stretch 1 pound **dough** into two thin 9-inch rounds. Top each with ½ cup crushed **San Marzano tomatoes, dried oregano, salt, pepper** and **olive oil;** bake until golden. Sprinkle each with ½ pound diced **mozzarella** and some **red pepper flakes, roasted red pepper,** torn **basil** and salt. Bake until the cheese melts.

PEPPERONI PIZZA
Press 1 pound **dough** into an oiled rimmed baking sheet. Cover and set aside until doubled. Top with ¾ cup **tomato sauce** and 1½ cups shredded **mozzarella;** drizzle with **olive oil** and bake until just crisp. Top with 6 ounces sliced **pepperoni** and 4 ounces **bocconcini,** then bake until bubbly. Sprinkle with torn **basil** and **pecorino.**

LAMB-FETA PIZZA
Stretch 1 pound **dough** into two thin 9-inch rounds; brush each with **olive oil.** Top each with **caramelized onions,** ⅓ cup cooked **ground lamb,** ¼ cup **feta** and some **pine nuts.** Bake until golden; top with torn **parsley** and **mint.**

POTATO-ROSEMARY PIZZA Stretch 1 pound **dough** into a 15-by-9-inch rectangle. Top with **olive oil, fresh rosemary, sea salt,** 1 thinly sliced **potato** and some **pecorino;** bake until crisp.

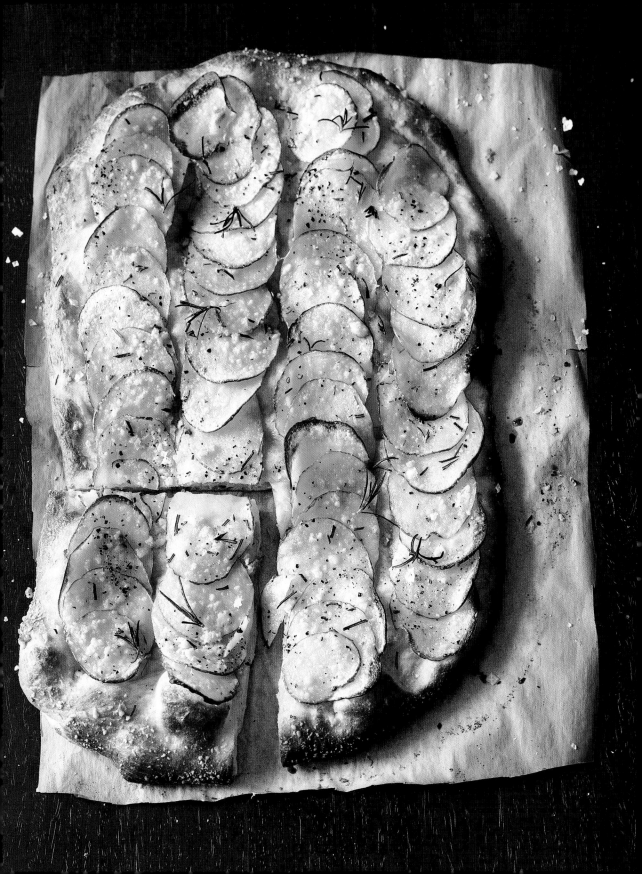

« BACON AND EGG PIZZA Stretch 1 pound **dough** into four 6-inch rounds. Top each with diced raw **bacon;** bake until crisp. Crack an **egg** onto each crust and top with **olive oil, salt** and **pepper;** bake until the eggs set. Top with **baby greens.**

SWEET POTATO PIZZA

Stretch 1 pound **dough** into a 15-by-9-inch rectangle. Top with **olive oil,** chopped **sage, sea salt** and 1 thinly sliced **sweet potato.** Sprinkle with **pecorino** and bake until crisp; top with crumbled **gorgonzola** and **pine nuts** 5 minutes before it's done.

PEPPERONI-MUSHROOM PIZZA

Press 1 pound **dough** into an oiled 15-inch pizza pan. Drizzle with **olive oil,** then top with ½ cup **tomato sauce,** some sautéed **mushrooms** and sliced **pepperoni,** and 2 cups shredded **mozzarella.** Bake, then top with **pecorino, dried oregano** and **olive oil.**

CAJUN SHRIMP PIZZA

Stretch 1 pound **dough** into two thin 9-inch rounds. Mix ¾ cup **tomato sauce** and 1 tablespoon **Cajun seasoning;** spread on the dough and top each with ½ cup shredded **manchego.** Bake until golden. Sauté chopped **scallions, green bell pepper, celery** and **shrimp;** season with **red pepper flakes.** Scatter over the pizzas.

PEPPER LATTICE PIZZA

Press 1 pound **dough** into an oiled 9-by-13-inch pan. Top with **caramelized onions.** Arrange sliced **roasted red peppers** on top in a lattice pattern; sprinkle with **olives** and bake until crisp. Drizzle with **olive oil.**

TOMATO PIE

Stretch 1 pound **dough** into two thin 9-inch rounds. Top each with ½ cup crushed **San Marzano tomatoes,** a generous amount of **dried oregano, salt, pepper** and **olive oil;** bake until golden. Drizzle with olive oil.

WHITE CLAM PIZZA

Stretch 1 pound **dough** into a 15-by-9-inch rectangle. Sprinkle with chopped **oregano** and 1 cup shredded **mozzarella,** then bake until crisp. Top with 8 ounces chopped **canned clams** and 4 ounces sliced mozzarella; bake until melted.

SALMON-POTATO PIZZA

Stretch 1 pound **dough** into a 15-by-9-inch rectangle. Top with **olive oil, rosemary, sea salt** and 1 thinly sliced **potato.** Bake until crisp. Top with **smoked salmon, crème fraîche** and chopped **chives.**

« BARBECUE CHICKEN PIZZA Stretch 1 pound **dough** into a 15-by-9-inch rectangle. Top with 1 cup shredded cooked **chicken,** ¼ cup **barbecue sauce,** some sliced **scallions, pickled jalapeños** and 1 cup shredded **cheddar.** Bake until golden.

WILD MUSHROOM PIZZA

Stretch 1 pound **dough** into a 15-inch round. Sauté 12 ounces **wild mushrooms** and 3 sliced **garlic cloves** in **olive oil;** scatter over the dough. Top with ½ cup each shredded **fontina, pecorino** and **mozzarella;** bake until golden.

OLIVE OIL–HERB PIZZA

Stretch 1 pound **dough** into a 15-inch round. Top with **olive oil, salt,** and chopped **thyme** and **oregano.** Bake until crisp, then brush with more olive oil.

NEW YORK–STYLE PIZZA

Press 1 pound **dough** into an oiled 15-inch pizza pan. Drizzle with **olive oil,** then top with ½ cup **tomato sauce** and 2 cups shredded **mozzarella.** Bake, then top with **pecorino, dried oregano** and olive oil.

SICILIAN PIZZA

Press 1 pound **dough** into an oiled rimmed baking sheet. Cover and set aside until doubled. Top with ¾ cup **tomato sauce** and 2 cups shredded **mozzarella;** drizzle with **olive oil** and bake.

TIP

Don't overload the toppings; you'll end up with a floppy crust.

HAWAIIAN PIZZA

Stretch 1 pound **dough** into a 15-inch round. Top with ½ cup each **tomato sauce,** shredded **mozzarella** and diced **pineapple,** 2 ounces sliced **ham,** and **red pepper flakes;** bake until golden.

FRESH VEGGIE PIZZA

Stretch 1 pound **dough** into a 15-inch round; bake until crisp. Mix 8 ounces **cream cheese,** ½ cup **sour cream,** 2 tablespoons chopped **basil** and 1 minced **garlic clove.** Spread over the crust. Top with chopped mixed **vegetables** and shredded **cheddar.** Sprinkle with **paprika.**

ZUCCHINI PIZZA

Stretch 1 pound **dough** into a 15-by-9-inch rectangle. Top with minced **garlic,** thinly sliced **zucchini, olive oil** and **red pepper flakes.** Bake until crisp.

ARTICHOKE-ASIAGO PIZZA

Stretch 1 pound **dough** into a 15-inch round; brush with **olive oil.** Top with 1 cup each shredded **asiago** and **jarred artichoke hearts.** Sprinkle with fresh **thyme;** bake until golden.

MEATBALL PIZZA Press 1 pound **dough** into an oiled 15-inch pizza pan. Top with **olive oil,** ½ cup **tomato sauce** and 6 ounces sliced **mozzarella.** Bake until just crisp, then top with sliced cooked **meatballs, pecorino,** torn **basil** and olive oil and bake until browned.

SAUSAGE-OLIVE PIZZA

Press 1 pound **dough** into an oiled 15-inch pizza pan. Top with **olive oil,** ½ cup **tomato sauce,** 6 ounces sliced **mozzarella,** 2 crumbled raw **sausages** and ⅓ cup chopped **kalamata olives.** Bake until just crisp, then top with sliced cooked **meatballs, pecorino,** torn **basil** and olive oil and bake until browned.

BROCCOLI RABE PIZZA

Press 1 pound **dough** into an oiled 15-inch pizza pan. Drizzle with **olive oil,** then top with ½ cup **tomato sauce,** 1½ cups shredded **mozzarella** and 2 crumbled raw **sausages.** Bake until just crisp, then top with 4 ounces **bocconcini,** sautéed **broccoli rabe** and **jarred cherry peppers.** Bake until the cheese melts.

FIG-ONION PIZZA

Stretch 1 pound **dough** into a 15-by-9-inch rectangle. Sprinkle with **cardamom.** Score into squares; top each with a **fig** half and a dollop of **robiola.** Bake; top with **caramelized onions.**

TIP

If you're using moisture-packed toppings, like zucchini or mushrooms, sauté them first.

APPLE-CHEDDAR PIZZA

Stretch 1 pound **dough** into two thin 9-inch rounds. Brush each with **olive oil** and season with **salt;** top each with ½ sliced **apple,** ½ teaspoon **fresh thyme** and ½ cup shredded **cheddar.** Bake until golden; top with crumbled cooked **bacon** and **maple syrup.**

PIZZA BIANCA

Press 1 pound **dough** into an oiled 15-inch pizza pan; top with **olive oil, salt, thyme, oregano** and ½ cup **robiola.** Bake until crisp; add 2 ounces each **ricotta** and **bocconcini,** olive oil and salt. Bake until the cheese melts.

STUFFED-CRUST PIZZA

Press 1 pound **dough** into an oiled 15-inch pizza pan and drizzle with **olive oil.** Place 8 **string-cheese sticks** along the edge and fold the dough over. Top with ½ cup **tomato sauce** and 2 cups shredded **mozzarella.** Brush the stuffed crust with olive oil and sprinkle with **dried oregano.** Bake, then top with **pecorino,** dried oregano and olive oil.

QUATTRO STAGIONI PIZZA Stretch 1 pound **dough** into two thin 9-inch rounds. Top each with ½ cup crushed **San Marzano tomatoes, dried oregano, salt, pepper** and **olive oil;** bake until golden. Top with **olives, jarred artichoke hearts,** sliced **ham** and sautéed **mushrooms** in four sections. Sprinkle each pizza with ½ pound diced **mozzarella,** torn **basil** and salt. Bake until the cheese melts, then drizzle with olive oil.

»

ONION-HERB FOCACCIA Press 1 pound **dough** into an oiled rimmed baking sheet. Mix ¼ cup **olive oil,** 2 tablespoons chopped **rosemary** and/or **oregano,** ½ teaspoon **red pepper flakes** and a big pinch of **sea salt,** and brush half over the dough; set aside until puffy, about 1 hour. Make dimples in the dough; top with thinly sliced **onion** and shaved **parmesan.** Bake until golden. Brush with the remaining herb oil.

HAM AND BRIE FOCACCIA

Press 1 pound **dough** into an oiled 8-inch-square pan. Top with 2 ounces sliced **ham,** 3 ounces sliced **brie** and ½ sliced **apple.** Add **olive oil, salt** and **pepper.** Bake until golden.

VERDE PIZZA

Stretch 1 pound **dough** into a 15-inch round; bake until crisp. Puree ¼ cup each **pistachios, basil, parsley** and **scallions,** 1 cup **arugula,** 2 **garlic cloves,** ½ cup **olive oil, salt** and **pepper.** Spread over the crust; top with **parmesan** and more arugula.

MORTADELLA PIZZA BIANCA

Stretch 1 pound **dough** into a 15-inch round; top with **olive oil, salt, thyme, oregano** and ½ cup **robiola.** Bake until crisp. Add 4 ounces each **ricotta** and **bocconcini,** olive oil and salt; bake until the cheese melts. Top with 2 ounces sliced **mortadella.**

BROCCOLI PIZZA

Press 1 pound **dough** into an oiled 15-inch pizza pan. Drizzle with **olive oil;** top with ½ cup **tomato sauce,** 2 cups shredded **mozzarella** and 1 cup blanched **broccoli.** Bake; top with **pecorino, dried oregano** and olive oil.

EGGPLANT PIZZA

Press 1 pound **dough** into an oiled 15-inch pizza pan. Top with **olive oil,** ½ cup **tomato sauce** and 6 ounces sliced **mozzarella.** Bake until crisp. Top with sliced **eggplant, ricotta, pecorino, basil** and olive oil and bake until browned.

RADICCHIO-PROSCIUTTO PIZZA

Stretch 1 pound **dough** into four 6-inch rounds. Divide ½ sliced **red onion** among the crusts; add **olive oil, salt** and **pepper.** Bake until crisp. Top with 2 ounces **prosciutto** and ½ head shredded **radicchio;** bake 1 more minute.

PISSALADIÈRE PIZZA

Press 1 pound **dough** into an oiled 9-by-13-inch pan. Top with **caramelized onions.** Arrange **anchovies** on top in a lattice pattern; sprinkle with **olives** and bake until crisp. Drizzle with **olive oil.**

SUN-DRIED TOMATO PIZZA

Stretch 1 pound **dough** into two thin 9-inch rounds; top each with **olive oil, salt, thyme, oregano** and ½ cup **robiola.** Bake until crisp, then add 2 ounces each **ricotta** and **bocconcini,** ¼ cup sliced **sun-dried tomatoes,** olive oil and salt to each; bake until the cheese melts. Top with **basil.**

CORN-RICOTTA PIZZA

Stretch 1 pound **dough** into two thin 9-inch rounds. Spread each with **caramelized onions.** Top with **thyme, corn, olive oil, salt** and **pepper.** Mix 2 tablespoons chopped **oregano** with ⅓ cup **ricotta** and dollop over the pizzas. Bake until golden; top with **basil.**

VEGETABLE PAPPARDELLE

Mince 4 **shallots,** 1 **carrot** and 1 **celery stalk.** Sauté in a skillet over medium heat with 2 tablespoons **butter** and 2 **thyme sprigs,** 6 minutes. Add ⅓ cup **white wine;** boil until evaporated. Add 4 cups **marinara sauce;** cook 3 minutes. Stir in 1 tablespoon butter and season with **salt** and **pepper.** Toss with 1 pound cooked **pappardelle.**

TUNA PUTTANESCA

Cook 4 sliced **garlic cloves** and a pinch of **red pepper flakes** in a skillet with **olive oil** over medium heat, 2 minutes. Add ½ cup chopped **kalamata olives** and 2 tablespoons **capers;** cook 2 minutes. Drain a 28-ounce can **plum tomatoes** (reserve the juice); crush into the skillet and cook 2 minutes. Add the tomato juice, some torn **basil,** and **salt;** cook 2 minutes. Add a 5-ounce can **oil-packed tuna.** Toss with 12 ounces cooked **linguine;** season with **pepper.**

LEEK-RADICCHIO RIGATONI

Heat 2 tablespoons **olive oil** in a skillet over medium-low heat; add 3 sliced **leeks** (white and light green parts) and season with **salt** and **sugar.** Cook, stirring, 10 minutes. Toss with 12 ounces cooked **rigatoni,** 1 cup pasta-cooking water, 2 tablespoons olive oil, 1 teaspoon **sugar** and 2 teaspoons **balsamic vinegar.** Add 1 small head sliced **radicchio** and 6 ounces cubed **fontina;** toss. Top with chopped toasted **hazelnuts.**

TIP

Add plenty of salt to pasta cooking water— at least 1 tablespoon for 4 quarts of water.

TOMATO-SALAMI FUSILLI

Cook 1 ounce diced **salami** and 4 minced **garlic cloves** in a skillet with 2 tablespoons **olive oil** over medium heat, 1 minute. Drain a 28-ounce can **plum tomatoes** (reserve the juice); crush into the skillet with your hands and cook 5 minutes. Add the tomato juice, 6 **basil leaves** and a pinch each of **sugar, salt** and **pepper;** cook 5 minutes. Stir in ¾ cup water and simmer until thick. Toss with 12 ounces cooked **fusilli.** Top with **parmesan** and **basil.**

PENNE ALLA VODKA

Cook 2 minced **shallots** in a skillet with **butter** over medium heat, 3 minutes. Add 1 minced **garlic clove** and a pinch of **red pepper flakes** and cook 30 seconds. Remove from the heat. Add ½ cup **vodka,** a 28-ounce can **crushed tomatoes** and **salt.** Simmer, stirring, 7 minutes. Stir in ⅔ cup **heavy cream;** simmer until thickened, 3 minutes. Stir in ½ cup grated **parmesan** and a handful of torn **basil.** Toss with 12 ounces cooked **penne,** adding some pasta-cooking water to loosen.

BLT PASTA Cook 8 slices **bacon;** drain and chop. Cook 1 chopped **red onion,** 3 sliced **garlic cloves,** some **red pepper flakes** and **salt** in 3 tablespoons drippings. Add 5 cups **grape tomatoes;** cook 12 minutes. Add ⅓ cup **cream;** cook 2 minutes. Toss with 12 ounces cooked **penne,** 4 cups **arugula,** the bacon, **basil** and some pasta-cooking water. Top with **parmesan.**

SPAGHETTI CARBONARA

Cook 6 chopped slices **bacon,** 2 tablespoons **olive oil,** 3 smashed **garlic cloves,** ½ teaspoon minced **rosemary,** 2 minced **jalapeños** and ¼ cup water in a skillet over medium-high heat until the water evaporates and the bacon crisps, 12 minutes. Discard the garlic. Add 12 ounces cooked **spaghetti** and toss. Whisk 3 **eggs,** ¾ cup grated **parmesan,** ½ cup grated **pecorino,** 2 tablespoons chopped **parsley** and some **pepper** in a bowl; whisk in ¼ cup pasta-cooking water. Add to the skillet and toss until creamy.

SEAFOOD PASTA

Heat 2 tablespoons **olive oil** and 3 sliced **garlic cloves** in a skillet over medium-high heat. Add a pinch of **red pepper flakes,** 1 cup **white wine** and 12 **littleneck clams;** cover and cook 5 minutes. Add 2 pounds **mussels** and 4 cups **marinara sauce.** Cook, uncovered, until the mussels open, 5 minutes. Toss with 1 pound cooked **bucatini** and **parsley.**

TIP

Save a bit of cooking water before you drain the pasta and use it to adjust your sauce, if needed.

PEA-PROSCIUTTO RAVIOLI

Cook 4 ounces chopped **prosciutto** in a skillet with **olive oil** over medium heat until crisp, 4 minutes. Stir in 3 sliced **garlic cloves** and 1 tablespoon **tomato paste;** cook 1 minute. Ladle in 1 cup pasta-cooking water; simmer until reduced by half, 4 minutes. Add ¼ cup **heavy cream;** simmer until thickened. Toss with 1 pound cooked **ravioli,** 1 cup blanched frozen **peas** and chopped **parsley.** Top with grated **parmesan.**

EGGPLANT-PARMESAN PASTA

Soak 1 pound cubed **eggplant** in warm salted water, 15 minutes. Drain; squeeze dry. Season 1 cup **flour** with **salt** and **pepper** in a bowl. Beat 2 **eggs** with ½ cup **milk** in another bowl. Mix 1½ cups flour and ½ cup grated **parmesan** in a third bowl. Dip the eggplant in the seasoned flour, the egg and then the flour-cheese mixture. Fry in **olive oil** over medium-high heat until golden; drain on paper towels. Mix with 4 cups **marinara sauce.** Toss with 1 pound cooked **rigatoni.**

RAVIOLI WITH SAGE-WALNUT BUTTER Combine ¼ cup **balsamic vinegar,** 2 teaspoons **honey** and a **bay leaf** in a saucepan over medium-high heat; cook until syrupy, 5 minutes. Melt 6 tablespoons **butter** in a large skillet over medium heat, then add ⅓ cup **sage leaves** and 1 cup chopped **walnuts;** cook 3 minutes. Add 1 cup pasta-cooking water and cook until reduced by half, 2 minutes. Toss with 1 pound cooked **ravioli,** some grated **parmesan** and **salt.** Drizzle with the balsamic syrup.

Perfect MARINARA SAUCE

Combine 3 tablespoons olive oil, 6 thinly sliced garlic cloves and a pinch of red pepper flakes in a large skillet; cook over medium-low heat until the garlic is golden, about 6 minutes. Crush a 28-ounce can of whole San Marzano tomatoes into the skillet with your hands; rinse the can with about 1 cup water and add to the sauce. Add a handful of torn basil leaves and season with salt. Increase the heat to medium and simmer, uncovered, until thick, 20 to 25 minutes. Toss with 1 pound cooked pasta (makes 4 cups sauce).

For extra-rich flavor, simmer the sauce with a parmesan rind or stir in a tablespoon of butter.

Pick a Pasta Match your sauce with the right shape.

| Capellini | Spaghetti | Fettuccine | Penne | Farfalle | Gemelli | Fusilli | Bucatini | Orecchiette | Rigatoni | Pappardelle |

Light, thin sauces ← — Medium-bodied sauces — → Thick, chunky sauces

Salads & Sides

Tossed Salads & Slaws

« CAESAR SALAD

Puree 1 minced **garlic clove,** 2 minced **anchovies,** the juice of ½ **lemon** and ½ teaspoon **Worcestershire sauce** in a blender. Add 1 **pasteurized egg yolk** and puree until smooth. With the motor running, slowly drizzle in ¼ cup **olive oil** and blend until smooth. Season the dressing with **salt** and **pepper.** Toss with torn **romaine;** top with shaved **parmesan** and **croutons.**

GREEN SALAD WITH BUTTERMILK DRESSING

Puree 2 chopped **scallions,** ½ minced **garlic clove,** ¼ cup each **buttermilk** and **plain yogurt,** 2 teaspoons **rice vinegar** and 1¼ teaspoons each **sugar** and **salt** in a blender until smooth. Toss 2 heads torn **butter lettuce,** ¼ cup shredded **carrots,** some **fresh cilantro** and **parsley,** and the buttermilk dressing in a large bowl; season with salt and **pepper.**

HERB SALAD

Whisk 1 teaspoon each **lemon juice** and **champagne vinegar** with **salt** and **pepper,** then whisk in 2 tablespoons **olive oil.** Toss with **fresh dill, basil, chives, tarragon** and **lettuce.**

SOUTHWESTERN COBB

Puree ⅓ cup each **mayonnaise** and **buttermilk,** 1 tablespoon **hot sauce,** 3 tablespoons **cilantro,** 1 sliced **scallion,** 1 teaspoon **orange zest,** 1 minced **garlic clove** and some **salt.** Toss with **romaine,** diced **avocado** and **jicama, orange segments** and **cotija cheese.**

CORNBREAD CAESAR

Toss 2 cups cubed **cornbread** with melted **butter, salt** and **cayenne pepper;** bake at 400°, 15 minutes. Puree 1 minced **garlic clove, 2 anchovies,** the juice of ½ **lemon** and ½ teaspoon **Worcestershire sauce** in a blender. Add 1 **pasteurized egg yolk.** With the motor running, slowly blend in ¼ cup **olive oil** until smooth; add salt and **pepper.** Toss with **romaine** and chopped **tomatoes;** top with the croutons.

TIP

Make vinaigrette in a jar: Just shake the ingredients to emulsify.

MISO-TOFU SALAD

Chop a 1-inch piece of fresh **ginger** in a blender; puree with 3 tablespoons **miso,** 2 tablespoons water, 1 tablespoon **rice vinegar,** 1 teaspoon **soy sauce** and ½ teaspoon **Sriracha.** Blend in ½ cup **peanut oil** until smooth. Toss the dressing with **baby spinach** and cubed **tofu.**

RED-AND-GREEN SALAD

Boil ¼ cup **balsamic vinegar,** 2 tablespoons **brown sugar** and the juice of 1 **lemon** in a saucepan until thickened, about 5 minutes. Whisk in ⅔ cup **olive oil** and season with **salt** and **pepper.** Combine torn **frisee, romaine** and **red endive** in a large bowl. Add sliced **red onion,** **scallions, parsley** and **candied walnuts.** Toss the salad with the dressing.

HERB-BIBB SALAD

Separate 1 large head **Bibb lettuce.** Combine in a large bowl with 2 tablespoons each torn **basil, dill, parsley** and **mint.** Toss with the juice of ½ **lemon** and 2 tablespoons **olive oil,** and season with **salt** and **pepper.**

BISTRO BACON SALAD Fry 4 strips chopped **bacon;** whisk 2½ tablespoons **cider vinegar** into the drippings. Pour into a bowl; whisk in 2 teaspoons **dijon mustard,** 2 tablespoons **olive oil,** and **salt** and **pepper.** Toss with **mesclun;** top with the bacon and a poached **egg.**

ESCAROLE-OLIVE SALAD

Mix ⅓ cup **olive oil,** a strip of **lemon zest,** 8 torn **basil leaves** and a pinch of **salt;** infuse 2 hours. Soak ½ thinly sliced **red onion** in cold water, 10 minutes; drain. Toss 1 head chopped **escarole,** the red onion slices, 2 sliced **celery stalks,** ¾ cup chopped **green olives** (plus a few tablespoons olive brine), 2 segmented **lemons** and ¼ cup each toasted **pine nuts** and **golden raisins** in a serving bowl. Discard the zest from the infused oil and drizzle the oil over the salad. Season with salt and **pepper.**

AVOCADO-ORANGE SALAD

Thinly slice ¼ **red onion;** soak in cold water 10 minutes. Whisk ¼ cup **orange juice,** the juice of 1 **lime,** 1 tablespoon **honey,** 2 teaspoons **dijon mustard,** ½ teaspoon **salt,** and **pepper** to taste in a bowl. Whisk in 3 tablespoons **olive oil.** Drain the onion; toss with 2 bunches **watercress,** 2 sliced **avocados,** 2 segmented **oranges** and the dressing. Top with **hazelnuts.**

MIX IT UP

Add some bite to your salad: Escarole, watercress, arugula and radicchio all have a peppery kick.

ARUGULA SALAD

Whisk 2 teaspoons each **whole-grain mustard** and **white wine vinegar,** ¼ teaspoon **salt,** and **pepper** to taste in a bowl. Slowly drizzle in 3 tablespoons **olive oil,** whisking until blended. Add 3 bunches torn **arugula** and ⅓ cup chopped toasted **walnuts** and toss.

SPINACH-WALNUT SALAD

Whisk 2 teaspoons **red wine vinegar** with 2 teaspoons minced **shallot,** and **salt** and **pepper** to taste. Slowly drizzle in 2 tablespoons **walnut oil,** whisking until smooth. Toss with 8 cups **baby spinach,** ⅓ cup crumbled **goat cheese** and ½ cup chopped toasted **walnuts.**

TRICOLOR SALAD

Whisk 2 teaspoons **balsamic vinegar** with **salt** and **pepper** to taste; slowly drizzle in 2 tablespoons **olive oil,** whisking until smooth. Toss the vinaigrette with 6 ounces **baby arugula,** ½ head torn **escarole** and ½ head torn **radicchio.** Season with salt and pepper.

WARM SPINACH-MUSHROOM SALAD Cook 1 sliced **red onion** in ¼ cup **olive oil** until soft and golden. Add 2 cups sliced **mushrooms** and cook until tender and browned; season with **salt.** Off the heat, stir in ½ cup torn **parsley,** 10 ounces **spinach** and the juice of 1 **lemon.** Season with salt and **pepper.** Sprinkle the salad with ½ cup crumbled **feta.**

SPANISH PIMIENTO SALAD

Brush 8 **scallions** with **olive oil;** season with **salt** and **pepper.** Grill until charred, about 4 minutes, then chop. Toss the scallions with ½ cup **olives,** 8 chopped **pimientos,** ¼ cup chopped **almonds,** 1 tablespoon **sherry vinegar,** 1½ teaspoons **smoked paprika** and some **romaine.** Grill thick **bread** slices; rub with **garlic.** Tear the bread into pieces and toss with the salad.

TOMATOES WITH MINT

Toss 2 pounds **heirloom tomato** chunks with **salt, pepper** and 1 thinly sliced **shallot.** Set aside 5 minutes. Top with **fresh mint;** drizzle with **olive oil** and **white wine vinegar.**

GREEK CUCUMBER SALAD

Mix 1 thinly sliced **red onion,** 4 cups chopped seeded **cucumbers,** 1 cup halved **kalamata olives,** ½ cup chopped **dill** and 1 cup crumbled **feta.** Toss with ½ cup **olive oil** and the juice of 1 **lemon;** season with **salt** and **pepper.**

TIP

To tame the bite of raw onion, soak thin slices in cold water for 10 minutes.

BEET–GOAT CHEESE SALAD

Whisk ½ cup **vegetable oil** with 2 tablespoons **sugar,** 2 tablespoons plus 1 teaspoon **lime juice,** ½ teaspoon each **mustard powder** and **salt,** 1 tablespoon finely chopped **onion** and 1 tablespoon **poppy seeds.** Toss with sliced **roasted beets** and **goat cheese.**

CELERY-SALAMI SALAD

Combine ½ bunch thinly sliced **celery,** ¼ thinly sliced **red onion,** the zest and juice of 1 **lemon** and a handful of torn **basil leaves.** Stir in some diced **salami.** Toss with ¼ cup **olive oil,** and **salt** and **pepper** to taste; shave some **parmesan** on top.

AVOCADO-JICAMA SALAD

Whisk 3 tablespoons **vegetable oil,** 1 tablespoon each **lime juice** and **orange juice,** 1 minced **shallot** and ½ teaspoon **salt** in a bowl. Add 2 diced **avocados,** 1½ cups cubed **jicama,** ½ cup each cubed **mango** and **pineapple,** and 2 tablespoons chopped **cilantro;** gently toss. Season with salt.

CUCUMBER–CHERRY PEPPER SALAD Toss 3 thinly sliced peeled **cucumbers** with 1 tablespoon **salt.** Chill 1 hour; drain and pat dry. Soak 3 tablespoons minced **onion** in cold water 15 minutes; drain. Mix 1½ cups **sour cream** and 1½ teaspoons **sugar,** then toss with the cucumbers, onion and ½ cup chopped **pickled cherry peppers;** season with **pepper.**

»

FENNEL SALAD
Core and thinly slice 2 **fennel bulbs** (use a mandoline if you have one); toss with sliced **red onion** and some of the fennel fronds. Drizzle with **olive oil** and **lemon juice** to taste, and season with **salt;** toss.

CREOLE GREEN BEAN SALAD
Combine 1 pound blanched thin **green beans** with 1 thinly sliced **red onion,** 1 tablespoon each **Creole mustard** and **red wine vinegar,** and 2 tablespoons **olive oil.** Season with **salt** and **pepper.**

GREEN BEAN–RADISH SALAD
Toss 1 cup blanched chopped **green beans** with 1 bunch thinly sliced **radishes** and 2 halved hard-boiled **eggs.** Drizzle with **olive oil;** season with **salt** and **pepper.**

CHAYOTE-LIME SALAD
Whisk the juice of 2 **limes,** 2 tablespoons **olive oil** and a pinch each of **sugar** and **salt.** Slice 1 peeled **chayote,** 1 **avocado** and 4 **radishes;** toss with the dressing.

TIP

The basic ratio for vinaigrette is 3 parts oil to 1 part acid (vinegar, lemon juice, etc.). Have fun and improvise!

CORN-SQUASH SALAD
Cut the kernels off 1 ear of **corn;** sauté in 2 tablespoons **olive oil** with 1 thinly sliced **yellow squash.** Toss the corn and squash with 1 chopped **yellow tomato** and a handful of torn **basil.** Season with **salt** and **pepper.**

PICKLED GREEK SALAD
Toss 3 quartered **tomatoes,** some **fresh oregano,** 2 tablespoons **capers** (plus 3 tablespoons brine), 1 tablespoon sliced **pickled peppers** (plus 1 tablespoon pickle juice), 3 tablespoons **olive oil,** and **salt** and **pepper.** Add some **watercress,** sliced **scallions** and **Greek olives;** toss.

SMOKED-TROUT SALAD
Whisk 1 tablespoon **cider vinegar** with 1 tablespoon minced **shallot,** 1 teaspoon **dijon mustard,** 1 teaspoon **honey,** and **salt** and **pepper.** Slowly whisk in 3 tablespoons **olive oil** until smooth. Toss the dressing with 6 ounces flaked **smoked trout,** 2 julienned **apples,** 1 julienned raw **beet,** 2 tablespoons **horseradish** and 2 bunches torn **arugula.**

HEIRLOOM TOMATO SALAD
Cut 1½ pounds **heirloom tomatoes** into wedges; season with **salt** and **pepper.** Cook 3 tablespoons **balsamic vinegar** and 2 teaspoons **brown sugar** in a skillet over medium heat until reduced by half, about 3 minutes. Remove from the heat; whisk in 2 tablespoons **olive oil.** Drizzle over the tomatoes; top with snipped **chives** and **basil.**

WATERCRESS-FRUIT SALAD

Cut 1 **peach** into wedges; toss with 1 cup seedless **watermelon** cubes, 2 tablespoons **olive oil** and 1 tablespoon **lemon juice**; season with **salt** and **pepper**.

JICAMA-ORANGE SALAD

Peel and segment 4 **oranges**. Squeeze the empty membranes over a bowl to release the juices. Whisk ¼ teaspoon **ancho chile powder, salt** and **pepper** to taste, 3 tablespoons **olive oil** and the juice of 1 **lime** into the orange juice. Toss in the orange segments and 1 peeled and diced **jicama**. Add 3 chopped **scallions**, 2 tablespoons **cilantro** and the seeds of ½ **pomegranate**.

ORANGES WITH MOZZARELLA

Toss 1 cup mini **bocconcini** and 1 cup **orange segments** with **olive oil**; season with **salt** and **pepper**. Top with torn **basil leaves**.

CANTALOUPE CARPACCIO

Slice ½ **cantaloupe** extra thin (use a mandoline if you have one). Toss with 2 tablespoons **olive oil**, 1 teaspoon **lemon juice**, and **pepper** to taste. Top with **ricotta**.

TIP

Invest in a mandoline: You'll get extra-thin, even veggie slices in no time!

WALDORF SALAD

Toss 3 chopped **apples** with 1½ tablespoons **lemon juice,** 2 sliced **celery stalks** and ¾ cup **walnuts**. Whisk ½ cup **mayonnaise**, 2 tablespoons **sour cream,** 2 tablespoons chopped **chives,** 1 tablespoon minced **parsley,** ¾ teaspoon **lemon zest,** 1 teaspoon **sugar,** and **pepper** to taste; toss with the apple mixture.

APPLE-HAM SALAD

Toss 3 sliced **apples** with the juice of 1 **lemon**. Cook 5 sliced **shallots** in 3 tablespoons **olive oil;** add **salt** and whisk in 2 tablespoons each **cider vinegar** and **dijon mustard**. Cool, then whisk in ¼ cup each **sour cream** and water. Toss with the apples, ½ pound chopped **ham,** 2 bunches **watercress** and 4 sliced **endives**.

NECTARINE-TOMATO SALAD

Toss 1 pound each **yellow tomatoes** and **nectarines** (both cut into wedges) with 2 ounces shaved **ricotta salata,** and **salt** and **pepper**. Toast 2 tablespoons **pine nuts** in 2 tablespoons **olive oil**. Off the heat, swirl in 2 teaspoons **balsamic vinegar;** drizzle over the tomato salad.

TOMATO-PEACH SALAD Toss 2 **tomatoes** and 2 **peaches** (both cut into wedges), ⅓ sliced **red onion**, 2 teaspoons **cider vinegar** and 1 tablespoon **olive oil**; add **sugar, salt** and **pepper**.

PEAR AND FENNEL SALAD

Whisk 3 tablespoons **white wine vinegar,** ½ teaspoon crushed **anise seeds,** and **salt** and **pepper** in a bowl, then whisk in ⅓ cup **olive oil.** Add 1 thinly sliced **fennel bulb,** 2 thinly sliced **pears** and some **parsley;** season with salt and **pepper** and toss. Top with shaved **pecorino.**

CURRIED TUNA SALAD

Toast 1 tablespoon **curry powder** in a skillet with 2 teaspoons **vegetable oil;** let cool. Mix with 6 tablespoons **mayonnaise,** ½ teaspoon **lime juice,** and **salt** and **pepper.** Toss with 2 cans flaked **tuna,** 3 tablespoons minced **red onion,** 1 tablespoon finely chopped **cilantro** and 1 tablespoon **golden raisins.**

BEET AND APPLE SALAD

Toss 2 thinly sliced **apples,** 4 thinly sliced **celery stalks,** 1 minced **shallot** and the juice of 1 **lemon.** Peel 1 raw **beet;** slice into matchsticks and add to the salad. Toss in 1 teaspoon **sugar,** 3 tablespoons each chopped **walnuts** and **olive oil,** and **salt** and **pepper.** Let stand 10 minutes.

TIP

To prevent soggy salads, dress your greens at the table right before serving.

SPICY SHRIMP SALAD

Whisk 2 tablespoons **rice vinegar,** 4 teaspoons **sesame oil,** 1½ teaspoons **sugar,** 1¼ teaspoons grated **ginger,** 1 teaspoon **lemon juice** and ½ teaspoon **salt** in a bowl. Julienne 5 **celery stalks,** a 4-inch piece **daikon,** 3 **carrots** and 2 **jalapeños.** Toss with the dressing; add ½ pound cooked **baby shrimp.** Top with **cilantro.**

ROAST BEEF SALAD

Whisk 2 tablespoons each **cider vinegar** and **honey mustard** with **salt, pepper** and 1 cup **hazelnut oil.** Toss with 2 sliced **endives,** 2 sliced **pears,** 8 cups **mesclun** and 10 ounces sliced **roast beef.** Top with **blue cheese** and **hazelnuts.**

PANZANELLA

Marinate 1½ pounds chopped **tomatoes** in ¼ cup **olive oil,** 2 tablespoons **red wine vinegar,** 4 minced **garlic cloves,** and **salt** and **pepper.** Soak cubed stale **bread** in water 5 minutes; drain, then toss with the tomatoes. Add sliced **red onion,** chopped **celery** and **basil;** toss.

WATERMELON-FETA SALAD
Whisk 2 tablespoons **white wine vinegar** with ⅓ cup **olive oil,** and **salt** and **pepper.** Toss with **baby arugula,** sliced **red onion,** cubed **watermelon,** crumbled **feta, niçoise olives** and **fresh oregano.**

CHICKEN-MANGO SALAD

Whisk 1 tablespoon each **lemon juice** and **honey,** 1 teaspoon grated **ginger** and ¼ cup **olive oil;** toss with 2 pounds shredded grilled **chicken,** 8 cups **mesclun** and 1 diced **mango.**

SPICY CARROT SLAW

Toss 4 grated **carrots** and 1 minced **garlic clove** with ¼ cup water; cover with plastic wrap and microwave until crisp-tender, 2 minutes, stirring once. Meanwhile, whisk 1 tablespoon **lemon juice** with 3 tablespoons **olive oil,** ¾ teaspoon **salt,** ¼ teaspoon **red pepper flakes,** and a pinch of **sugar.** Drain the carrots; toss with the dressing, 3 tablespoons chopped **parsley,** and salt and **pepper.**

CARROT-COCONUT SLAW

Mix 1 teaspoon **sugar,** ⅓ cup chopped **cilantro,** the juice of 1 **lime** and **salt.** Add 3 shredded **carrots.** Toast ½ teaspoon **cumin seeds** in a skillet with ¼ cup **vegetable oil,** 30 seconds. Add ⅓ cup **unsweetened shredded coconut** and swirl until golden. Let cool. Toss with the carrots.

TIP

Assemble and chill slaws a few hours before serving so the flavors have a chance to combine.

GRAPE-CABBAGE SLAW

Whisk 2 tablespoons **cider vinegar,** 1 tablespoon **dijon mustard,** 2 teaspoons **sugar,** 1 teaspoon **salt,** and ½ teaspoon **pepper.** Gradually add ¼ cup **olive oil,** whisking until smooth. Add 1 small head shredded **red cabbage,** ⅓ cup chopped **parsley,** 6 chopped **scallions** and 2 cups chopped **seedless red grapes;** toss to coat.

ASIAN APPLE SLAW

Mix ¼ cup **rice vinegar** and 3 tablespoons **lime juice** with 2 teaspoons each **sugar** and **fish sauce,** and a pinch of **salt.** Toss with 1 each julienned **jicama** and **apple,** 2 chopped **scallions** and some **mint.**

CREAMY SLAW

Toss 1 grated **carrot,** 1 head shredded **cabbage,** ⅓ minced **red onion** and 1 tablespoon chopped **parsley.** Whisk ½ cup each **mayonnaise** and **sour cream,** 3 tablespoons **pineapple juice,** 1 tablespoon **sugar** and 1 teaspoon **celery seeds.** Toss the vegetables with the dressing and season with **salt** and **pepper.**

JICAMA-MANGO SLAW

Toss 1 julienned **mango,** 2 cups julienned **jicama,** ½ cup thinly sliced **red onion,** 1 cup thinly sliced **radishes** and some **cilantro;** drizzle with **olive oil** and **lime juice.** Sprinkle with 1 teaspoon **ground cumin** and a pinch each of **salt** and **cayenne;** toss.

WATERCRESS WITH ORANGES
Whisk the grated zest and juice of 1 **orange,** 1 teaspoon **honey** and ½ cup **olive oil** in a bowl. Add 12 cups **watercress,** 3 sliced oranges, ⅔ cup toasted **walnuts** and ¼ cup thinly sliced **fennel** and toss.

TOMATO–BELL PEPPER SALAD
Toss 1 cup each diced **cucumber, tomato, green bell pepper** and **scallions** with 3 tablespoons chopped **dill,** 2 tablespoons chopped **parsley,** the juice of 1 **lemon** and ½ cup **olive oil.** Season with **salt.**

HEARTS OF PALM SALAD
Soak ¼ cup sliced **red onion** in cold water, 10 minutes; drain. Toss with 2 cups sliced **hearts of palm,** 1 cup sliced **celery** and some chopped **parsley.** Add 3 tablespoons each **lemon juice** and **olive oil,** and **salt** and **pepper.** Serve over **arugula.**

ESCAROLE-BACON SALAD
Cook 6 strips diced **bacon** in a skillet; drain on paper towels. Whisk 2 teaspoons **dijon mustard,** 3 tablespoons **red wine vinegar,** 1 teaspoon **honey,** and **salt** and **pepper** into the drippings. Whisk in 2 tablespoons **olive oil.** Toss the dressing with 1 head torn **escarole,** some sliced **radishes,** shaved **gouda** and the bacon.

BEET-ORANGE SALAD

Boil 1 pound **beets** in salted water until tender, 30 to 40 minutes. Drain, then peel and slice. Toss with ¼ cup **olive oil,** 2 tablespoons **sherry vinegar,** 2 tablespoons chopped **chives,** and **salt** and **pepper.** Add 1 bunch **arugula** and 2 segmented **blood oranges** and toss.

Potato & Pasta Salads

EGG-PICKLE POTATO SALAD

Boil, peel and cube 2 pounds **russets;** toss with 2 tablespoons **cider vinegar** and ½ teaspoon **salt.** Mix 2 cups **mayonnaise,** 2 finely chopped **scallions,** 1 finely chopped **celery stalk,** 3 chopped hard-boiled **eggs,** ½ cup finely chopped **red bell pepper,** ¼ cup diced **pickles** (plus 1 tablespoon pickle juice), 1 tablespoon **dijon mustard,** 1 teaspoon **sugar** and salt to taste. Toss with the potatoes.

GARDEN POTATO SALAD

Boil 2 pounds sliced **red potatoes,** adding 1 sliced **carrot** during the last minute of cooking. Drain; toss with 1 cup sliced **radishes,** 1 chopped **cucumber,** 3 chopped **scallions** and ½ cup chopped mixed **parsley** and **chives.** Mix ½ cup **mayonnaise,** ¼ cup **white wine vinegar,** and **salt** and **pepper;** toss with the potatoes.

THAI POTATO SALAD

Mix ⅓ cup each **mayonnaise** and **unsweetened coconut milk,** 1 tablespoon each **curry paste** and **lime juice,** and **salt.** Toss with 2 pounds boiled cubed **russets,** 1 sliced **bell pepper,** and some shredded **basil** and **mint.**

PATRIOTIC POTATO SALAD

Boil 2 pounds mixed cubed **red, white and blue or purple potatoes** with 2 tablespoons **cider vinegar.** Drain; toss with ½ cup chopped **celery** and ¼ cup chopped **scallions.** Mix ¼ cup **olive oil,** 2 tablespoons each cider vinegar and **whole-grain mustard,** and **salt** and **pepper;** toss with the potatoes.

CAVIAR POTATO SALAD

Whisk ½ cup **crème fraîche,** 2 tablespoons each **white wine vinegar** and **olive oil,** 1 tablespoon **dijon mustard,** some minced **red onion, chives** and **chervil,** and **salt** and **pepper.** Toss with 2 pounds boiled halved **new potatoes.** Top with **salmon caviar.**

TIP

For the best flavor, boil potatoes with the skins on; drain and cool slightly, then peel, if desired.

DILL POTATO SALAD

Mix ½ cup each **sour cream** and **mayonnaise,** ¼ cup each chopped **dill** and **scallions,** 1 teaspoon **sugar,** 2 tablespoons **cider vinegar,** and **salt.** Toss with 2 pounds boiled cubed **russets.**

PESTO-PEA POTATO SALAD

Boil 2 pounds cubed **Yukon golds,** adding 1 cup frozen **peas** during the last 4 minutes. Drain; toss with a mix of 6 tablespoons **white wine vinegar,** ¼ cup **pesto,** some **pine nuts,** and **salt** and **pepper.**

PROVENÇAL POTATO SALAD

Mix 1 cup chopped mixed **parsley, chives** and **tarragon,** ½ cup chopped **shallots,** ⅓ cup **white wine,** ¼ cup **olive oil,** 2 tablespoons each **white wine vinegar** and **dijon mustard,** and **salt** and **pepper** to taste. Toss with 2 pounds boiled halved **fingerlings,** 2 cups halved **grape tomatoes,** 1 shaved **fennel bulb,** ½ cup halved **kalamata olives** and some chopped fennel fronds.

BACON-RANCH POTATO SALAD Mix ⅔ cup **mayonnaise,** ¼ cup **buttermilk,** 2 tablespoons **cider vinegar,** 1 minced **garlic clove,** ½ cup chopped **celery,** 2 chopped **scallions,** 1 teaspoon **sugar,** and **salt** and **pepper.** Toss with 2 pounds boiled cubed **red potatoes** and 6 slices crumbled cooked **bacon.**

»

SICHUAN POTATO SALAD

Cut 2 **russets** into matchsticks; boil 1 minute. Cook 2 sliced **garlic cloves,** 1 teaspoon each **sugar** and **salt,** and 2 **dried red chiles** in a skillet with **peanut oil,** 30 seconds. Add 3 chopped **scallions.** Drain the potatoes; toss with the flavored oil, 1½ teaspoons **balsamic vinegar** and 1 teaspoon **sesame oil.**

SALT COD POTATO SALAD

Cook 3 sliced **garlic cloves** in a skillet with ¼ cup **olive oil** until soft. Mix with ¾ cup grated **tomato,** ½ cup flaked **salt cod** and 1 pound boiled cubed **Yukon golds.** Top with chopped **parsley.**

INDIAN POTATO SALAD

Cook 1 tablespoon each **garam masala,** grated **ginger** and **canola oil** in a skillet, 30 seconds. Mix with 1 cup **Greek yogurt,** ½ cup **mayonnaise,** 1 cup **chickpeas** and 2 pounds boiled cubed **russets.** Season with **salt** and **pepper;** top with **cilantro.**

TIP

Slice waxy spuds like Yukon golds and red potatoes before you boil them. If you slice them after, the skins may fall off.

GREEK POTATO SALAD

Mix 1 cup **Greek yogurt,** ¼ cup **olive oil,** and **salt** and **pepper.** Toss with 2 pounds boiled cubed **Yukon golds,** 1 cup chopped **cucumber,** ½ cup crumbled **feta,** 3 tablespoons each chopped **red onion** and **mint,** and some chopped **oregano.**

SALMON POTATO SALAD

Arrange 4 boiled sliced **Yukon golds,** ½ cup sliced **red onion,** 6 ounces **smoked salmon** and 2 sliced **tomatoes** on a platter. Mix ¼ cup **crème fraîche,** 1 tablespoon **lemon juice** and some **lemon zest;** drizzle over the salad. Top with **capers.**

HAM-CHEESE POTATO SALAD

Mix 1 cup **mayonnaise** with 2 tablespoons **mustard,** 8 ounces cubed **ham,** 6 ounces shredded **cheddar,** ½ cup each diced **red onion** and **pickles,** and 2 tablespoons chopped **pickled green chiles.** Toss with 2 pounds boiled cubed **Yukon golds.**

NIÇOISE POTATO SALAD

Boil 2 pounds halved **fingerlings,** adding 2 cups chopped **green beans** during the last 4 minutes. Mix 1 cup chopped mixed **parsley, chives** and **tarragon,** ½ cup chopped **shallot,** ⅓ cup **white wine,** ¼ cup **olive oil,** 2 tablespoons each **white wine vinegar** and **dijon mustard,** and **salt** and **pepper** to taste. Toss with the potatoes, green beans, 1 can **oil-packed tuna** (drained) and ½ cup halved **kalamata olives.**

GERMAN POTATO SALAD

Fry 4 slices **bacon;** cook ¾ cup chopped **onion** in the drippings. Add 1 tablespoon each **flour, sugar** and **whole-grain mustard,** ¼ cup each **white wine vinegar** and water, and **salt;** cook 2 minutes. Toss with 2 pounds boiled sliced **russets.** Crumble the bacon on top. Serve the salad warm.

CLASSIC RED POTATO SALAD

Boil 2 pounds cubed **red potatoes;** toss with 2 tablespoons **cider vinegar** and ½ teaspoon **salt.** Mix 2 cups **mayonnaise,** 2 chopped **scallions,** 1 chopped **celery stalk,** 1 tablespoon each **dijon mustard** and **cider vinegar,** 1 teaspoon **sugar,** and salt. Toss with the potatoes.

ROASTED POTATO SALAD

Halve 2 pounds **red potatoes.** Toss with ¼ cup **olive oil,** 6 **garlic cloves** and some chopped **rosemary;** roast at 400°, 25 minutes. Toss with chopped **parsley, salt** and 2 teaspoons each **dijon mustard** and **lemon juice.**

TIP

Dress potatoes while they are still warm so they'll absorb the dressing better.

CHIPOTLE POTATO SALAD

Mix ⅔ cup **mayonnaise,** ¼ cup **buttermilk,** 2 tablespoons each **chipotle hot sauce** and **cider vinegar,** 1 minced **garlic clove,** 2 teaspoons **orange zest,** ½ cup chopped **celery,** ¼ cup chopped **cilantro,** 2 chopped **scallions,** 1 teaspoon **sugar,** and **salt** and **pepper.** Toss with 2 pounds boiled cubed **red potatoes.**

WALDORF POTATO SALAD

Boil, peel and cube 2 pounds **russets;** toss with 2 tablespoons **cider vinegar** and ½ teaspoon **salt.** Mix 2 cups **mayonnaise,** 2 chopped **scallions,** 2 chopped **celery stalks,** 1 chopped **apple,** ½ cup chopped **walnuts,** 1 tablespoon cider vinegar, 1 teaspoon **sugar,** and salt. Toss with the potatoes.

RELISH POTATO SALAD

Boil, peel and cube 2 pounds **russets;** toss with 2 tablespoons **white wine vinegar** and ½ teaspoon **salt.** Mix 1 cup **whipped salad dressing,** ½ cup **relish,** 2 tablespoons **yellow mustard** and 1 chopped **scallion;** toss with the potatoes.

CRAB BOIL POTATO SALAD
Mix ½ cup each **corn** and chopped **celery,** 1 cup **mayonnaise,** 1 tablespoon **lemon juice** and 1½ teaspoons **Old Bay Seasoning.** Toss with 2 pounds boiled cubed **red potatoes** and 1 cup **crabmeat.**

CARROT-SESAME POTATO SALAD Boil 2 pounds sliced **red potatoes,** adding 4 matchstick-cut **carrots** during the last 2 minutes. Drain and toss with 4 chopped **scallions** and ½ cup bottled **sesame-ginger dressing.** Top with **sesame seeds.**

GREEN GODDESS POTATO SALAD

Puree 1 cup **mayonnaise,** ¼ cup mixed **parsley, tarragon** and **basil,** 1 **scallion,** 1 teaspoon **sugar,** and some **lemon juice** and **salt.** Toss with 2 pounds boiled halved **fingerlings.**

AVOCADO-SHRIMP POTATO SALAD

Puree 1 cup **mayonnaise,** ¼ cup mixed **parsley, tarragon** and **basil,** 1 **scallion,** 1 teaspoon **sugar,** and some **lemon juice** and **salt.** Toss with 2 pounds boiled halved **fingerlings,** some halved cooked **shrimp** and diced **avocado.**

DUTCH POTATO SALAD

Mix ½ cup **sour cream,** ¾ cup **mayonnaise,** 2 tablespoons each **horseradish** and **cider vinegar,** 2 teaspoons **caraway seeds,** 1 teaspoon **sugar,** 2 chopped **cucumbers** and 4 chopped **scallions.** Toss with 2 pounds boiled cubed **russets.**

BAGNA CAUDA POTATO SALAD

Cook 6 **anchovies,** 4 smashed **garlic cloves** and ½ teaspoon **red pepper flakes** in ⅓ cup **olive oil,** 5 minutes. Add ¼ cup each chopped **parsley** and **scallions,** 1 tablespoon chopped **oregano,** and the zest and juice of 1 **lemon.** Drizzle over 1 pound boiled sliced **red potatoes.**

COLESLAW POTATO SALAD

Mix ⅓ cup each **mayonnaise** and **olive oil** with ¼ cup **whole-grain mustard.** Season with **salt** and **pepper.** Add 3 cups **coleslaw mix,** 3 chopped **scallions** and 2 pounds boiled quartered **new potatoes.**

BEET-DILL POTATO SALAD

Mix ½ cup each **sour cream** and **mayonnaise,** ¼ cup each chopped **dill** and **scallions,** 1 teaspoon **sugar,** 2 tablespoons **cider vinegar,** and **salt.** Toss with 2 pounds boiled cubed **russets** and 1 cup sliced roasted **beets.**

GRILLED POTATO SALAD

Boil 2 pounds sliced **russets,** 5 minutes. Toss with ¼ cup **olive oil** and 1 tablespoon chopped **rosemary.** Grill the potatoes, ½ **lemon** and 1 sliced **red onion.** Chop the potatoes and onion; toss with more olive oil, some **parsley, salt** and the juice from the grilled lemon.

RANCH POTATO SALAD

Mix ⅔ cup **mayonnaise,** ¼ cup **buttermilk,** 2 tablespoons **cider vinegar,** 1 minced **garlic clove,** ½ cup chopped **celery,** 2 chopped **scallions,** 1 teaspoon **sugar,** and **salt** and **pepper.** Toss with 2 pounds boiled cubed **red potatoes.**

GRILLED VEGETABLE POTATO SALAD Boil 2 pounds sliced **russets,** 5 minutes. Toss with ¼ cup **olive oil** and 1 tablespoon chopped **rosemary.** Grill the potatoes, some sliced **zucchini** and **eggplant,** ½ **lemon** and 1 sliced **red onion.** Chop the potatoes and vegetables; toss with **grape tomatoes,** olive oil, **parsley, salt** and the juice from the grilled lemon.

PERUVIAN POTATO SALAD

Blend ½ cup **evaporated milk,** ⅓ cup **queso fresco** and 1 tablespoon each **aji amarillo paste** (or other chile paste) and **vegetable oil.** Toss with 2 pounds boiled cubed **Yukon golds** and ¼ cup chopped **olives.** Top with sliced hard-boiled **eggs.**

FRENCH POTATO SALAD

Mix 1 cup chopped mixed **parsley, chives** and **tarragon,** ½ cup chopped **shallots,** ⅓ cup **white wine,** ¼ cup **olive oil,** 2 tablespoons each **white wine vinegar** and **dijon mustard,** and **salt** and **pepper** to taste. Toss with 2 pounds boiled halved **fingerlings.**

GRILLED CHICKEN POTATO SALAD

Mix 1½ tablespoons each **champagne vinegar** and **dijon mustard,** ⅓ cup **olive oil,** ¼ cup chopped **cornichons,** some chopped **parsley,** and **salt** and **pepper.** Toss the mixture with 1½ cups diced grilled **chicken** and 2 pounds boiled halved **fingerlings.**

SALSA VERDE POTATO SALAD

Toss 2 pounds boiled cubed **Yukon golds** with 1 cup each sliced **red onion** and **bell pepper,** 1½ cups **salsa verde,** 1 chopped **avocado** and **salt** to taste. Top with **cilantro** and **cotija cheese.**

SWEET POTATO–BEET SALAD

Thinly slice 1 pound boiled **sweet potatoes** and 1 roasted **beet.** Whisk 1½ tablespoons **champagne vinegar,** 2 tablespoons **walnut oil,** and some **salt, pepper** and chopped **parsley.** Drizzle over the vegetables.

MEXICAN POTATO SALAD

Toss 2 pounds boiled cubed **Yukon golds,** 2 tablespoons **olive oil,** 1 tablespoon **cider vinegar,** 3 cups **salsa,** and **salt** to taste.

TOMATO-HERB POTATO SALAD

Soak ½ cup sliced **red onion** in ice water; drain. Toss the onion with 1 cup chopped mixed **parsley, dill** and **chives,** ½ cup chopped **shallots,** 6 tablespoons each **white wine vinegar** and **olive oil,** and **salt** and **pepper.** Toss with 2 pounds boiled quartered **new potatoes** and 2 cups halved **grape tomatoes.**

AMERICAN POTATO SALAD

Whisk ½ cup **mayonnaise,** 1 tablespoon **mustard** and 2 tablespoons each chopped **parsley** and **relish.** Toss with 2 pounds boiled quartered **new potatoes,** 2 sliced **celery stalks,** ½ chopped **red onion** and 2 chopped hard-boiled **eggs.** Season with **salt** and **pepper.**

CURRIED POTATO SALAD

Heat ⅓ cup each **olive oil** and **golden raisins** in a skillet. Add 2 teaspoons **curry powder** and stir 30 seconds. Off the heat, mix with 1 cup **Greek yogurt,** 2 cups blanched **green beans** and 2 pounds boiled cubed **russets.** Season with **salt.**

STEAKHOUSE PASTA SALAD

Toss ½ pound cooked **pasta shells** with 1 cup chopped cooked **steak**, 1 cup each chopped **bell pepper** and blanched **green beans,** and ½ cup crumbled **bacon.** For the dressing, mix ¼ cup each **mayonnaise** and **sour cream,** 1¼ teaspoons grated **garlic,** ¾ cup **parmesan,** 1 tablespoon **lemon juice,** and **salt** and **pepper.** Toss with the pasta mixture.

THAI NOODLE SALAD

Soak 8 ounces **rice vermicelli** in hot water 10 minutes. Drain and rinse under cold water. Mix 6 tablespoons **lime juice,** 3 tablespoons each **soy sauce, peanut butter, brown sugar** and **vegetable oil.** Toss with the noodles and some sliced **red bell pepper, scallions, basil, cilantro** and **mint.**

GREEK PASTA SALAD

Toss ½ pound cooked **penne** in a bowl with 1 cup chopped cooked **chicken,** 1 cup each chopped **cucumber** and **cherry tomatoes,** and ½ cup crumbled **feta.** For the dressing, cook 3 thinly sliced **garlic cloves** and a pinch of **red pepper flakes** in ⅓ cup **olive oil** over medium heat, 3 minutes; let cool and season with **salt** and **pepper.** Toss with the pasta mixture.

MACARONI SALAD

Whisk 1½ teaspoons **sugar,** ½ cup **mayonnaise,** 3 tablespoons **sour cream,** ¾ teaspoon **mustard powder,** 1½ tablespoons **cider vinegar,** and **salt** and **pepper.** Toss with 4 cups cooked **macaroni,** and some **sliced celery, red onion** and **parsley.**

TIP

It's best to slightly undercook pasta for a salad—it'll soak up the dressing and soften as it sits.

TUNA NIÇOISE PASTA SALAD

Toss ½ pound cooked **wagon wheel pasta** in a bowl with 1 cup canned **tuna,** 1 cup each chopped **celery** and **white beans,** and ½ cup **olives.** For the dressing, mix ⅓ cup **mayonnaise,** 3 tablespoons **sour cream,** 1½ tablespoons **lemon juice,** ½ cup chopped mixed **herbs,** and **salt** and **pepper.** Toss with the pasta mixture.

VEGGIE PASTA SALAD

Toss ½ pound cooked **penne** in a bowl with 1 cup chopped **baked tofu,** 1 cup each blanched **broccoli** and shredded **carrots,** and ½ cup each chopped **roasted red peppers** and chopped **walnuts.** For the dressing, mix ⅓ cup **mayonnaise,** 3 tablespoons **sour cream,** 1½ tablespoons **lemon juice,** ½ cup chopped mixed **herbs,** and **salt** and **pepper.** Toss with the pasta mixture.

PESTO PASTA SALAD

Toss 12 ounces cooked **penne** with 4 cups cooked **broccoli,** 1 cup diced **mozzarella,** ¾ cup pesto and ¼ cup **parmesan.** Top with sliced **almonds.**

SQUASH AND ORZO SALAD Sauté chopped **zucchini, yellow squash** and **scallions** in **olive oil.** Toss with cooked **orzo, parsley, dill, goat cheese, salt** and **pepper.**

ASPARAGUS PASTA SALAD

Toss ½ pound cooked **fusilli** with 1 cup each chopped blanched **asparagus** and **corn,** and ½ cup **sun-dried tomatoes.** For the dressing, mix ¼ cup each **mayonnaise** and **sour cream,** 1 tablespoon **lemon juice,** ¼ teaspoon grated **garlic,** ¾ cup **parmesan,** and **salt** and **pepper.** Toss with the pasta mixture.

SUMMER PASTA SALAD

Toss ½ pound cooked **fusilli** with 1 cup each **corn** and chopped blanched **green beans.** Add ½ cup chopped **sun-dried tomatoes.** For the dressing, whisk ⅓ cup **mayonnaise,** 1½ tablespoons **lemon juice,** 3 tablespoons **sour cream** and ½ cup chopped mixed **herbs.** Toss with the pasta mixture.

PASTA CAPRESE

Mix 1 pound cooked **fusilli,** 1½ cups diced **mozzarella,** 2 pounds chopped **tomatoes,** 2 cups chopped **basil,** 3 tablespoons **pine nuts** and 2 minced **garlic cloves;** season with **salt** and **pepper.**

TIP

Pasta salad tastes best at room temperature or even slightly warm—not straight out of the fridge.

SEAFOOD PASTA SALAD

Toss ½ pound cooked **pasta shells** in a large bowl with ½ cup **crabmeat** and ½ cup chopped cooked **shrimp.** Add 1 cup each blanched frozen **peas** and chopped blanched **asparagus.** Add ½ cup chopped **almonds.** For the dressing, whisk ⅓ cup **olive oil,** 2 tablespoons **white wine vinegar,** 1 minced **shallot,** ½ teaspoon **salt,** and **pepper** to taste until smooth. Toss with the pasta mixture.

PIZZA PASTA SALAD

Toss ½ pound cooked **wagon wheel pasta** in a large bowl with 1 cup cubed **salami,** 1 cup halved **cherry tomatoes,** 1 cup diced **red bell pepper,** ½ cup chopped pitted **kalamata olives** and ½ cup shredded **mozzarella.** For the dressing, whisk ⅓ cup **olive oil,** 2 tablespoons **white wine vinegar,** 1 minced **shallot,** ½ teaspoon **salt,** and **pepper** to taste until smooth. Add the dressing to the pasta mixture and toss.

BELL PEPPER–PASTA SALAD Broil 2 halved, seeded **bell peppers** and 6 unpeeled **garlic cloves** until charred. Peel the peppers; cut into strips. Peel the garlic and mash with **salt;** toss with the bell peppers and **olive oil.** Add 1 teaspoon **lemon zest** and the juice from the lemon. Mix in 12 ounces cooked **rigatoni,** some chopped toasted **almonds, bocconcini** and torn **basil.** Season with salt and **pepper.**

Beans & Grains

« **BALSAMIC BEANS**

Sauté 4 ounces diced **pancetta.** Add 2 minced **garlic cloves,** a small can of crushed **tomatoes** and 1 cup water; bring to a boil. Add 2 cans **white beans,** 2 tablespoons each **honey** and **balsamic vinegar,** 1 **thyme sprig** and a pinch of **red pepper flakes.** Simmer 20 minutes. Season with **salt;** top with chopped **parsley.**

TUNA-BEAN SALAD

Mix 1 can **cannellini beans,** 1 tablespoon **capers,** ½ cup **pickled mushrooms,** 4 sliced **celery stalks** and ¼ cup chopped **kalamata olives;** stir in 1 tablespoon **dijon mustard,** the juice of 1 **lemon,** and **salt** and **pepper.** Toss with a handful of sliced **cherry tomatoes** and 1 can **oil-packed tuna.**

THREE-BEAN SALAD

Bring ⅓ cup **cider vinegar,** ¼ cup each **sugar** and **vegetable oil,** and a pinch of **salt** to a boil. Meanwhile, blanch 8 ounces each **green and wax beans** in salted boiling water; drain. Toss with the vinegar mixture, 1 can **kidney beans** and some sliced **red onion;** marinate off the heat 1 hour. Add salt, **pepper** and chopped **parsley.**

BLACK-EYED PEA SALAD

Whisk the juice of 1½ **limes** with 1 minced **garlic clove** and some **cumin, salt** and **cilantro;** whisk in ¼ cup **olive oil.** Toss with 1 pound **black-eyed peas,** ½ minced **jalapeño,** and some diced **tomato, red onion** and **avocado.**

COWBOY BEANS

Brown 2 ounces diced **dried chorizo** in **olive oil.** Add ½ diced **onion;** cook 4 minutes. Stir in ½ diced **jalapeño,** 1 teaspoon each **dried oregano, chili powder** and minced **garlic,** and 1 chopped **tomato;** cook 1 minute. Add 1 can **pinto beans** (undrained) and ¾ cup water; cook 15 minutes. Add **salt, pepper** and **hot sauce.**

RICE-PASTA PILAF

Toast ½ cup broken **spaghetti** in 2 tablespoons **butter.** Stir in 1 cup **rice;** add 2 cups **chicken broth,** 1 cup water, 2 **garlic cloves** and 1 teaspoon **salt.** Boil 3 minutes, then stir, cover and simmer 15 minutes. Let sit 5 minutes; fluff with a fork and smash the garlic. Stir in some butter and **cilantro.**

TIP

Always drain and rinse canned beans to remove excess salt, unless a recipe says otherwise.

COCONUT RICE

Sauté 2 tablespoons minced **ginger** in a saucepan with **butter.** Add 1 cup rinsed **basmati rice,** 1 cup **coconut milk,** 1 cup water and a pinch of **salt.** Bring to a boil, then reduce the heat; cover and simmer until the liquid is absorbed, 15 minutes. Let stand 10 minutes off the heat; fluff with a fork. Top with chopped **cilantro** and **cashews.**

PASTA WITH FARRO

Toast 1 cup **farro** in a saucepan with **olive oil** over medium-high heat. Add 2 cups water and **salt.** Bring to a boil, then cover and simmer until the water is absorbed, 20 to 25 minutes. Meanwhile, cook 1 pound **orecchiette** as directed; drain. Brown 3 tablespoons **butter;** toss with the pasta and farro. Season with salt.

BULGUR-PINE NUT SALAD

Mix 2 cups cooked **bulgur,** ⅓ cup **pine nuts,** the juice of 1 **lemon,** ⅓ cup each chopped **scallions, mint** and **parsley,** and ¼ cup **olive oil;** add 2 diced **tomatoes,** and **salt** and **pepper.**

CHICKPEAS AND RADICCHIO
Fry 1 cup **parsley** in ¼ cup **olive oil** until crisp. Toss with 1 can **chickpeas,** 1 small head **radicchio** (cut into wedges) and the juice of 1 **lemon;** season with **salt** and **pepper.**

GREEK RICE SALAD

Whisk ⅓ cup **olive oil,** the juice of 1½ **lemons,** and a pinch each of **salt** and **allspice.** Toss with 1 diced **cucumber,** 2 diced **tomatoes,** 2 sliced **scallions,** ¼ cup each chopped **parsley, dill** and **mint,** and some **lemon zest.** Add 4½ cups cooked **rice** and a dash of **hot sauce;** top with **feta.**

GORGONZOLA POLENTA

Bring 4 cups salted **water** to a boil. Whisk in 1 cup **instant polenta.** Simmer, stirring, until thick, 10 minutes. Add 1 tablespoon **butter,** ¼ cup crumbled **gorgonzola,** 1 tablespoon chopped **oregano** and a dash of **nutmeg.** Top with more cheese and some **pepper.**

TABBOULEH

Cook 1 cup **bulgur** as the label directs; cool. Mix with 1 diced peeled **cucumber,** 1 cup chopped **parsley,** ½ cup each chopped **mint** and **scallions,** ¼ cup **olive oil,** 3 tablespoons **lemon juice,** 1¼ teaspoons **salt,** ½ teaspoon **allspice** and some **pepper.** Top with minced **jalapeño** and **feta.**

MIX IT UP

Try a new grain: Barley, bulgur and quinoa are all nutty-tasting, healthful choices.

CAULIFLOWER COUSCOUS

Cook 1½ cups **Israeli couscous** as the label directs. Drain, then rinse under cold water and toss with **olive oil.** Cook 3 cups **cauliflower** florets and 1 sliced **shallot** in olive oil, 6 minutes. Season with **salt** and **pepper.** Add a pinch of **cinnamon** and ¼ cup chopped **dates;** cook 2 more minutes. Add the cauliflower mixture to the couscous along with a splash of **red wine vinegar,** some chopped **parsley,** and salt and pepper.

SPICED LENTILS

Bring 1 cup **red or yellow lentils,** 4 cups water, a pinch of **turmeric** and a 1-inch piece chopped **ginger** to a boil; simmer 15 to 20 minutes. Whisk vigorously; season with **salt.** Cook 1 teaspoon **cumin seeds,** 2 sliced **garlic cloves** and 2 **dried red chiles** in a skillet with 3 tablespoons **olive oil** over medium-high heat, 2 minutes. Add 1 cup halved **cherry tomatoes;** cook 1 minute. Stir into the lentils. Add some chopped **cilantro.**

MUSHROOM BARLEY Cook 2 sliced **onions** in 2 tablespoons **olive oil** until caramelized, 20 to 25 minutes. Meanwhile, sauté ¾ pound sliced **cremini mushrooms** in 2 tablespoons **butter.** Cook 1½ cups **quick-cooking barley** in **chicken broth** as the label directs, then toss with the mushrooms, onions, some **dill** and **salt.**

OLIVE-DILL BULGUR

Toast 2 cups **bulgur** in 1 to 2 tablespoons each **butter** and **olive oil** over medium heat until golden. Add 4 cups water and season with **salt;** cover and simmer until the liquid is absorbed and the bulgur is just tender, about 20 minutes. Cut a seedless **cucumber** into chunks; toss with 2 teaspoons **red wine vinegar,** 2 teaspoons **olive oil,** ¼ cup chopped **dill** and a small handful of halved pitted **black olives.** Serve the cucumber mixture on top of the bulgur.

PILAF WITH CRANBERRIES

Cook 1¼ cups **wild rice blend** as the label directs, using **chicken broth** instead of water and adding ½ **cinnamon stick.** Cook ½ minced **onion** in a skillet with 3 tablespoons **butter,** about 5 minutes. Add ⅓ cup sliced **almonds;** cook 2 minutes. Add ⅓ cup **dried cranberries** and cook 2 more minutes. Toss with the rice. Top with chopped **parsley.**

TRY THIS

For extra flavor, cook your rice in chicken broth or use a bit of wine or beer in place of some of the water.

EDAMAME-SHIITAKE RICE

Soak 1 ounce **dried shiitake mushrooms** in 2 cups boiling water, covered, until soft, about 40 minutes. Drain, reserving the soaking liquid. Discard the shiitake stems and chop the caps. Cook 2 cups **sushi rice** as the label directs, using ½ cup soaking liquid in place of ½ cup water. Cook 1½ cups **frozen edamame** in salted boiling water until tender, about 6 minutes; drain. Add the edamame and mushrooms to the rice; season with **salt** and toss.

WILD RICE WITH HAZELNUTS

Prepare 1 cup **wild rice blend** as the label directs. Cook 1 thinly sliced **leek** in 2 tablespoons **butter** with a few **thyme sprigs** until tender, about 8 minutes; season with **salt** and **pepper.** Toss the cooked rice with half of the leek mixture, then top with the rest. Top with chopped **hazelnuts** and season with salt and pepper.

SPICED RICE WITH NECTARINES

Preheat a grill to medium high. Cut 2 **nectarines** into wedges and toss with **olive oil** and a big pinch each of **cumin, cinnamon, cayenne pepper** and **salt.** Grill until marked, 2 to 3 minutes per side. Chop and toss with 3 cups cooked **rice,** the juice of ½ **lemon,** a splash of olive oil, a pinch each of cumin and cinnamon, and ¼ cup each sliced **almonds** and chopped **dill.**

PASTA AND BEANS

Cook 8 ounces **small pasta** as the label directs, adding 1½ cups thawed frozen **fava or lima beans** in the last minute of cooking. Drain and toss with 1 cup chopped **parsley,** 1 bunch sliced **scallions,** ¼ cup **olive oil,** ¾ cup grated **parmesan,** ½ teaspoon grated **lemon zest,** and **salt** and **pepper.**

HUSHPUPPIES

Whisk ¾ cup **cornmeal,** ¼ cup **flour,** 2 tablespoons **sugar** and ¾ teaspoon each **baking soda** and **salt** in a bowl. Stir in 1 beaten **egg,** ½ cup each **buttermilk** and **corn,** 1 minced **jalapeño,** 4 minced **scallions,** and **pepper** to taste. Deep-fry spoonfuls of the batter in 350° **vegetable oil** until golden, 2 to 3 minutes.

LEMON ORZO

Simmer 1 cup **orzo** in a saucepan with 2½ cups water, 2 tablespoons **olive oil,** 1 teaspoon **dried mint,** 1 teaspoon **salt,** ½ teaspoon **paprika** and 2 strips **lemon zest,** stirring occasionally, until the orzo is tender, 12 to 15 minutes. Let cool slightly. Stir in 2 chopped **scallions,** the juice of 1 **lemon,** and salt to taste.

CURRY PILAF

Sauté 1 chopped **onion,** 2 smashed **garlic cloves,** 1 **cinnamon stick,** a strip of **lemon zest,** a pinch of **turmeric** and ½ teaspoon **curry powder** with **butter** and **olive oil** until golden. Add 1 cup **basmati rice;** stir until toasted. Stir in 1⅓ cups water and **salt;** bring to a boil. Cover and simmer 15 minutes. Let sit, then fluff. Add **lemon juice, cilantro** and **cashews.**

Vegetable Sides

« **BABY BELL PEPPERS WITH FETA AND MINT**

Toss 1 pound **baby bell peppers** or quartered regular peppers with 2 tablespoons **olive oil;** season with **salt** and **red pepper flakes.** Grill over high heat, turning, until blistered, about 10 minutes. Transfer to a bowl and toss with 1 tablespoon olive oil, some chopped **mint** and the juice of ½ **lemon.** Top with crumbled **feta.**

ROASTED POTATOES AND TOMATOES

Put a baking sheet in the oven and preheat to 450°. Cut 1½ pounds large **red potatoes** lengthwise into wedges. Toss with 2 tablespoons **olive oil,** 1 pint **cherry tomatoes,** 3 **rosemary sprigs,** 3 smashed **garlic cloves,** and **salt** and **pepper.** Put cut-side down on the hot baking sheet; roast 15 minutes. Flip and roast 10 more minutes.

GLAZED MIXED VEGETABLES

Cook 4 each sliced **carrots** and **celery stalks** in salted boiling water, 5 minutes. Add 1½ cups frozen **pearl onions;** cook 1 more minute, then drain. Cook 2 tablespoons each **butter** and **sugar,** and the juice of ½ **lemon** in a skillet until syrupy. Add the vegetables and **salt** and **pepper;** toss.

INDIAN CAULIFLOWER

Toss 7 cups small **cauliflower** florets and 3 chopped **plum tomatoes** with ¼ cup **olive oil,** 2 minced **garlic cloves,** 1½ teaspoons **cumin seeds,** ¼ teaspoon **turmeric,** a pinch of **cayenne pepper,** ½ teaspoon **salt,** and **pepper** to taste on a baking sheet. Roast at 450° until tender, about 25 minutes. Sprinkle with **lemon juice** and chopped **cilantro.**

GARLICKY BROCCOLI RABE

Cook ⅓ cup **olive oil,** 6 whole **garlic cloves** and a **rosemary sprig** over medium-low heat, stirring, until the garlic is golden, about 7 minutes. Season with **salt** and **pepper.** Meanwhile, cook 2 bunches **broccoli rabe** in salted boiling water until wilted, about 5 minutes. Drain and return to the pot, then pour in the garlic oil. Cover and cook, stirring occasionally, until the broccoli rabe is tender, about 5 minutes. Season with salt and pepper and top with shaved **parmesan.**

TIP

Don't toss your broccoli or cauliflower stems: Peel, slice into sticks and serve as crudité.

BROCCOLI WITH ANCHOVIES

Chop 1 bunch **broccoli** into florets; peel and slice the stems. Cook in 1 to 2 inches salted boiling water until tender, about 5 minutes; drain. Cook 1 chopped **garlic clove,** 3 to 5 minced **anchovy fillets** and a pinch of **red pepper flakes** in a skillet with 3 tablespoons **olive oil** over medium heat, 30 seconds. Add the broccoli, the juice of ½ **lemon** and **salt.** Drizzle with olive oil.

QUICK PICKLED VEGETABLES

Blanch ⅓ pound each halved **baby carrots, green beans** and **wax beans** until crisp-tender, 2 to 4 minutes. Cool the vegetables in ice water, then drain and put in a glass bowl with ½ sliced **red onion.** Make the brine: Boil 2 cups each **white vinegar** and water, ¼ cup **kosher salt,** 2 **bay leaves,** ¾ cup **sugar,** the zest and juice of 1 **lemon,** and 1 teaspoon each **peppercorns** and **coriander seeds;** pour the brine over the vegetables, then let cool. Chill at least 4 hours or up to 1 week.

BROCCOLI RABE WITH CHERRY PEPPERS
Cook 2 bunches **broccoli rabe** in a steamer basket until tender, about 7 minutes. Meanwhile, cook 2 sliced **garlic cloves** in a deep skillet with 1 tablespoon **olive oil** over medium heat until golden; add ¼ cup sliced **pickled cherry peppers** and 2 tablespoons liquid from the jar. Toss in the broccoli rabe and season with **salt** and **pepper.** Drizzle with olive oil and top with shaved **parmesan.**

CURRIED CORN

Mix 1 teaspoon each **ground ginger, paprika** and **coriander** with ½ teaspoon each **ground cumin** and **turmeric.** Brush 4 ears of **corn** with **vegetable oil.** Sprinkle with the spices and grill over high heat, turning, 12 minutes. Serve with **yogurt** mixed with **salt** and **cilantro.**

LEMON-BASIL CORN

Bring 4 cups water, ½ cup **basil leaves,** ½ **lemon,** 3 tablespoons **olive oil** and a pinch of **salt** to a boil. Add 4 ears of **corn;** cook about 5 minutes. Mix ½ cup torn basil, 1 teaspoon **lemon zest,** 1 tablespoon **lemon juice** and 3 tablespoons olive oil. Drain the corn and toss with the flavored oil and a splash of the cooking water.

LIME-SAGE CORN

Mix ½ stick softened **butter,** 1½ tablespoons chopped **sage** and 1 tablespoon each **lime zest** and **lime juice.** Season with **salt** and **pepper.** Boil 4 ears of **corn** about 5 minutes; drain and spread with the butter.

TIP

Don't buy prehusked corn—it deteriorates quickly once it's shucked.

TEX-MEX CORN

Pull back the husks from 4 ears of **corn** and remove the silk; sprinkle each ear with 1 teaspoon **chili powder.** Cover with the husks and grill over medium-high heat, turning, about 20 minutes. Combine ½ cup **mayonnaise** and 1 teaspoon chili powder in a bowl. Fold back the husks and spread the corn with the mayonnaise mixture. Sprinkle with grated **cheddar** and crumbled cooked **bacon.**

ARTICHOKES PROVENÇAL

Cook ½ chopped **onion,** 2 chopped **garlic cloves** and a pinch of **salt** in a skillet with 1 tablespoon **olive oil,** 5 minutes. Pour in ½ cup **white wine** and simmer until reduced by half. Add 2 chopped **tomatoes,** two 9-ounce packages frozen **artichoke hearts,** 3 tablespoons water, 1 strip **lemon zest** and ½ teaspoon salt. Cover and cook until the artichokes are tender, 6 minutes. Stir in some chopped **olives** and **basil.** Season with salt and **pepper.**

BARBECUED CORN Pulse 6 tablespoons softened **butter** with 1 **garlic clove,** ¼ cup **barbecue sauce** and 1 tablespoon **ancho chile powder** in a food processor until smooth. Brush 4 ears of **corn** with three-quarters of the spiced butter and wrap in foil. Grill over medium-high heat, turning often, until tender, 15 minutes. Brush with the remaining spiced butter and season with **salt.**

FENNEL WITH TOMATOES

Core and thinly slice 2 **fennel bulbs;** chop some of the fronds. Peel the cloves from 1 head of **garlic** and toss with the fennel and fronds, 1 quartered **lemon,** 3 tablespoons **olive oil** and 1 teaspoon each **salt** and **sugar** on a baking sheet. Roast at 500° until golden, about 20 minutes. Toss in 1 pint **grape tomatoes.** Continue roasting until the tomatoes burst, about 7 more minutes.

ASPARAGUS WITH GARLIC DIP

Trim 3 bunches **asparagus** and peel the bottoms. Boil until tender, 4 to 5 minutes; drain and cool. Peel the cloves from 4 heads **garlic** and cook in ½ cup **olive oil** over low heat until soft, 30 minutes. Drain, reserving the oil. Puree the garlic with 2 tablespoons **lemon juice,** 1 teaspoon **mayonnaise,** 1½ teaspoons **sugar,** 1 teaspoon **dijon mustard** and ¼ cup water. Blend in ¼ cup of the garlic oil. Season with **salt, pepper** and chopped **chives;** serve with the asparagus.

TIP

Peel the bottoms of thick asparagus with a vegetable peeler to get rid of the tough, woody parts.

LEMON ASPARAGUS

Boil 2 bunches **asparagus** 4 to 5 minutes; drain. Mix ½ cup chopped **parsley,** 1 tablespoon each **lemon zest** and **lemon juice,** 1 minced **garlic clove,** 2 tablespoons **olive oil,** and **salt** and **pepper** in a bowl. Drizzle the asparagus with olive oil and top with the parsley mixture.

CHEESE-CRUSTED SQUASH

Mix 2 minced **garlic cloves,** 8 minced **sage leaves,** the zest of 1 **lemon,** ½ cup grated **parmesan,** 3 tablespoons each **breadcrumbs** and **olive oil,** and **salt** and **red pepper flakes.** Pat onto thin wedges of **acorn squash.** Bake in a single layer at 450°, 15 to 20 minutes.

GRILLED BOK CHOY

Halve 1 pound **bok choy** lengthwise; microwave, covered, 3 to 5 minutes. Whisk ¼ cup **sweet chili sauce** with 1 tablespoon **rice vinegar** and 1 teaspoon each **brown sugar, sesame oil** and **soy sauce.** Toss with the bok choy. Grill over medium heat, 1 to 2 minutes per side.

GRILLED SUMMER SQUASH Toss 1½ pounds sliced **yellow squash** and 1 sliced **onion** with **olive oil, salt** and **pepper.** Grill over medium-high heat, 3 to 5 minutes per side. Toss with more olive oil, the zest and juice of 1 **lemon,** and some chopped **parsley** and **mint.** Top with shaved **ricotta salata.**

CREAMED SCALLIONS

Combine 4 bunches **scallions** and ¼ cup water in a saucepan; bring to a simmer, cover and cook 5 to 7 minutes. Add ½ cup **cream** and 1 chopped **garlic clove;** uncover and simmer until the liquid is reduced by half, about 5 minutes. Season with **salt** and **pepper.**

ROASTED TURNIPS

Toss 1 pound halved **baby turnips** and 10 ounces small **white mushroom caps** on a baking sheet with 2 teaspoons chopped **rosemary,** 2 tablespoons **olive oil,** and **salt** and **pepper.** Turn the turnips cut-side down and roast at 425° until tender, 25 to 30 minutes.

GRILLED RED ONIONS

Cut 4 **red onions** into wedges and quarter 8 **bacon** strips. Toss with 6 **oregano sprigs,** 1 tablespoon **olive oil,** 2 teaspoons **red wine vinegar,** 8 smashed **garlic cloves,** and **salt** and **pepper.** Divide between 2 pieces of foil; seal into flat packets. Grill over high heat, 15 minutes.

TIP

Remove leaves from root vegetables when you get home from the store; they leech moisture from the vegetables.

SPICED CARROT RELISH

Remove the zest from 1 **orange** and 1 **lemon** in strips using a vegetable peeler; thinly slice the strips. Bring the zest strips, the juice from the orange and lemon, 5 cups grated **carrots,** ¾ cup **sugar,** ¾ cup **cider vinegar,** 1½ cups water and 1½ teaspoons each crushed **coriander seeds, mustard seeds** and **salt** to a simmer in a large saucepan over medium heat. Cook until the carrots are soft and the liquid is syrupy, about 45 minutes. Let cool to room temperature.

CRANBERRY CARROTS

Cook 1½ pounds thinly sliced **carrots** in a skillet with 2 tablespoons **olive oil** until beginning to soften, 5 to 7 minutes. Add 1½ cups **no-sugar-added cranberry juice,** ¾ teaspoon **cumin** and a pinch each of **cinnamon** and **salt.** Simmer until the carrots are tender and glazed, stirring often, about 25 minutes. Sprinkle with chopped **parsley** and season with salt and **pepper.**

ONION GRATIN Toss 2 sliced **sweet onions** with 3 tablespoons **Worcestershire sauce,** 2 tablespoons **olive oil,** ¼ cup water, and **salt** and **pepper** in a baking dish. Cover; bake at 425° until tender, 25 minutes. Toss 1 cup **croutons** and ½ cup grated **gruyère** with some chopped **parsley,** olive oil, salt and pepper; sprinkle on the onions and bake 5 more minutes.

STEWED GREEN BEANS

Cook ½ chopped **onion** in a pot with 3 tablespoons **olive oil,** 5 minutes. Add 1¼ pounds **green beans,** a small can **crushed tomatoes,** 1¼ cups water, 1 teaspoon **salt,** ¼ teaspoon **pepper** and a pinch of **cinnamon.** Partially cover and simmer, 35 to 40 minutes.

BUTTERED SNAP PEAS

Cook 1¼ pounds **sugar snap peas** in boiling water until bright green, about 3 minutes; drain. Cook 1 minced **shallot** in a skillet with 2 tablespoons **butter** until soft, about 3 minutes. Whisk in a splash of water, then add the peas and cook 2 to 3 minutes. Add chopped **tarragon** and **parsley;** season with **salt** and **pepper.**

CHILE-GARLIC EDAMAME

Cook 1 pound frozen **edamame** in the pods in salted boiling water until tender, 5 minutes; drain. Heat 1 tablespoon **olive oil,** ¼ teaspoon **red pepper flakes** and 2 sliced **garlic cloves** in a skillet, 1 to 2 minutes. Stir in the edamame, **lime juice** and **salt.**

TIP

To avoid trimming green beans, buy thinner haricots verts instead.

EGGPLANT SALAD

Soak ¼ cup minced **red onion** in water. Pierce 2 **eggplants** with a fork; microwave until soft, 20 to 25 minutes. Cool the eggplants slightly, then halve, scoop out the flesh and chop. Drain the onion; toss with the chopped eggplant, 3 tablespoons **olive oil,** some chopped **cilantro** and **parsley,** a squeeze of **lemon juice,** and **salt** and **pepper.** Drizzle with more olive oil.

EGGPLANT CAPONATA

Cook 1 chopped **onion** in a skillet with ¼ cup **olive oil** until starting to soften, about 3 minutes. Add 1 chopped **celery stalk** and 1 chopped **eggplant** and cook 4 minutes. Add 1 chopped **red bell pepper;** cook 3 minutes. Add 3 tablespoons **golden raisins,** some chopped **oregano** and ½ cup water; simmer 8 minutes. Add 1 cup halved **grape tomatoes** and 1 tablespoon each **cider vinegar** and **capers;** cook 7 minutes. Stir in some chopped **basil.** Season with **salt** and **pepper.**

GREEN BEANS WITH PINE NUTS Sauté 1 sliced **red onion** in a skillet with **olive oil,** 5 minutes. Add 1 tablespoon olive oil and 1 pound **green beans;** cook 5 minutes. Add ¼ cup water, and **salt** and **pepper** to taste; cook until the beans are tender, about 7 minutes. Stir in 3 tablespoons toasted **pine nuts** and season with salt and pepper.

CLASSIC MASHED POTATOES

Cover 2 pounds whole **russet or Yukon gold potatoes** with cold water; add **salt** and simmer 45 minutes. Drain, peel and mash with ½ to 1 stick **butter.** Add 1 cup hot **milk,** and salt and **pepper;** mash until smooth.

BROCCOLI-CHEESE MASH

Cover 2 pounds whole **russet or Yukon gold potatoes** with cold water; add **salt** and simmer 45 minutes. Drain, peel and mash with ½ to 1 stick **butter.** Add 1 cup hot **milk,** and salt and **pepper;** mash until smooth. While the potatoes are cooking, boil 1 head **broccoli** florets until tender; drain. Add to the mashed potatoes with ½ pound grated **cheddar.**

SPICY MASHED POTATOES

Cover 2 pounds whole **russet or Yukon gold potatoes** with cold water; add **salt** and simmer 45 minutes. Drain, peel and mash with ½ to 1 stick **butter.** Add 1 cup hot **milk,** 1 tablespoon chopped **chipotles in adobo sauce,** and salt and **pepper;** mash until smooth. Top with chopped **scallions** and **cilantro.**

TIP

Use warm milk and room-temperature butter for mashed potatoes. Cold ingredients tighten the starches and make the potatoes gluey.

PESTO SMASHED POTATOES

Cover 2 pounds whole **red potatoes** with cold water; add **salt** and simmer 40 minutes. Drain; do not peel. Smash with ½ stick butter, ¾ cup hot **milk,** and salt and **pepper.** Stir in ½ cup **pesto** and top with **pine nuts.**

TWO-CHEESE MASH

Cover 2 pounds whole **russet or Yukon gold potatoes** with cold water; add **salt** and simmer 45 minutes. Drain, peel and mash with ½ to 1 stick **butter.** Add 1 cup hot **milk, pepper** and a tiny pinch of salt; mash. Stir in ½ cup each grated **parmesan** and **pecorino.**

ROSEMARY MASH

Cover 2 pounds whole **russet or Yukon gold potatoes** with cold water; add **salt** and simmer 45 minutes. Drain, peel and mash with ½ to 1 stick **butter.** Add 1 cup hot **milk, pepper,** and a tiny pinch of salt; mash until smooth. Stir in ½ cup each grated **parmesan** and **pecorino;** top with 2 teaspoons minced **rosemary** mixed with the grated zest of 1 **lemon.**

TANGY MASHED POTATOES Cover 2 pounds whole **russet or Yukon gold potatoes** with cold water; add **salt** and simmer 45 minutes. Drain, peel and mash with ½ to 1 stick **butter.** Add 1 cup **sour cream,** and salt and **pepper;** mash until smooth. Top with chopped **dill.**

ROASTED TOMATO MASH

Toss 1 pint **grape tomatoes** with **olive oil** and **salt** on a baking sheet; roast 20 to 30 minutes at 450°, stirring often. Meanwhile, cover 2 pounds whole **russet or Yukon gold potatoes** with cold water; add salt and simmer 45 minutes. Drain, peel and mash with ½ to 1 stick **butter.** Add 1 cup hot **milk,** and salt and **pepper;** mash until smooth. Stir the tomatoes into the potatoes.

SQUASH-MUSHROOM MASH

Cover 2 pounds whole **russet or Yukon gold potatoes** with cold water; add **salt** and simmer 45 minutes. Drain, peel and mash with ½ to 1 stick **butter.** Add 1 cup hot **milk,** and salt and **pepper;** mash until smooth. Meanwhile, peel and cube 1 pound **butternut squash;** boil 8 minutes. Drain, puree and swirl into the mashed potatoes. Sauté 12 ounces sliced **shiitake mushroom caps** in butter until golden; serve on the mashed potatoes and top with chopped **parsley.**

TIP

Avoid mashing potatoes in a food processor or with an electric mixer; a fork or potato masher works best.

TEX-MEX MASH

Cover 2 pounds whole **red potatoes** with cold water; add **salt** and simmer 45 minutes. Drain and mash with ½ to 1 stick **butter,** ¾ cup hot **milk,** and salt and **pepper.** Add ½ pound grated **jack cheese,** ¼ cup sliced **scallions** and 2 minced seeded **jalapeños.** Top with **sour cream.**

MASHED SWEET POTATOES

Roast 2 pounds **sweet potatoes** at 400° until tender, 1 hour. Halve; scoop out the flesh. Mash with ½ stick **butter** and add **salt.** Cook ½ cup diced **prosciutto** in **olive oil** 6 minutes. Spoon on the potatoes.

SAUSAGE-CHEESE MASH

Sauté ½ pound crumbled **sweet Italian sausage** until crisp. Cover 2 pounds whole **russet or Yukon gold potatoes** with cold water; add **salt** and simmer 45 minutes. Drain, peel and mash with ½ to 1 stick **butter.** Add 1 cup hot **milk,** salt and **pepper,** and 1 cup **parmesan;** mash. Top with the sausage.

BLUE CHEESE–WALNUT MASH Cover 2 pounds whole **russet or Yukon gold potatoes** with cold water; add **salt** and simmer 45 minutes. Drain, peel and mash with ½ to 1 stick **butter.** Add 1 cup hot **milk,** and salt and **pepper;** mash. Brown ½ stick butter with ½ cup chopped **walnuts,** 2 tablespoons each chopped **rosemary** and **parsley,** and ½ teaspoon salt; add a pinch of **sugar.** Crumble **blue cheese** over the potatoes; drizzle with the walnut butter.

TOMATO-CHARD POTATOES

Toss 1 pint **grape tomatoes** with **olive oil** and **salt;** roast 20 to 30 minutes at 450°, stirring. Cover 2 pounds whole **russet potatoes** with cold water; add salt and simmer 45 minutes. Drain, peel and mash with ½ to 1 stick **butter.** Add 1 cup hot **milk,** ½ pound grated **gruyère,** and salt and **pepper.** Mix in the tomatoes and some cooked **Swiss chard.**

CREAMY DIJON LEEKS

Halve 1 bunch **leeks** lengthwise; cut into pieces. Steam until tender, 10 minutes. Cook 1 minced **shallot** in 1 tablespoon **olive oil,** 2 minutes; season with **salt.** Add 1 tablespoon **flour** and cook 1 minute. Whisk in 1 cup **chicken broth;** cook until thickened, 4 minutes. Whisk in 1½ tablespoons **dijon mustard** and 3 tablespoons **parsley.** Spoon on the leeks.

ROASTED BEETS WITH FETA

Peel and dice 4 **beets.** Toss on a rimmed baking sheet with 1 tablespoon **olive oil,** 1 teaspoon **salt,** and **pepper** to taste. Roast at 450°, stirring once or twice, until tender, 35 minutes. Transfer to a bowl; toss with 4 chopped **scallions** and 2 teaspoons **lemon juice.** Top with crumbled **feta.**

TOMATO-GARLIC CORN

Slice the top off 2 heads **garlic;** drizzle with **olive oil,** wrap in foil and roast at 400°, 45 minutes. Squeeze out the cloves; mash with 1 grated **tomato** and 2 tablespoons grated **parmesan;** season with **salt, pepper** and **fresh thyme.** Grill 4 ears of **corn,** turning, 12 minutes. Cover with the tomato mixture.

BROCCOLI AND PEPPERS

Cook 1 pound **broccoli** and 1 sliced **red bell pepper** in salted boiling water until just tender, 3 minutes; drain. Transfer to ice water to cool; drain. Heat 2 tablespoons **olive oil** over medium heat. Add ½ cup chopped **walnuts,** 2 sliced **garlic cloves** and 2 crushed **dried red chiles;** cook about 30 seconds. Add the vegetables and cook 2 more minutes. Season with **salt.**

PEPPER-SWIRLED POTATOES

Cover 2 pounds whole **russet or Yukon gold potatoes** with cold water; add **salt** and simmer 45 minutes. Drain, peel and mash with ½ to 1 stick **butter.** Add 1 cup hot **milk,** and salt and **pepper;** mash until smooth. Sauté 2 chopped **red bell peppers** and 1 teaspoon **fresh thyme** in **olive oil,** covered, until tender. Puree and swirl into the potatoes.

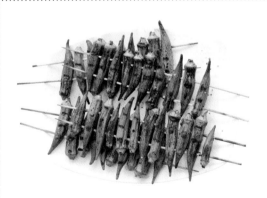

GREEK SMASHED POTATOES

Cover 2 pounds whole **red potatoes** with cold water; add **salt** and simmer 40 minutes. Drain; do not peel. Smash with ½ stick **butter,** ¾ cup hot **milk,** and salt and **pepper.** Mix in ½ pound **feta,** ¼ cup each minced **dill, parsley** and **scallions,** and some **fresh oregano.**

SMOKY OKRA

Toss 1 pound **okra** with 1 tablespoon **vegetable oil** and ¾ teaspoon each **salt** and **smoked paprika.** Thread the okra across 2 skewers, leaving a bit of space between each piece. Grill over medium-high heat until tender and charred, 4 to 5 minutes per side.

CRANBERRY SAUCE

Empty a 12-ounce bag of fresh or frozen cranberries into a saucepan and transfer ½ cup to a small bowl.

Add 1 cup sugar, 1 strip orange or lemon zest and 2 tablespoons water to the pan; cook over low heat, stirring occasionally, until the sugar dissolves and the cranberries are soft, about 10 minutes. Increase the heat to medium and cook until the cranberries burst, about 12 minutes. Reduce the heat to low and stir in the reserved cranberries. Add sugar, salt and pepper to taste and cool to room temperature before serving.

Extra, Extra... Polish off your leftover cranberry sauce.

Stir into champagne.

Spread on a chicken salad sandwich.

Serve with blue cheese or brie and crackers.

Spoon over store-bought cheesecake.

Whisk into vinaigrette and drizzle over greens.

Refrigerate cranberries in an airtight container for up to 1 month or freeze for up to 1 year.

Drinks & Desserts

Cold Drinks

PEACH-GINGER ICED TEA
Steep 4 **black tea bags** in 6 cups hot water, 4 minutes. Remove the tea bags; let the tea cool. Mash 6 **canned peach halves** with 1½ cups of the peach juice, ⅓ cup **sugar** and 1 tablespoon grated **ginger** in a pitcher. Add ice and the tea.

BLACKBERRY ICED TEA
Steep 6 **black tea bags** in 8 cups hot water, 4 minutes. Remove the tea bags and let the tea cool; chill. Combine ¾ cup **sugar,** ½ cup water and 1 cup **blackberries** in a saucepan; bring to a simmer over medium heat, stirring until the sugar dissolves. Remove from the heat and let cool, then strain. Fill a pitcher with ice, then add the tea and the blackberry syrup.

MINT ICED TEA
Steep 6 **black tea bags** in 8 cups hot water, 4 minutes. Remove the tea bags and let the tea cool; chill. Combine ¾ cup each **sugar** and water and 3 **mint sprigs** in a saucepan; bring to a simmer over medium heat, stirring until the sugar dissolves. Remove from the heat and let cool, then strain. Fill a pitcher with ice, then add the tea and the mint syrup.

LAVENDER ICED TEA
Steep 6 **black tea bags** in 8 cups hot water, 4 minutes. Remove the tea bags and let the tea cool; chill. Simmer ¾ cup each **sugar** and water and 3 tablespoons **dried lavender** in a saucepan over medium heat, stirring until the sugar dissolves. Remove from the heat and let cool, then strain. Fill a pitcher with ice; add the tea and the lavender syrup.

ORANGE ICED TEA
Steep 6 **black tea bags** in 8 cups hot water, 4 minutes. Remove the tea bags and let the tea cool; chill. Simmer ¾ cup each **sugar** and water and 6 strips **orange zest** in a saucepan over medium heat, stirring until the sugar dissolves. Remove from the heat and let cool, then strain. Fill a pitcher with ice; add the tea and the orange syrup.

GUAVA ICED TEA
Steep 3 **green tea bags** in 4 cups hot water, 4 minutes. Remove the tea bags and let the tea cool; chill. Mix with 4 cups **guava juice** in a pitcher with ice; garnish with **lemon** slices.

TIP

Don't squeeze tea bags when you remove them: The tannins will make your iced tea taste bitter.

THAI ICED TEA
Combine 8 cups cold **black tea** and ⅓ to ¼ cup **sweetened condensed milk** in a pitcher. Serve over ice.

ICED CHAI
Brew 6 **black tea bags** in 4 cups hot water with a 1-inch piece **ginger** and 2 teaspoons **chai spice blend.** Let cool, then remove the tea bags and ginger and stir in ¼ cup **honey.** Serve over ice with **sweetened condensed milk** to taste.

VIETNAMESE ICED COFFEE
Pour 3 tablespoons **sweetened condensed milk** in a glass over ice; add 1 cup cold strong **coffee.**

CARAMEL-JAVA FREEZE
Puree 1 cup cold **espresso,** 1 cup **milk,** ¼ cup each **caramel sauce** and **sugar** and 2 cups crushed ice. Pour into 4 glasses; top with **whipped cream** and more caramel.

ARNOLD PALMER
Mix 4 cups **lemonade** and 4 cups cold **black tea** in a pitcher. Serve on ice with **lemon** slices.

BERRY-GUAVA LEMONADE For each drink, mash 4 diced **strawberries** with 2 tablespoons **sugar** and 4 tablespoons **guava juice** in a glass. Fill with ice, then add 6 tablespoons **lemon juice** and some **lemon** slices.

STRAWBERRY LIMEADE

Bring 1 cup **sugar** and 1 cup water to simmer in a saucepan over medium heat; let cool. Combine in a pitcher with 1 cup **lime juice,** 2 cups cold water, some frozen chopped **strawberries** and ice. Add a few **lime slices.**

HIBISCUS LEMONADE

Bring 1 cup **dried hibiscus** and 1½ cups each **sugar** and water to a simmer in a saucepan over medium heat, stirring until the sugar dissolves. Let cool, then strain the syrup into an ice-filled pitcher. Add 2 cups each **lemon juice** and cold water.

LAVENDER ORANGEADE

Bring ¼ cup **dried lavender** and 1½ cups each **sugar** and water to a simmer in a saucepan over medium heat, stirring until the sugar dissolves. Let cool, then strain into an ice-filled pitcher. Stir in 2 cups each **orange juice** and cold water, then add a few strips of **orange zest** or some **orange slices.**

TIP

To get the most juice out of your citrus, press and roll the fruit on the counter before squeezing.

PINK LEMONADE

Boil 1 cup **sugar,** 1 cup water and 2 cups **raspberries;** let cool. Strain into an ice-filled pitcher, then stir in 1 cup **lemon juice** and 2 cups cold water.

CINNAMON GRAPEFRUITADE

Bring 4 **cinnamon sticks** and 1½ cups each **sugar** and water to a simmer in a saucepan over medium heat, stirring until the sugar dissolves. Let cool, then pour the syrup into an ice-filled pitcher. Stir in 2 cups each **grapefruit juice** and cold water and add a handful of **raspberries.**

INSTANT HORCHATA

Sweeten a pitcher of **rice milk** with **sugar,** then add a pinch of **cinnamon.** Serve over ice with diced **cantaloupe** and **pecans.**

KIWI PUNCH

Peel and cube 7 **kiwis;** puree with ¼ cup **sugar,** the juice of 2 **limes** and 1 cup cold water; strain. Serve over ice with lime slices.

SAGE LIMEADE Heat 1½ cups each **sugar** and water in a saucepan over medium heat, stirring until the sugar dissolves; let cool. Mix 2 cups of the sugar syrup with 1½ cups **lime juice,** ½ cup **lemon juice** and 2 cups water in a pitcher; divide among ice-filled glasses. Add a sprig of **sage** to each glass.

APPLE-PEAR PUNCH

Simmer 3 cups each **apple cider** and **pear nectar, 2 cinnamon sticks** and ½ teaspoon each whole **allspice** and **cloves** in a saucepan, about 5 minutes. Chill, then strain into a punch bowl of ice. Add 1 bottle **sparkling cider.**

PINK GRAPEFRUIT PUNCH

Bring 1 cup each **sugar** and water to a simmer in a saucepan with 6 **cinnamon sticks;** let cool. Mix with 4 cups each **pink grapefruit juice** and **seltzer** in a punch bowl. Serve over ice. Garnish with a **grapefruit twist.**

GINGER JUICE

Soak 1 cup grated **ginger** in 8 cups water overnight. Transfer to a saucepan, add 1 cup **sugar** and simmer 1 hour. Strain into a pitcher and chill. Stir in a dash of **almond extract** and serve over ice; top with **seltzer.**

RUSSIAN CHERRY SODA

Boil 1 cup water, 1 cup **sugar** and 1 cup pitted **cherries** until syrupy. For each drink, stir a spoonful of the syrup into a glass of **seltzer.**

TIP

Keep simple syrup on hand for sweetening drinks: Simmer equal parts sugar and water, then let cool. Refrigerate up to a month.

LAVENDER-PEACH COOLERS

Bring ½ cup **sugar** and ½ cup water to a simmer in a saucepan over medium heat; stir ¼ cup **dried lavender** into the hot syrup, then let cool. Puree ½ cup of the syrup with 1½ pounds **peaches** and 1 cup water; strain into a pitcher. Stir in some **lemon juice** and serve over ice.

MEXICAN SQUASH COOLERS

Peel, seed and cube 4 **sweet dumpling squash.** Combine in a saucepan with 10 cups water, 1 pound **brown sugar** and 2 **cinnamon sticks;** simmer until the squash is falling apart. Strain, pressing to squeeze out the liquid, then pour through a cheesecloth-lined sieve into a pitcher. Add a few strips of **lime zest;** chill. Serve on ice with diced **pineapple** and **pecans.**

RUBY STRAWBERRY COOLERS

Toss 1 pint roughly chopped **strawberries** and ½ cup **sugar;** let sit 1 hour. Puree the strawberries with 2 cups cold strong **hibiscus tea.** Strain through a cheesecloth-lined sieve into a pitcher. Serve over ice.

SPARKLING GINGER CIDER Combine ½ pound peeled, sliced **ginger** and 4 cups **apple cider** in a pitcher; chill 1 hour. Pour into 4 ice-filled glasses and top with **ginger ale** and **fresh mint.**

HONEYDEW SLUSH
Freeze 2 cups each **honeydew melon** and diced **cucumber** until firm. Puree with the juice of 1 **lime** and **sugar** to taste. Pour into 4 glasses.

POMEGRANATE SLUSH
Blend 1 cup **pomegranate juice** and 2 tablespoons **honey** with 3 cups ice until slushy. Pour into 4 glasses; top with more juice.

PISTACHIO SLUSH
Puree ½ cup **pistachios,** 1 cup each water and **milk,** ⅓ cup **sugar,** 2 teaspoons **vanilla** and a pinch of **salt** with 1½ cups ice. Pour into 4 glasses.

RASPBERRY SODA
Fill a jar with **raspberries;** cover with **cider vinegar** and steep overnight. Strain into a saucepan; add 1 cup **sugar** per 1 cup liquid. Boil 15 minutes, then cool. Combine 3 tablespoons raspberry syrup in a glass with ice; add some **lime juice** and top with **seltzer.**

CUCUMBER WATER
Combine 1 gallon ice water, 1 sliced **lemon** and ½ sliced **cucumber** in a pitcher; chill.

TRY THIS

Garnish your drinks with fruit kebabs: Just skewer berries or cut fruit on cocktail picks.

AGUA FRESCA
Puree 2 unpeeled **cucumbers** with the juice of 2 **limes,** 3 tablespoons **sugar,** 1 cup water and ¼ **serrano pepper;** strain. Pour into 4 ice-filled glasses.

WATERMELON COOLERS
Puree 1 cup cubed **watermelon,** 2 cups **cranberry juice** and ¼ cup each **grenadine** and **lemon juice** in a blender. Strain, then divide among 4 ice-filled glasses; top with **seltzer.**

FAUX CHAMPAGNE
Squeeze ½ **lime** into a flute. Add 1 dash **bitters;** fill with **sparkling apple cider.**

ELDERFLOWER SPRITZER
Stir 1 to 2 tablespoons **elderflower syrup** into a glass of **seltzer** on ice. Add a **lemon or lime slice.**

SUGAR PLUM SPRITZER
Combine 1 cup **plum juice** with ½ cup **ginger ale** and 2 pieces chopped **crystallized ginger.** Moisten the rim of a glass with water and dip in **cinnamon sugar.** Pour in the spritzer.

WHITE GRAPE SPRITZER Mix equal parts **white grape juice** and **lemon-lime soda** in a pitcher; serve over ice with sliced **fruit.**

CHERRY COOLERS

Puree ½ pound pitted **cherries,** ½ cup **sugar** and 1 cup strong **hibiscus tea.** Serve over ice; top with **cherries.**

COLD-BREWED ICED TEA

Combine 8 cups cold water and 6 tablespoons **loose black tea** or 10 **black tea bags** in a pitcher. Cover and refrigerate 15 to 36 hours, until it's the strength you like. Strain loose tea with a fine-mesh sieve or remove the tea bags. Serve on ice with **lemon wedges.**

BLACKBERRY LEMONADE

Bring 1½ cups each **sugar** and water to a simmer, stirring until the sugar is dissolved. Let cool. Muddle 2 cups **blackberries** with the sugar syrup in a pitcher. Stir in 2 cups each **lemon juice** and cold water; add ice and **lemon slices.**

NUTELLA EGG CREAM
Mix 2 tablespoons room-temperature
Nutella and ¾ cup **milk** in a glass. Quickly
stir, then pour in ½ cup cold **seltzer.**

MINT LIMEADE
Bring 1½ cups each **sugar** and water to a
simmer, stirring until dissolved. Let cool.
Muddle 2 **lime wedges** and some **mint
leaves** in each glass and add ice. Mix the
sugar syrup, 2 cups water, 1½ cups **lime
juice** and ½ cup **lemon juice** in a pitcher;
pour into the glasses.

CLASSIC LEMONADE
Remove strips of zest from 2 **lemons** with a
vegetable peeler. Bring the zest and 1½ cups
each **sugar** and water to a boil, stirring until
the sugar dissolves. Let cool, then strain
into an ice-filled pitcher. Stir in ½ teaspoon
salt, 2 cups each **lemon juice** and cold
water, and some **lemon slices.**

Hot Drinks

WHITE CHOCOLATE CHAI
Heat 4 cups **milk,** 1 cup **cream,** 8 ounces chopped **white chocolate** and 4 teaspoons **chai spice blend** in a saucepan, whisking. Pour into 4 mugs; top with **whipped cream,** shaved white chocolate and chai spice.

MEXICAN HOT CHOCOLATE
Heat 4 disks (about 3 ounces each) chopped **Mexican chocolate** in a saucepan with 1 cup water until melted. Gradually add 3 cups **milk,** whisking until frothy. Pour into 4 mugs and top with **chili powder.**

HAZELNUT HOT CHOCOLATE
Heat 1 cup **milk** and ¾ cup **Nutella** in a saucepan, whisking. Add 4 cups milk and whisk until frothy. Pour into 4 mugs; top with **whipped cream** and chopped **hazelnuts.**

SUGAR-AND-SPICE HOT COCOA
Whisk 1 cup each boiling water and **sugar** and ½ cup **unsweetened cocoa powder** in a saucepan. Whisk in 3 cups **milk,** 1 cup **cream** and 1 teaspoon **vanilla** and heat through. Pour the cocoa into 4 mugs; top with **whipped cream** and dust with **ground cardamom.** Sprinkle with chopped **chocolate.**

WHITE HOT COCOA

Bring 4 cups **milk,** ½ teaspoon **pepper,** 1 split **vanilla bean** and 7 ounces chopped **white chocolate** to a simmer, whisking to melt the chocolate. Remove from the heat; steep 1 hour. Discard the vanilla bean and reheat. Pour into 4 mugs; top with more pepper.

COCONUT COCOA

Heat 8 ounces chopped **bittersweet chocolate,** 3 cups **unsweetened coconut milk,** 1 cup water and 2 to 3 tablespoons **sugar** in a saucepan, whisking. Pour into 4 mugs; top with **whipped cream** and **coconut.**

CREAMY BANANA COCOA

Bring 3 cups **milk,** 1 chopped **banana,** 2 tablespoons **sugar** and 1 teaspoon **cinnamon** to a simmer. Add 4 ounces chopped **milk chocolate** and 1 ounce chopped **bittersweet chocolate.** Remove from the heat. Let sit 1 minute, then puree. Pour into 4 mugs.

CAFÉ MOCHA

Bring 2 cups **milk** to a simmer, then whisk in ½ cup **unsweetened cocoa powder** and ⅓ cup **superfine sugar** until smooth; puree. Stir about 2 tablespoons into a cup of hot **coffee** in place of cream.

MIX IT UP

Serve hot cocoa with an edible swizzle stick: Use rock candy, a peppermint stick or skewered doughnut holes.

MULLED HIBISCUS PUNCH

Simmer 2 cups **dried hibiscus,** 8 cups water, 1 cup **sugar,** 6 **cloves,** 2 **cinnamon sticks,** 1 teaspoon **vanilla** and a dash of **nutmeg** in a saucepan, 30 minutes. Strain. Pour into 6 to 8 mugs and serve with cinnamon sticks.

MAPLE CHAI

Bring 2 cups **milk** just to a boil; add 2 **chai tea bags** and steep 10 minutes. Pour into 2 mugs; stir in **maple syrup** to taste.

HONEY-LEMON TEA

Steep 1 **black tea bag** and 1 **star anise pod** in a mug with ¾ cup hot water. Add 2 teaspoons **honey,** some **lemon juice** and a pinch of **cinnamon.**

LAYERED MOCHA

Microwave 4 ounces chopped **bittersweet chocolate** with ¼ cup water on 50 percent power until melted, 2 minutes, stirring once. Divide among 4 small mugs and top each with a spoonful of **sweetened condensed milk** and a shot of hot **espresso.**

HOT DULCE DE LECHE

Heat 4 cups **milk** and 1 cup **dulce de leche** in a saucepan, whisking until frothy. Pour into 4 mugs; sprinkle with **cinnamon.**

Cocktails

≪ FROZEN STRAWBERRY MARGARITAS
Puree 3 cups **strawberries** in a blender with ¼ cup **orange liqueur,** ⅓ cup **lime juice,** ¾ cup **tequila** and a pinch of **salt** until smooth. Add 1 to 2 tablespoons **honey,** then add 3 cups ice and blend until frothy. Divide among 4 glasses and garnish with strawberry halves dipped in **sugar.**

≪ MARGARITAS ON THE ROCKS
Rub the rims of 4 rocks glasses with **lime** and dip in **coarse salt,** if desired. Fill the glasses three-quarters of the way with ice. Combine 1 cup **tequila,** ⅔ cup **lime juice,** ⅓ cup **orange liqueur** and 2 teaspoons **superfine sugar** in a large shaker filled with ice. Shake well and pour into the glasses. Garnish with lime wedges.

REAL-MAN MARGARITAS
Rub the rims of 4 beer mugs with **lime** and dip in **coarse salt.** Fill the mugs with ice. Add **Mexican beer,** a squeeze of **lime juice** and a splash of **tequila** to each mug. Add **hot sauce** to taste.

HIBISCUS MARGARITAS
Combine ¾ cup each cold **hibiscus tea** and **tequila,** ½ cup each **orange liqueur** and **lime juice,** and 1 heaping tablespoon **superfine sugar** in a shaker filled with ice. Shake well and strain into 4 glasses.

SLUSHY MARGARITAS

Mix 1½ cups water with 1¼ cups each **orange liqueur** and **lime juice,** and ⅔ cup **sugar;** freeze in 2 ice cube trays until solid. For each drink, blend 6 margarita ice cubes with 2 ounces **tequila;** add 6 plain ice cubes, one at a time, blending until slushy.

WATERMELON MARGARITAS

Puree 1½ cups cubed **watermelon,** 1 cup **tequila,** ½ cup each **lime juice** and **orange liqueur,** 1 tablespoon **confectioners' sugar** and ½ teaspoon **salt.** Divide among 4 glasses.

CRANBERRY MARGARITAS

Simmer 3 cups **cranberries** in a saucepan with ½ cup **sugar** and ¼ cup water until they burst. Strain, reserving the syrup. For each drink, shake 3 tablespoons each cranberry syrup and **tequila** and 2 tablespoons each **orange liqueur** and **lime juice** in a shaker filled with ice. Strain into a glass.

BLUEBERRY MARGARITAS

Puree 8 ounces **tequila,** 4 ounces **blue curaçao,** 1 cup **blueberries,** the juice of 6 **limes,** 2 tablespoons **sugar** and 6 cups ice until slushy; pour into 4 glasses.

TIP

Use 100% agave silver tequila for margaritas on the rocks: It's clear, unaged and clean-tasting, so it's ideal for mixing.

PALOMA MARGARITAS

Pour ½ teaspoon **grenadine** into each of 4 ice-filled glasses. Shake 1 cup **grapefruit juice,** 1 cup **tequila,** ¼ cup **lime juice,** 2 teaspoons **superfine sugar** and a pinch of **salt** in a shaker filled with ice. Strain into the glasses; top with **grapefruit soda.**

PINEAPPLE MARGARITAS

Rub the rims of 4 glasses with **lime,** then dip in **coarse salt** mixed with **chili powder.** Fill a shaker with ice. Add 1 cup **tequila,** 1 cup **pineapple juice,** ½ cup **lime juice** and 1½ tablespoons **agave nectar.** Shake; strain into the glasses.

JALAPEÑO MARGARITAS

Steep ½ sliced **jalapeño** in 1¼ cups **tequila,** 1 hour. Rub the rims of 4 glasses with **lime,** then dip in **sugar** and **coarse salt.** Fill with ice. Shake the tequila, ½ cup **lime juice,** 3 tablespoons **orange liqueur** and 2 teaspoons **superfine sugar** in a shaker filled with ice; strain into the glasses.

PASSION FRUIT MARGARITAS

Shake 1 cup **tequila,** 1 cup **passion fruit nectar,** ¼ cup **orange liqueur,** 2 teaspoons **superfine sugar** and a pinch of **salt** in a shaker filled with ice; strain into 4 ice-filled glasses.

LILLET COCKTAILS
For each drink, pour ⅓ cup **Lillet or dry vermouth** into an ice-filled wine glass. Add 2 dashes **orange bitters.** Top with **sparkling wine or seltzer** and garnish with an **orange slice.**

LYCHEE LILLET
Puree half of the **lychees** from a 20-ounce can with all of the syrup; strain. Mix with 2½ cups **Lillet** and a few dashes of **rose water** and **bitters.**

PIMM'S GINGER CUP
Pour 2 ounces **Pimm's No. 1** over ice. Squeeze in some **lemon juice;** top with **ginger ale** and garnish with a **cucumber** stick.

CHAMPAGNE PUNCH
Mix 1 bottle **champagne,** 2 cups **seltzer,** 1 cup **peach nectar** and ½ cup **brandy** in a punch bowl; add sliced **peaches** and **berries.**

KIR ROYALE
Pour ½ ounce **crème de cassis** into a flute. Top with **champagne** and garnish with a **lemon twist.**

TIP

For champagne cocktails, use Spanish cava or Italian prosecco instead; they're great low-cost alternatives to champagne.

BUBBLY ON THE ROCKS
Put a few **strawberry slices or raspberries** in an ice cube tray. Fill with water; freeze until firm. Drop the berry ice cubes into flutes and fill with **prosecco.**

CHAMPAGNE COCKTAIL
Saturate a **sugar cube** with **bitters** and drop into a flute. Top with **champagne.**

SPARKLING PORT
Pour 1 ounce **tawny port** into a flute and top with **champagne.**

SPARKLING ROSÉ COCKTAILS
Combine 2 ounces each **orange juice** and **raspberry liqueur** in a shaker filled with ice. Shake well and strain into 2 flutes. Top with **sparkling rosé** and garnish with **raspberries.**

SAKE SPRITZER
Shake 1 **basil leaf,** 6 **mint leaves,** 2 **lemon twists,** 1 **orange wedge,** ¼ cup diced **cucumber** and 1½ ounces **orange liqueur** in a shaker filled with ice. Strain into a glass. Top with **sparkling sake.**

LYCHEE-MINT SPRITZERS Muddle 8 **mint leaves** with 2 teaspoons **sugar** in a shaker. Add 4 canned **lychees,** ¼ cup syrup from the can, 3 ounces **vodka** and a squeeze of **lime juice;** add ice and shake. Strain into 2 ice-filled glasses and top with **seltzer,** then garnish with mint and lime.

WHITE SANGRIA

Mix 1 bottle **dry white wine,** ¼ cup **light rum,** 3 tablespoons **elderflower liqueur** and 2 tablespoons **sugar** in a pitcher, stirring to dissolve the sugar, then add 2 sliced **nectarines,** 2 sliced **plums** and 1 sliced **lemon.** Refrigerate at least 1 hour and up to 1 day. Add 1½ cups **seltzer** just before serving.

ROSÉ SANGRIA

Mix 1 bottle **dry rosé,** ¼ cup **brandy,** 2 tablespoons **raspberry liqueur** and 2 tablespoons **sugar** in a pitcher, stirring to dissolve the sugar, then add 1½ cups **raspberries,** 1½ cups quartered **strawberries** and 1 sliced **lemon.** Refrigerate at least 1 hour and up to 1 day. Add 1½ cups **seltzer** just before serving.

MELON SANGRIA

Mix 1 bottle **white wine,** ½ cup **green melon liqueur,** the juice of 3 **limes** and ¼ cup **sugar** in a pitcher; chill. Garnish with **melon** balls.

TIP

Sangria is the perfect make-ahead party drink: Prepare the base the night before so the fruit soaks up the flavors.

FRESH CHILE MICHELADA

Mix equal parts **coarse salt** and **chipotle chile powder.** Moisten the rim of a glass with a **lime wedge,** then dip in the chile salt. Muddle 1 or 2 thin slices **serrano chile pepper** with the juice of 1 lime in the glass, then mix in ¼ teaspoon **Worcestershire sauce,** 2 teaspoons **hot sauce** and a pinch of salt. Fill the glass halfway with ice. Fill with 1 bottle chilled **lager** and serve with a lime wedge.

BLACK FOREST BEER

Pour 1 bottle chilled **lager** into a glass. Stir in 2 tablespoons **sour cherry preserves** until mostly dissolved, then add 2 teaspoons **cherry liqueur** and a splash of **grenadine.**

STOUT FLIP

Dissolve 1 cup **sugar** in 1 cup water in a saucepan over low heat, stirring; let cool. Shake 4 ounces **stout beer,** 2 ounces **dark rum,** 1 **pasteurized egg** and 2 teaspoons of the sugar syrup in a shaker filled with ice. Strain into a glass.

RED SANGRIA Stir 1 bottle **dry red wine,** ¼ cup **brandy,** ¼ cup **orange liqueur** and 2 tablespoons **sugar** in a pitcher. Add 2 sliced **oranges** and 1 sliced **green apple.** Refrigerate at least 1 hour and up to 1 day. Add 1½ cups **seltzer** just before serving.

BOURBON COOLERS

Combine 6 ounces each **bourbon** and **orange juice** in a shaker filled with ice. Add 5 tablespoons **maple syrup,** cover and shake 1 minute; strain into 6 champagne flutes. Top with **dry sparkling white wine** and garnish each drink with an **orange twist.**

PORT MANHATTAN

Shake 2 ounces **whiskey,** 2 ounces **tawny port** and 3 dashes **orange bitters** in a shaker filled with ice. Strain into a glass and garnish with a **lemon twist.**

CHERRY-LIME COCKTAIL

Muddle 6 pitted fresh or thawed frozen **cherries,** 3 **lime wedges** and 2 teaspoons **sugar** in a tall glass. Add 3 ounces **gin** and ice.

PEPPERMINT STRIPE

Pour ½ ounce **crème de cacao** into a shooter glass. Pour in ½ ounce **crème de menthe** over the back of a spoon to form a separate layer. Pour in ½ ounce **Irish cream liqueur** the same way.

TIP

You don't need a bartender's muddler to make cocktails: Use the handle of a wooden spoon or a rolling pin.

BRANDY SLUSH

Heat 1 cup each water and **sugar** in a saucepan over medium heat, stirring until the sugar dissolves. Mix with 1½ cups **brandy,** 2 cups **orange juice** and ½ cup **lemon juice** in a small baking dish; freeze until slushy. Scoop into glasses, top with **seltzer** and stir.

CIDER PUNCH

Combine 4 cups **apple cider,** 1 **cinnamon stick,** 3 **cloves** and a pinch of **salt** in a saucepan. Halve 1 **orange;** squeeze the juice into the pan and add the peels. Bring to a simmer, then let steep 10 to 15 minutes. Strain into a pitcher and add ¾ cup **apple brandy or bourbon.** Chill at least 2 hours or overnight. Serve on the rocks. Garnish with orange slices.

SPARKLING SIDECAR

Moisten the rim of a tumbler and dip in **coarse sugar;** fill with ice. Combine 1 ounce each **cognac, orange liqueur** and **lemon juice** in a shaker filled with ice. Shake well, then strain into the glass. Top with a splash of **seltzer.**

« ROSEMARY GIN AND TONIC Muddle a **lime wedge** with 4 **cucumber slices** in a glass. Add 2 ounces **gin,** a sprig of **rosemary** and some ice; top with **tonic.**

DARK CHOCOLATE MARTINI

Mix 2 tablespoons each **raw sugar** and finely chopped **dark chocolate** on a plate. Moisten the rim of a chilled martini glass, then dip it in the sugar-chocolate mixture. Combine 2 ounces each **chocolate liqueur** and **vodka,** 1 ounce chilled **espresso,** ½ teaspoon **orange juice** and a strip of **orange zest** in a shaker filled with ice; strain into the glass and garnish with an **orange wedge.**

DERBY MARTINI

Combine 1½ ounces **bourbon,** ¾ ounce **Lillet,** ½ ounce **cherry brandy,** 1 teaspoon **lemon juice** and a dash of **bitters** in a shaker filled with ice. Shake well, then strain into a martini glass.

ELDERFLOWER FIZZ

Fill a tall glass halfway with ice and **cranberry juice.** Add a splash each of **vodka** and **elderflower liqueur,** then top with **seltzer** and garnish with **fresh mint.**

TIP

If a cocktail is pure alcohol, stir with ice for 30 seconds, then strain. Stirring dilutes a drink less than shaking.

CUCUMBER-MINT GIMLETS

Peel, seed and chop 6 **English cucumbers.** Puree, then strain through a sieve into a bowl, pressing to extract the juice; chill. Combine ⅓ cup **lemon juice,** 8 **mint sprigs** and ¼ cup **sugar** in a pitcher; muddle with a wooden spoon. Stir in 2 cups **gin,** the cucumber juice and some cucumber and **lemon slices.** Divide among 6 to 8 ice-filled glasses.

SWEET TEA MOJITOS

Stir 5 **black tea bags,** 2 cups **turbinado sugar** and 2 handfuls of **mint** in 3 cups simmering water and steep 5 minutes. Strain into a pitcher; add the juice of 3 **limes,** 1½ cups **light rum,** 1 cup water and a handful of mint. Stir, crushing the mint. Chill; serve over ice with more mint.

CAMPARI FIZZ PUNCH

Mix 1 cup each **Campari, gin** and **sweet vermouth,** 2 bottles **prosecco** and ½ cup **grenadine** in a punch bowl. Garnish with **orange slices.**

MINT MARTINI Combine 2 **cucumber slices,** 4 **mint leaves,** 1 tablespoon **lime juice** and 1 teaspoon **sugar** in a shaker and muddle with a wooden spoon. Add 3 ounces **gin or vodka** and fill with ice. Cover and shake, then strain through a sieve into a chilled martini glass. Garnish with a cucumber slice.

ITALIAN BITTER PUNCH

Mix equal parts **herbal liqueur** (such as Strega), **gin** and **orange juice** in a pitcher. Serve over ice and top with a splash of **lemon-lime soda.** Garnish with **orange slices.**

HONEY PUNCH

Dissolve ½ cup **honey** in ½ cup boiling water. Let cool, then pour into a pitcher; add the juice of 2 **lemons,** 2 cups **apricot nectar** and 1 cup **vodka.** Chill. Add 1 bottle **sparkling apple juice.** Serve over ice with **lemon slices.**

MULLED RED WINE

Heat ¾ cup each **sugar** and water until the sugar dissolves. Off the heat, add 2 strips **lemon zest,** 3 whole **cloves,** 10 **black peppercorns, 2 cinnamon sticks,** 1 bottle **red wine** and ½ cup each **gin** and **orange liqueur.** Steep 5 minutes.

MOCHACCINO COCKTAIL

Combine ½ cup hot strong **coffee** and ¼ cup each warmed **vanilla vodka, chocolate liqueur** and **half-and-half** in a glass. Top with **whipped cream.**

TRY THIS

Turn some of your punch mix into ice cubes and use them for serving.

HOT BUTTERED RUM

Mix 4 tablespoons softened **butter** with ½ teaspoon each **vanilla, cinnamon** and **allspice,** and a pinch of **nutmeg.** Heat ½ cup **pineapple juice** in a mug; stir in 1 tablespoon **brown sugar** and 1 ounce **rum.** Top with a pat of the spiced butter.

HOT TEA TODDY

Steep 1 **tea bag** and 1 **star anise pod** in ¾ cup hot water, 5 minutes. Add 1 ounce **brandy,** 2 teaspoons **honey,** some **lemon juice** and 1 **cinnamon stick.**

HOT GINGERMAN

Steep 1 tablespoon grated **ginger** in 1 cup hot water, 15 minutes. Add a shot of **bourbon** and garnish with a **lemon wedge.**

WHITE WINE WASSAIL

Boil ½ cup each water and **sugar** in a saucepan with ½ **orange** and ½ **lemon** (sliced), a 1-inch piece sliced peeled **ginger,** 5 **cardamom pods,** 5 **black peppercorns** and 1 **cinnamon stick.** Add 2 bottles **white wine** and the juice of the remaining citrus halves; warm through.

RED-WINE PUNCH Combine 1 bottle **red wine,** 6 ounces **brandy,** 6 ounces **raspberry or orange liqueur** and the juice of 2 **lemons** in a large pitcher and refrigerate at least 2 hours or overnight. Serve over ice and garnish with **raspberries** and **orange slices.**

GODFATHER

Put 2 ounces **scotch** and 1 ounce **amaretto** in a shaker filled with ice; stir. Strain into a short glass with ice.

CLASSIC GIN AND TONIC

Fill a highball glass with **ice.** Pour in 3 ounces **gin.** Top with **tonic water.** Garnish with a **lime wedge.**

PEPPERED WHISKEY

Wet the rim of a martini glass; dip in **pepper.** Brew strong **hibiscus tea;** sweeten heavily with **sugar** to make a syrup. Cool. Combine 1 ounce hibiscus syrup, 2 ounces **whiskey** and the juice of ½ **orange** in a shaker filled with ice. Shake and strain into the glass.

CLASSIC MICHELADA

Combine the juice of 1 **lime,** ¼ teaspoon **Worcestershire sauce,** 2 teaspoons **hot sauce** and a pinch of **salt** in a tall glass. Fill the glass halfway with ice, then fill with 1 bottle chilled **lager** and stir. Serve with a **lime wedge.**

WATERMELON-COCONUT COOLERS

Dissolve 1 cup **sugar** in 1 cup water in a saucepan over low heat, stirring; let cool. Blend 8 cups frozen cubed **watermelon** with 8 ounces **lemon vodka,** 7 ounces of the sugar syrup and a 17.5-ounce can **coconut juice.** Divide among 4 glasses; serve with watermelon wedges.

ICE

You need the right size ice for the right drink, so bartenders start with a giant block and chisel off what they need. To do the same—and impress your friends—order a block from a local ice distributor (small 10-pound blocks can cost as little as $1.50). Or freeze your own: Line a small, sturdy cooler (like one for a six-pack) with a clean, clear plastic tarp and fill three-quarters of the way with water, being careful not to get water between the tarp and cooler. Freeze until completely solid, at least 24 hours. Pull out the ice block, then follow the instructions below and start chipping away.

Flavored Ice

Spice up a drink with one of these tasty, colorful cubes.

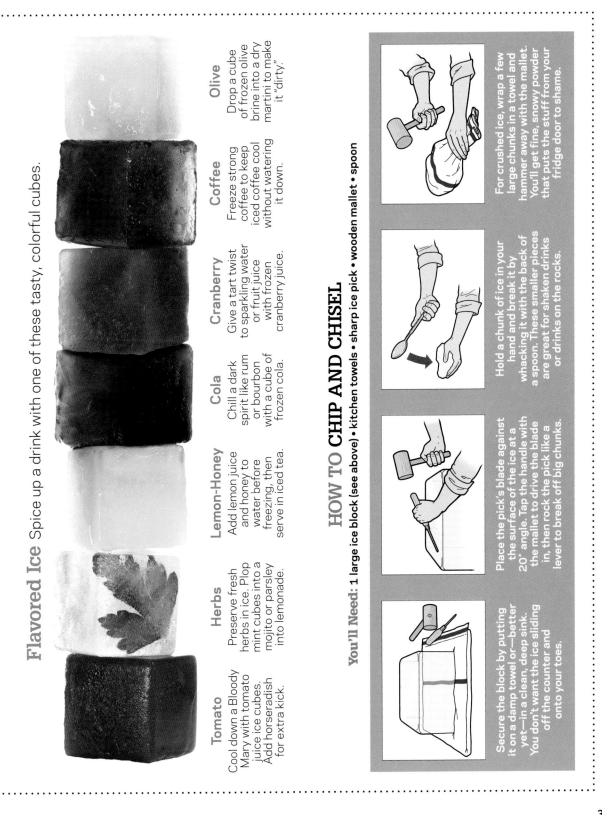

Tomato
Cool down a Bloody Mary with tomato juice ice cubes. Add horseradish for extra kick.

Herbs
Preserve fresh herbs in ice. Plop mint cubes into a mojito or parsley into lemonade.

Lemon-Honey
Add lemon juice and honey to water before freezing, then serve in iced tea.

Cola
Chill a dark spirit like rum or bourbon with a cube of frozen cola.

Cranberry
Give a tart twist to sparkling water or fruit juice with frozen cranberry juice.

Coffee
Freeze strong coffee to keep iced coffee cool without watering it down.

Olive
Drop a cube of frozen olive brine into a dry martini to make it "dirty."

HOW TO CHIP AND CHISEL

You'll Need: 1 large ice block (see above) • kitchen towels • sharp ice pick • wooden mallet • spoon

Secure the block by putting it on a damp towel or—better yet—in a clean, deep sink. You don't want the ice sliding off the counter and onto your toes.

Place the pick's blade against the surface of the ice at a 20° angle. Tap the handle with the mallet to drive the blade in, then rock the pick like a lever to break off big chunks.

Hold a chunk of ice in your hand and break it by whacking it with the back of a spoon. These smaller pieces are great for shaken drinks or drinks on the rocks.

For crushed ice, wrap a few large chunks in a towel and hammer away with the mallet. You'll get fine, snowy powder that puts the stuff from your fridge door to shame.

Brownies & Cookies

◀◀ FUDGY BROWNIES

Melt 1 stick **butter** with 2 cups **chocolate chips.** Whisk in ¾ cup each **light brown and granulated sugar.** Whisk in 4 **eggs,** one at a time, then 1 teaspoon **vanilla.** Stir in 1 cup **flour** and ½ teaspoon **salt.** Pour into a 9-by-13-inch pan lined with foil; bake at 325°, 45 minutes.

BLONDIES

Melt 1 stick **butter;** whisk in 2 cups **dark brown sugar.** Cool slightly. Whisk in 2 **eggs,** one at a time, 2 tablespoons **bourbon** and 2 teaspoons **vanilla.** Stir in 1½ cups **flour,** 2 teaspoons **baking powder** and 1 teaspoon **salt;** add ¾ cup **chocolate chips** and ½ cup chopped **walnuts.** Pour into a 9-by-13-inch pan lined with foil; bake at 325°, 45 minutes.

S'MORES BROWNIES

Melt 1 stick **butter** with 2 cups **chocolate chips.** Whisk in ¾ cup each **light brown and granulated sugar.** Whisk in 4 **eggs,** one at a time, then 1 teaspoon **vanilla.** Stir in 1 cup **flour** and ½ teaspoon **salt.** Lay **graham crackers** in a 9-by-13-inch pan lined with foil. Add the batter; bake at 325°, 35 minutes. Sprinkle with 2 cups **mini marshmallows** and ¾ cup **mini chocolate chips;** bake 10 more minutes.

MARBLE BROWNIES

Make the brownie batter: Melt 1 stick **butter** with 2 cups **chocolate chips.** Whisk in ¾ cup each **light brown and granulated sugar.** Whisk in 4 **eggs,** one at a time, then 1 teaspoon **vanilla.** Stir in 1 cup **flour** and ½ teaspoon **salt.** Make the blondie batter: Melt 1 stick butter. Whisk in 2 cups **dark brown sugar.** Cool slightly. Whisk in 2 eggs, one at a time, 2 tablespoons **bourbon** and 2 teaspoons vanilla. Stir in 1½ cups flour, 2 teaspoons **baking powder** and 1 teaspoon salt, then add ¾ cup chocolate chips and ½ cup chopped **walnuts.** Pour the brownie batter into a 9-by-13-inch pan lined with foil; drop the blondie batter on top and swirl. Bake at 325°, 45 minutes.

TROPICAL BROWNIES

Whisk 1¾ cups **flour,** 3 tablespoons **unsweetened cocoa powder** and 1 teaspoon each **salt** and **baking powder** in a bowl. Bring 2½ cups **light brown sugar,** 2 sticks **butter** and 1 cup water to a simmer in a saucepan. Remove from the heat and whisk in 6 ounces chopped **unsweetened chocolate;** let cool. Whisk in 5 **eggs** and 2 teaspoons **vanilla.** Stir in the flour mixture, then add 1¼ cups chopped **hazelnuts.** Pour into a 9-by-13-inch pan lined with foil; bake at 325°, 30 to 35 minutes. For the frosting, beat 1 stick softened butter, 2 teaspoons vanilla, 2 tablespoons **milk** and 1¼ cups **confectioners' sugar.** Spread on the cooled brownies; top with toasted **coconut.**

MOCHA BROWNIES

Whisk 1¾ cups **flour**, 3 tablespoons **unsweetened cocoa powder** and 1 teaspoon each **salt** and **baking powder** in a bowl. Bring 2½ cups **light brown sugar**, 2 sticks **butter** and 1 cup water to a simmer in a saucepan. Remove from the heat and whisk in 6 ounces chopped **unsweetened chocolate;** let cool. Whisk in 5 **eggs** and 2 teaspoons **vanilla.** Add the flour mixture. Pour into a 9-by-13-inch pan lined with foil; bake at 325°, 30 to 35 minutes. For the frosting, beat 1 stick softened butter, 1 teaspoon **instant espresso** dissolved in 1 tablespoon water, and 1¼ cups **confectioners' sugar.** Spread on the cooled brownies; top with shaved **chocolate.**

RED VELVET BROWNIES

Whisk 1 cup **flour**, 3 tablespoons **unsweetened cocoa powder** and ½ teaspoon each **salt** and **baking powder** in a bowl. Bring 1½ cups **dark brown sugar**, 1 stick **butter** and ⅔ cup water to a simmer in a saucepan. Remove from the heat and whisk in 2 ounces chopped **unsweetened chocolate;** let cool. Whisk in 3 **eggs,** 1½ teaspoons **vanilla** and 2 teaspoons **red food coloring.** Stir in the flour mixture. Pour into a 9-by-13-inch pan lined with foil; bake at 325°, 20 to 25 minutes. For the frosting, beat 8 ounces softened **cream cheese,** 4 tablespoons softened butter, 1½ cups **confectioners' sugar** and 1 teaspoon vanilla. Spread on the cooled brownies.

LEMON SHORTBREAD

Beat 2 sticks **butter,** 1 teaspoon **lemon zest,** ¼ cup **granulated sugar** and ½ cup **confectioners' sugar** until fluffy. Whisk 2 cups **flour** and 1 teaspoon **salt,** then stir into the butter mixture. Press into a buttered 8-inch-square or 9-inch-round tart pan. Score into pieces with a fork, then chill 30 minutes. Bake at 300°, 1 hour. Cool. Mix 2 cups confectioners' sugar with the zest and juice of 1 **lemon.** Spread over the finished shortbread and sprinkle with **yellow decorating sugar.** Slice along the scored lines.

BAR-SNACK BLONDIES

Beat 2 sticks **butter,** ¾ cup **dark brown sugar** and ¾ cup **granulated sugar** until fluffy; beat in 1 teaspoon **vanilla** and 2 **eggs.** Whisk 2½ cups **flour,** ½ teaspoon **baking soda** and 1 teaspoon **salt,** then stir into the butter mixture. Stir in 2 cups **chocolate chunks,** ½ cup broken **thin pretzels** and ½ cup **peanuts** and chill 30 minutes. Press the dough into a 9-by-13-inch pan; sprinkle with more pretzels. Bake at 350°, 40 to 45 minutes.

HAZELNUT LINZER BARS

Beat 2 sticks **butter,** ¼ cup
granulated sugar and ½ cup
confectioners' sugar until fluffy.
Whisk 1 cup **flour,** 1 cup **ground
oats,** ¾ cup finely ground **hazelnuts**
and 1 teaspoon **salt,** then stir into
the butter mixture. Mix one-third
of the dough with ¼ cup chopped
hazelnuts; squeeze into clumps
and freeze 30 minutes. Press the
remaining dough into a buttered
8-inch-square pan. Spread with
raspberry preserves and top with
the frozen clumps. Bake at 350°,
50 minutes.

ORANGE-ANISE SHORTBREAD

Beat 2 sticks **butter,** the seeds
from 1 **vanilla bean,** ½ teaspoon
crushed toasted **anise seeds,**
¼ cup **granulated sugar** and
½ cup **confectioners' sugar** until
fluffy. Whisk 2 cups **flour** and
1 teaspoon **salt,** then stir into the
butter mixture. Press into a buttered
8-inch-square or 9-inch-round
tart pan. Score into pieces with
a fork, then chill 30 minutes.
Bake at 300°, 1 hour. Cool. Whisk
2 cups confectioners' sugar and
2½ tablespoons **orange juice;**
spread over the finished shortbread
and slice along the scored lines. Top
with **candied orange slices.**

CLASSIC CHOCOLATE COOKIES

Beat 1¼ cups **sugar** and 1 stick **butter** until fluffy, then beat in 1 **egg** and 1 teaspoon **vanilla.** Whisk 1½ cups **flour,** ½ cup **unsweetened Dutch-process cocoa powder,** ¾ teaspoon **salt** and ¼ teaspoon **baking powder;** stir into the butter mixture. Chill 30 minutes, then roll into balls and bake at 350˚, 12 to 15 minutes.

CLASSIC SUGAR COOKIES

Beat 2 sticks **butter,** ½ cup **confectioners' sugar** and ¾ cup **granulated sugar.** Beat in 1 teaspoon each **orange zest** and **vanilla,** and 2 **egg yolks.** Whisk 2¼ cups **flour,** ½ teaspoon **baking powder** and ¼ teaspoon **salt;** stir into the butter mixture. Chill 30 minutes. Roll into balls; flatten. Top with granulated sugar. Bake at 350˚, 15 minutes.

BUTTERSCOTCH COOKIES

Beat 1 cup **vegetable oil** and 1½ cups **granulated sugar;** beat in 1 teaspoon **vanilla** and 2 **eggs.** Whisk 2½ cups **flour,** ¾ teaspoon **baking soda** and 1 teaspoon **salt,** then stir into the butter mixture. Add 2 cups **butterscotch chips** and chill 30 minutes. Drop by tablespoonfuls and bake at 350˚, 14 to 16 minutes.

CHOCOLATE-MALTED COOKIES

Beat 1¼ cups **dark brown sugar** and 1 stick **butter.** Beat in 1 **egg** and 1 teaspoon **vanilla.** Whisk 1½ cups **flour,** ½ cup **unsweetened Dutch-process cocoa powder,** ¼ cup **malted milk powder,** ¾ teaspoon **salt** and ¾ teaspoon **baking soda;** stir into the butter. Chill 30 minutes; roll into balls. Top with halved **malt balls.** Bake at 350˚, 12 minutes.

CLASSIC CHOCOLATE-CHIP COOKIES

Beat 2 sticks **butter,** ¾ cup **dark brown sugar** and ¾ cup **granulated sugar** until fluffy; beat in 1 teaspoon **vanilla** and 2 **eggs.** Whisk 2½ cups **flour,** ¾ teaspoon **baking soda** and 1 teaspoon **salt,** then stir into the butter mixture. Add 2 cups **chocolate chips** and chill 30 minutes. Roll into balls and bake at 350˚, 8 to 12 minutes.

FIG PINWHEELS

Trim store-bought **pie dough** into an 8-inch square. Pulse 1 cup **dried figs,** ½ cup **pitted dates,** a pinch of **cinnamon,** ½ teaspoon **orange zest,** 1½ teaspoons **orange juice** and 1 tablespoon **butter** in a food processor. Spread over the dough; roll into a log. Chill 30 minutes. Cut into ½-inch slices and bake at 375˚, 12 to 15 minutes.

PEANUT BUTTER COOKIES

Beat 2 sticks **butter,** 1 cup **peanut butter,** ½ cup **granulated sugar** and ¾ cup **confectioners' sugar.** Beat in 2 **egg yolks** and 1 teaspoon **vanilla.** Whisk 2¼ cups **flour,** ½ teaspoon **baking powder** and ¼ teaspoon **salt;** add to the butter. Chill 30 minutes. Roll into balls; press with a fork. Top with **coarse sugar;** bake at 350˚, 12 minutes.

COCONUT CHUNK COOKIES

Beat 1¼ cups **sugar** and 1 stick **butter.** Beat in 1 **egg** and 1 teaspoon **vanilla.** Whisk 1½ cups **flour,** ½ cup **unsweetened Dutch-process cocoa powder** and ¾ teaspoon **salt;** stir into the butter mixture. Add 1 cup **coconut,** ½ cup chopped **cashews** and 1 cup **chocolate chunks.** Chill 30 minutes. Drop by tablespoonfuls; bake at 350˚, 20 to 25 minutes.

WALNUT-LAVENDER SHORTBREAD
Beat 2 sticks **butter,** ¼ cup
granulated sugar and ½ cup
confectioners' sugar until fluffy.
Whisk 2 cups **flour,** ¾ cup finely
ground **walnuts** and 1 teaspoon
salt, then stir into the butter mixture.
Press into a buttered 8-inch-square
or 9-inch-round tart pan and score
into pieces with a fork, then chill
30 minutes. Sprinkle ½ teaspoon
dried lavender over the dough and
bake at 300°, 1 hour. Cool, then slice
along the scored lines.

CHOCOLATE–PB SANDWICHES
Beat 1¼ cups **dark brown sugar**
and 1 stick **butter** until fluffy,
then beat in 1 **egg** and 1 teaspoon
vanilla. Whisk 1½ cups **flour,**
½ cup **unsweetened Dutch-process
cocoa powder,** ¾ teaspoon **salt** and
¾ teaspoon **baking soda;** stir into the
butter mixture. Chill 30 minutes, then
roll out to ⅛ inch thick and cut into
shapes. Bake at 350°, 8 to 12 minutes.
Beat 1 cup creamy **peanut butter,**
6 tablespoons softened butter and
¾ cup **confectioners' sugar** until
smooth, then sandwich between the
cooled cookies.

OATMEAL-RAISIN COOKIES

Melt 2 sticks **butter** over medium heat until browned, then cool. Beat the butter, ¾ cup **dark brown sugar** and ¾ cup **granulated sugar** until fluffy; beat in 1 teaspoon **vanilla** and 2 **eggs.** Whisk 2½ cups **flour,** ¾ cup **oats,** ¾ teaspoon **baking soda** and 1 teaspoon **salt,** then stir into the butter mixture. Add 1 cup **golden raisins** and chill 30 minutes. Drop the dough by tablespoonfuls and bake at 350°, 12 to 15 minutes.

GINGER CRACKLES

Beat 1½ sticks **butter,** ¼ cup **dark brown sugar** and ½ cup **granulated sugar.** Add 1 **egg yolk,** 1 teaspoon **vanilla,** ½ cup **molasses** and 2 tablespoons **ginger preserves.** Whisk 2¼ cups **flour,** 1¼ teaspoons **baking soda,** a pinch of **pepper,** 2 teaspoons **ground ginger** and ½ teaspoon each **allspice, mustard powder** and **salt.** Stir into the butter mixture and chill 30 minutes. Roll into balls, sprinkle with **coarse sugar** and bake at 375°, 15 to 20 minutes.

RUGALACH

Cut store-bought **pie dough** into 16 wedges (like a pizza). Starting from the tip, spread **apricot jam** over the top two-thirds of each wedge; sprinkle with chopped **pecans.** Roll up from the fat end to form a crescent shape. Brush with beaten **egg,** sprinkle with **coarse sugar** and chill 30 minutes. Bake at 325°, 30 to 35 minutes.

CHUBBY CHIP COOKIES

Beat 2 sticks **butter,** ¾ cup **dark brown sugar** and ¾ cup **granulated sugar** until fluffy; beat in 1 teaspoon **vanilla** and 3 **egg yolks.** Whisk 2½ cups **flour,** ¾ teaspoon **baking soda** and 1 teaspoon **salt,** then stir into the butter mixture. Add 2 cups **chocolate chunks.** Roll into 1-inch balls; chill 1 hour. Bake at 350°, 15 to 20 minutes.

SAVORY LEMON COOKIES

Beat 2 sticks **butter,** ½ cup **parmesan,** 1 tablespoon **lemon zest,** 2 teaspoons **pepper,** ¼ cup **granulated sugar** and ½ cup **confectioners' sugar** until fluffy. Whisk 2 cups **flour** and 1 teaspoon **salt,** then stir into the butter mixture. Roll into small balls; bake at 300°, 8 to 12 minutes.

RICE PETITS FOURS

Melt 3 tablespoons **butter** and a 10-ounce bag of **marshmallows** in a saucepan over low heat. Remove from the heat and stir in 6 cups **crisp rice cereal.** Press into a 9-by-13-inch baking pan. Spread with 12 ounces melted **chocolate** and sprinkle with **nonpareils,** then let harden. Cut into small squares.

SNOWSTORMS

Beat 1¼ cups **dark brown sugar** and 1 stick **butter;** beat in 1 **egg** and 1 teaspoon **vanilla.** Whisk ½ cup **unsweetened Dutch-process cocoa powder,** 1½ cups **flour,** ¾ teaspoon **salt** and ¾ teaspoon **baking soda;** stir into the butter mixture. Chill 30 minutes. Roll into balls; bake at 350°, 12 to 15 minutes. Roll in **confectioners' sugar.**

CINNAMON-SUGAR ROLLS

Trim store-bought **pie dough** into a rectangle. Spread with softened **butter** and sprinkle with a mixture of **cinnamon** and **sugar.** Roll into a log, then flatten slightly. Brush with beaten **egg,** sprinkle with **coarse sugar** and bake at 375°, 15 to 20 minutes. Cool, then slice the log into thin pieces.

MIXED CHIP COOKIES

Beat 1½ sticks melted **butter,** ¾ cup **dark brown sugar** and ¾ cup **granulated sugar;** beat in 1 teaspoon **vanilla** and 2 **eggs.** Whisk 2½ cups **flour,** ¾ teaspoon **baking soda** and 1 teaspoon **salt;** stir into the butter mixture. Add **assorted chips;** chill 30 minutes. Roll into balls; bake at 350°, 8 to 12 minutes.

COCONUT MACAROONS

Whisk ⅔ cup **granulated sugar,** 2 beaten **egg whites,** 2 teaspoons **vanilla** and ½ teaspoon **salt.** Stir in 2⅔ cups **unsweetened shredded coconut.** Drop by tablespoonfuls, then form into pyramids with your fingers. Bake at 350°, 15 to 20 minutes.

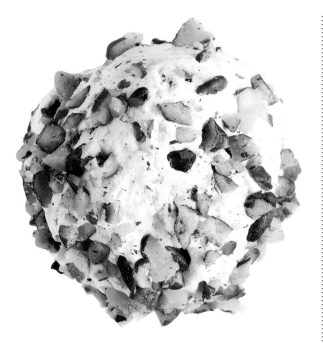

DIVINITIES

Mix 4 cups **sugar,** 1 cup **light corn syrup** and ¾ cup water in a saucepan, then cook over medium heat, without stirring, until a candy thermometer reaches 250°. Beat 3 **egg whites** until firm; drizzle the hot syrup into the egg whites and beat until stiff. Stir in 1 teaspoon **vanilla** and 2 cups chopped **hazelnuts or pecans.** Shape into small balls with buttered hands, then roll in more chopped nuts and cool.

CHOCOLATE-CHERRY COOKIES

Beat 1 cup **dark brown sugar** and 1 stick **butter** until fluffy, then beat in 3 **eggs,** 4 ounces melted **semisweet chocolate,** 2 tablespoons **buttermilk** and 1 teaspoon **vanilla.** Whisk 1½ cups **flour,** ½ cup **unsweetened Dutch-process cocoa powder,** ¾ teaspoon **salt** and ¼ teaspoon **baking powder;** stir into the butter mixture. Add 2 cups **chocolate chunks** and 1 cup **dried cherries.** Drop by tablespoonfuls and chill 30 minutes; bake at 350°, 8 to 12 minutes.

OAT-WALNUT THINS
Beat 2 sticks **butter,** ¼ cup
granulated sugar and ½ cup
confectioners' sugar until fluffy.
Whisk 2 cups **flour,** 1 cup **ground
oats,** ¾ cup finely ground **walnuts**
and 1 teaspoon **salt,** then stir
into the butter mixture. Divide
between two 8-inch-square pans,
score into pieces and bake at 300˚,
1 hour. Cool and slice along the
scored lines; drizzle with melted
bittersweet chocolate.

BLACK AND WHITES
Beat 2 sticks **butter,** ½ cup
granulated sugar and ¾ cup
confectioners' sugar until fluffy.
Beat in 2 **egg yolks,** 1 teaspoon
vanilla and 1 teaspoon **orange zest.**
Whisk 2¼ cups **flour** and ¼ teaspoon
salt; stir into the butter mixture,
then chill 2 hours. Roll out to
⅛ inch thick, cut into 2-inch rounds
and chill 30 minutes. Bake at 350˚,
8 to 10 minutes. Cool, then spread
vanilla frosting on one half and
chocolate frosting on the other.

NUTTY CHOCOLATE COOKIES

Beat 1 cup **dark brown sugar** and 1 stick **butter** until fluffy, then beat in 3 **eggs,** 4 ounces melted **semisweet chocolate,** 2 tablespoons **buttermilk** and 1 teaspoon **vanilla.** Whisk 1½ cups **flour,** ½ cup **unsweetened Dutch-process cocoa powder,** ¾ teaspoon **salt** and ¼ teaspoon **baking powder;** stir into the butter mixture. Add 1 cup **oats,** ½ cup **Grape-Nuts cereal** and 2 cups chopped **mixed nuts** to the batter. Drop by tablespoonfuls and chill 30 minutes. Bake at 350˚, 8 to 12 minutes.

MEXICAN WEDDING COOKIES

Beat 2 sticks **butter,** ½ cup **granulated sugar** and ¾ cup **confectioners' sugar** until fluffy. Beat in 2 **egg yolks,** 1 teaspoon **almond extract** and 1 teaspoon **orange zest.** Whisk 2¼ cups **all-purpose flour,** 1 cup **almond flour,** ½ teaspoon **baking powder** and ¼ teaspoon **salt;** stir into the butter mixture, then chill 30 minutes. Scoop into small balls and bake at 325˚, 20 to 25 minutes. Cool, then toss in confectioners' sugar.

PECAN SANDIES

Beat 2 sticks **butter,** ¼ cup **granulated sugar** and ½ cup **confectioners' sugar** until fluffy. Whisk 2 cups **flour,** ¾ cup ground **pecans** and 1 teaspoon **salt,** then stir into the butter mixture. Roll into two 1-inch-thick logs and chill 30 minutes. Slice into ½-inch-thick rounds and press a pecan into each. Brush the cookies with beaten **egg** and chill 30 minutes. Bake at 375°, 12 to 15 minutes.

CHOCOLATE GINGERBREADS

Beat 1¼ cups **dark brown sugar** and 1 stick **butter** until fluffy, then beat in 1 **egg,** ¼ cup **molasses,** 2 tablespoons minced **crystallized ginger,** 1 teaspoon **vanilla** and a large pinch each of **cinnamon** and **cloves.** Whisk 1½ cups **flour,** ½ cup **unsweetened Dutch-process cocoa powder,** ¾ teaspoon **salt** and ¾ teaspoon **baking soda;** stir into the butter mixture. Do not chill. Drop the dough by tablespoonfuls, sprinkle with **coarse sugar** and bake at 350°, 8 to 12 minutes.

COCOA WAFERS

Beat 1¼ cups **sugar** and 1 stick **butter,** then beat in 1 **egg** and 1 teaspoon **vanilla.** Whisk 1½ cups **flour,** ½ cup **unsweetened Dutch-process cocoa powder,** ¾ teaspoon **salt** and ¼ teaspoon **baking powder;** stir into the butter mixture. Chill 30 minutes. Roll out to ⅛ inch thick; cut into 2-inch rounds. Bake at 350˚, 8 to 12 minutes.

CLASSIC SHORTBREAD

Beat 2 sticks **butter,** ¼ cup **granulated sugar** and ½ cup **confectioners' sugar** until fluffy. Whisk 2 cups **flour** and 1 teaspoon **salt,** then stir into the butter mixture. Press into a buttered 8-inch-square or 9-inch-round tart pan. Score into pieces with a fork, then chill 30 minutes. Bake at 300˚, 1 hour. Cool, then slice along the scored lines.

SUGAR SANDWICH COOKIES

Beat 2 sticks **butter,** ½ cup **granulated sugar** and ¾ cup **confectioners' sugar** until fluffy. Beat in 2 **egg yolks,** 1 teaspoon **vanilla** and 1 teaspoon **orange zest.** Whisk 2¼ cups **flour** and ¼ teaspoon **salt;** stir into the butter mixture, then chill 2 hours. Roll out to ¼ inch thick; cut into 2-inch rounds. Chill 30 minutes, then bake at 350˚, 8 to 10 minutes. Cool; sandwich with **jam or frosting.**

MAPLE-WALNUT TRUNKS

Beat 2 sticks **butter,** ¾ cup **dark brown sugar** and ¾ cup **maple sugar;** beat in 1 teaspoon **vanilla** and 2 **eggs.** Whisk 1¼ cups **all-purpose flour,** 1¼ cups **whole-wheat flour,** ¾ teaspoon **baking soda** and 1 teaspoon **salt;** stir into the butter mixture. Chill. Spoon 1 teaspoon chopped **walnuts** and ¼ teaspoon **maple syrup** into mini muffin cups; top with dough. Bake at 350˚, 20 minutes.

SPICED SHORTBREAD

Beat 2 sticks **butter**, ¼ cup **granulated sugar**, ½ cup **confectioners' sugar**, 1½ teaspoons **cinnamon** and ½ teaspoon **cardamom** until fluffy. Whisk 2 cups **flour** and 1 teaspoon **salt**, then stir into the butter mixture. Pat into a ¼-inch-thick square on parchment paper; cut into 1-inch squares and chill 30 minutes. Sprinkle with cinnamon and sugar. Bake at 375˚, 12 to 15 minutes.

PISTACHIO LINZER COOKIES

Beat 2 sticks **butter**, ½ cup **granulated sugar** and ¾ cup **confectioners' sugar**. Beat in 2 **egg yolks**, 1 teaspoon **vanilla** and 1 teaspoon **orange zest**. Whisk 2¼ cups **flour**, ¾ cup ground **pistachios**, ½ teaspoon **baking powder** and ¼ teaspoon **salt**; stir into the butter mixture; chill 30 minutes. Roll out and cut into rounds. Bake at 350˚, 10 to 15 minutes. Cool; sandwich with **jam**.

MOVIE-CONCESSION COOKIES

Beat 2 sticks **butter**, ¾ cup **dark brown sugar** and ¾ cup **granulated sugar** until fluffy; beat in 1 teaspoon **vanilla** and 2 **eggs**. Whisk 2½ cups **flour**, ¾ teaspoon **baking soda** and 1 teaspoon **salt**; stir into the butter mixture. Add 1 cup **chocolate-covered peanuts**, ½ cup **chocolate-covered raisins** and ½ cup **M&M's**; chill 30 minutes. Press into muffin cups. Bake at 350˚, 20 to 25 minutes.

CHOCOLATE-DIPPED SHORTBREAD

Beat 2 sticks **butter**, ¼ cup **granulated sugar** and ½ cup **confectioners' sugar** until fluffy. Whisk 2 cups **flour** and 1 teaspoon **salt**, then stir into the butter mixture. Press into a buttered 8-inch-square pan and score into pieces; chill 30 minutes. Bake at 300˚, 1 hour. Cool, then slice along the scored lines. Dip in melted **chocolate** and sprinkle with **coarse sea salt**.

LEMON VOLCANOES

Beat 2 sticks **butter** and 1 cup **sugar** until fluffy. Beat in 2 **egg yolks,** 1 teaspoon **vanilla** and 1 teaspoon **lemon zest.** Whisk 2¼ cups **flour** and ¼ teaspoon **salt;** stir into the butter mixture, then chill 30 minutes. Pulse ¼ cup sugar and 1 tablespoon lemon zest in a food processor. Roll the dough into two 1-inch-thick logs and roll in the lemon sugar. Freeze the logs 20 minutes, then slice 1 inch thick. Bake at 325˚, 20 to 25 minutes.

EASY WHOOPIE PIES

Beat 1¼ cups **sugar** and 1 stick **butter** until fluffy, then beat in 3 **eggs,** 6 ounces melted **semisweet chocolate** and 1 teaspoon **vanilla.** Whisk 1½ cups **flour,** ½ cup **unsweetened Dutch-process cocoa powder,** ¾ teaspoon **salt** and ¾ teaspoon **baking powder;** stir into the butter mixture. Chill 30 minutes. Roll into balls and bake at 375˚, 6 to 8 minutes. Cool slightly. Flip over half the cookies, top each with a **marshmallow** and return to the oven to soften, 2 minutes. Top with the remaining cookies.

LIME COOKIES
Beat 2 sticks **butter,** ½ cup
granulated sugar and ¾ cup
confectioners' sugar until fluffy.
Beat in 2 **egg yolks,** 1 teaspoon
vanilla and 1 teaspoon **lime zest.**
Whisk 2¼ cups **flour,** ½ teaspoon
baking powder and ¼ teaspoon
salt; stir into the butter mixture, then
chill 30 minutes. Roll tablespoonfuls
into balls and flatten; sprinkle with
coarse sugar and bake at 350°,
15 to 20 minutes. Whisk 1½ cups
confectioners' sugar, 2 tablespoons
green decorating sugar and
3 tablespoons **lime juice;** spread
over the cooled cookies.

BROWN-BETTY BUTTONS
Melt 2 sticks **butter** over medium
heat until browned, then cool. Beat
the browned butter and ¾ cup
granulated sugar until fluffy. Beat
in 1 **egg yolk,** 1 teaspoon **vanilla**
and 1 teaspoon **orange zest.** Whisk
2¼ cups **flour,** ½ teaspoon **baking
powder** and ¼ teaspoon **salt;** stir
into the butter mixture, then chill
30 minutes. Scoop into small balls;
bake at 325°, 10 to 12 minutes. Cool,
then sandwich with **raspberry jam**
and dust with **confectioners' sugar.**

No-Bake Desserts

NEAPOLITAN ICE CREAM SANDWICHES
For each sandwich, spread **neapolitan ice cream** between 2 thin slices of **pound cake.** Smooth the edges so the ice cream is flush with the cake. Place the sandwiches on a baking sheet and pour 2 tablespoons melted **dark chocolate** over each, letting it drip down the sides. Freeze until hard. Top with **whipped cream** and chopped **pistachios.**

COFFEE-DOUGHNUT ICE CREAM SANDWICHES
Split **mini chocolate-covered doughnuts** in half crosswise. Sandwich with **coffee ice cream,** arranging spoonfuls on the doughnut ring and keeping the hole empty; freeze.

ALMOND CROISSANT ICE CREAM SANDWICHES
Cut **almond croissants** in half, then split open. Lightly toast and let cool. Sandwich with **cherry-vanilla ice cream;** freeze.

SALTED CARAMEL ICE CREAM SANDWICHES
Spread **dulce de leche** on small **butter crackers.** Sandwich with **vanilla ice cream;** freeze.

CHOCO-BANANA ICE CREAM SANDWICHES
Arrange thin slices of **banana** on slices of **banana bread.** Sandwich with **chocolate ice cream;** freeze.

ICE CREAM PB&Js
Break **graham crackers** into squares. Spread half of the squares with **peanut butter** and the other half with **raspberry jam.** Sandwich with **black raspberry ice cream;** freeze.

ICE CREAM WAFFLEWICHES
Prepare toaster waffles or make homemade: Whisk 2 cups **flour,** 4 teaspoons **baking powder,** 2 tablespoons **sugar** and 1 teaspoon **salt.** Mix in 2 **eggs,** 1½ cups **milk,** 5 tablespoons melted **shortening** and 4 tablespoons melted **butter.** Cook in a waffle iron until crisp. Let the waffles cool. Sandwich with **ice cream.** Dust with **confectioners' sugar;** freeze.

AFFOGATO
Put a scoop of **vanilla ice cream** in a mug; top with **espresso.**

CONCORD FLOAT
Scoop some **vanilla ice cream** into a glass. Mix equal parts **concord grape juice** and **lemon-lime soda,** then slowly pour over the ice cream.

TIP

Use firm ice cream, not softened, to make sandwiches: Scrape thin strips of the ice cream, then smooth it out.

BOOZY MILKSHAKES
Blend 1 quart softened **vanilla ice cream,** ½ cup **malted milk powder** and ⅓ cup **scotch** in a blender until smooth (in batches, if necessary). Divide the mixture among 8 chilled glasses.

PB EGG CREAM
Puree 1 cup **peanut butter** with 4 cups **milk.** Pour some **chocolate syrup** into 4 glasses; top with the peanut-butter milk. Slowly add **seltzer** and stir.

BIRTHDAY CAKE SHAKES
Blend 1½ cups **vanilla ice cream,** 1 crumbled **vanilla cupcake** (unfrosted), 1 cup **milk** and ¼ teaspoon **almond extract.** Pour into 4 glasses and top with rainbow **sprinkles.**

PEPPERMINT SHAKES
Puree ½ pint each **vanilla and mint chip ice cream** with 1 cup **milk** in a blender. Pour into 4 glasses and garnish with **peppermint sticks.** Add a shot of **peppermint schnapps** to each glass, if desired.

PRALINE ICE CREAM SANDWICHES Sandwich a scoop of **praline or butter pecan ice cream** and a spoonful of **caramel sauce** between **chocolate wafers or chocolate graham crackers.** Run a knife around the edge to smooth the ice cream, then roll in chopped **pecans,** if desired. Freeze.

PUMPKIN PIE SHAKES
Blend 2 slices store-bought **pumpkin pie,** 1 cup **milk** and 1 cup **vanilla ice cream** until smooth. Pour into 4 glasses.

CHOCOLATE-BERRY SHAKES
Blend 1 pint **chocolate ice cream,** 2 cups **raspberries,** 2 tablespoons **sugar** and ¾ cup each **milk** and ice. Pour into 4 glasses.

BLACK AND WHITE SHAKES
Blend 1½ cups each **vanilla and chocolate ice cream** with 2 cups **milk** and 6 crumbled **chocolate sandwich cookies.** Pour into 4 glasses.

CHOCO-BANANA SHAKES
Blend 2 **bananas,** 1 pint **chocolate ice cream,** 1 cup **milk,** a pinch of **salt** and 1 cup ice. Pour into 4 glasses.

WHITE RUSSIAN SHAKES
Blend 1 pint **vanilla ice cream,** ¼ cup each **vodka** and **coffee liqueur** and 2 tablespoons chilled **espresso.** Pour into 4 glasses.

TRY THIS

Blend a spoonful of dry milk or malted milk powder into your shake to make it taste extra creamy.

CHOCOLATE-CHERRY SHAKES
Puree 1 pint **vanilla ice cream,** ½ cup **milk,** 1 cup **frozen cherries** and 16 **chocolate wafers.** Pour into 4 glasses.

GINGERSNAP SHAKES
Crush 8 **gingersnaps,** then put in a blender and add 1 cup **milk;** soak 5 minutes. Add 2 cups **vanilla ice cream,** 4 teaspoons **molasses** and 2 teaspoons **ground ginger;** blend. Pour into 4 glasses.

OATMEAL COOKIE SHAKES
Blend 1 pint **vanilla ice cream** and 2 cups each **milk** and crumbled **oatmeal cookies** with a pinch of **cinnamon.** Pour into 4 glasses.

MEZCAL-ORANGE FLOAT
Put 2 scoops **vanilla ice cream** in a glass; add 1 ounce **mezcal** and 6 ounces **orange soda.**

STOUT FLOAT
Put 1 scoop each **chocolate and vanilla ice cream** in a mug. Pour cold **stout beer** on top.

CARAMEL–ROOT BEER FLOAT Bring 1 cup **sugar** and 2 teaspoons **lemon juice** to a boil over medium-high heat, stirring. Continue to cook, swirling but not stirring, until amber. Remove from the heat and carefully stir in ¾ cup **cream** and 2 tablespoons **bourbon.** Return to the heat and whisk until smooth; swirl in 2 tablespoons **butter.** For each float, put 2 scoops **vanilla ice cream** in a glass and fill with **root beer;** drizzle with the caramel.

APRICOT SUNDAES

Combine 2 cups **dried apricots,** 2 cups water, 2 tablespoons **sugar** and 1 strip **lemon zest** in a baking dish. Cover; microwave 5 minutes. Let sit 5 minutes; let cool. Spoon over 4 bowls **frozen yogurt.**

PRETZEL SUNDAES

Mash 1 pint **vanilla ice cream** and ½ cup chopped **chocolate-covered pretzels.** Cover and freeze; scoop into 4 bowls. Top with chocolate-covered pretzels.

BERRY-GRAPE SUNDAES

Cook ¾ cup each **blackberries** and **seedless red grapes,** ⅓ cup **sugar** and 2 teaspoons water, 10 minutes. Remove the fruit; simmer the liquid until syrupy, 2 minutes. Stir the fruit back into the syrup and spoon over 4 bowls **vanilla ice cream.**

BERRY-WAFFLE SUNDAES

Simmer 1 cup **blueberries,** ½ cup **maple syrup,** ¼ teaspoon **vanilla** and a strip of **lemon zest.** Prepare 4 **toaster waffles;** top with **butter-pecan ice cream** and the blueberry sauce.

MIX IT UP

Design your own ice cream flavor: Mash chopped cookies, nuts, candy or fruit into softened ice cream and freeze.

RASPBERRY SHERBET

Puree 6 cups **raspberries,** ⅓ cup **grape or apple juice** and 1 cup **superfine sugar** until smooth. Strain; discard the raspberry seeds. Stir in 1½ cups **buttermilk,** ¼ cup **heavy cream** and a pinch of **salt;** cover and refrigerate until cold, about 1 hour. Transfer to an ice cream maker and freeze according to the manufacturer's instructions. Transfer to an airtight container and freeze until firm, at least 2 hours. Scoop into 4 to 6 bowls; sprinkle with **pepper.**

GRILLED BANANA SPLITS

Cut a small piece off the curved side of 4 unpeeled **bananas,** then make a deep slit down the center of each through the peel; place on separate sheets of foil. Open the slits and brush with melted **butter;** sprinkle with **sugar** and 1 ounce chopped **semisweet chocolate.** Fold up the foil around the bananas. Grill over high heat until the chocolate melts, 6 to 8 minutes. Open the peels and top with **ice cream, whipped cream** and a **cherry.**

PEANUT BUTTER MOUSSE Puree one 12-ounce package **silken tofu** and ⅓ cup each **creamy peanut butter** and **confectioners' sugar** in a blender until smooth. Divide among 4 glasses, cover with plastic wrap and refrigerate until set, at least 30 minutes. Top with **marshmallow cream** and sprinkle with chopped **peanuts and/or chocolate.**

MANGO RICE PUDDING

Divide prepared **rice pudding** among 4 bowls and top with chopped peeled **mango.** Drizzle with warm **dulce de leche** and sprinkle with toasted **shredded coconut.**

PEPITA RICE PUDDING

Combine ⅓ cup each **golden raisins** and **rum** in a bowl and microwave 3 minutes. Heat ½ stick **butter,** ½ cup **pepitas** (green pumpkin seeds) and a pinch of **salt** in a skillet until the seeds are golden and the butter is speckled brown. Stir in the raisin-rum mixture and 1 tablespoon **dark brown sugar.** Spoon over 4 bowls of prepared **rice pudding.**

CHERRY RICE PUDDING

Bring 2 cups cooked **rice,** 1⅔ cups **milk,** ½ teaspoon **vanilla** and a pinch of **salt** to a simmer in a saucepan over medium heat. Cook, stirring occasionally, until creamy, 6 to 8 minutes. Remove from the heat, stir in ¾ cup **white chocolate chips** and let sit a few minutes. Spoon the rice pudding over 4 bowls of **cherries.**

TRY THIS

Make chocolate curls: Soften a bar of chocolate in the microwave for 5 seconds, then scrape with a vegetable peeler.

ZABAGLIONE WITH BERRIES

Toss 1 quart sliced **strawberries** with 1 tablespoon **sugar** in a bowl; let macerate 10 minutes. Divide among 4 bowls. Put 5 **egg yolks,** 1 **egg white,** 3 tablespoons sugar, 1 tablespoon **marsala wine,** ½ teaspoon **vanilla** and a pinch of **salt** in a large heatproof bowl. Set the bowl over a saucepan of simmering water (do not let the bowl touch the water) and whisk vigorously over medium to medium-high heat until thick, 8 to 10 minutes. Pour over the berries.

RHUBARB COMPOTE

Combine 1 pound chopped **rhubarb,** ½ cup **sugar,** ¼ cup **honey,** 3 tablespoons chopped **butter** and ½ teaspoon **cinnamon** in a large microwave-safe bowl; cover with plastic wrap and pierce once or twice to allow steam to escape. Microwave until the rhubarb is tender, about 6 minutes. Carefully remove the plastic wrap and stir. Cool slightly, then spoon the rhubarb compote into 6 to 8 bowls. Top with **vanilla ice cream or frozen yogurt.**

« **MOCHA MOUSSE** Stir 1 tablespoon chilled **espresso or strong coffee** into 2 cups prepared **chocolate pudding.** Beat ¾ cup **cream** with 1 tablespoon **sugar** until soft peaks form. Fold into the mocha pudding. Top with shaved **chocolate.**

STRAWBERRY PARFAITS

Toss 1 quart quartered **strawberries** with 1 teaspoon **sugar** in a bowl. Sprinkle a layer of crushed **gingersnaps** in 4 parfait glasses. Top with the berries. Mix 1 cup **Greek yogurt** with 2 tablespoons **honey** and ½ teaspoon **cinnamon;** spoon over the berries.

ORANGE CREAM PARFAITS

Fold a scoop of **confectioners' sugar** and a splash of **vanilla** into 4 cups freshly **whipped cream.** Spoon some **orange marmalade** into 4 wine glasses; top with the whipped cream, cover and chill. Top with shaved **chocolate.**

PEACHES AND CREAM

Toss 3 sliced **peaches** with 1 tablespoon **brown sugar** and ½ teaspoon **vanilla;** set aside until juicy, about 30 minutes. Whip 1 cup **cream** until it thickens, then beat in 4 teaspoons brown sugar. Add 4 teaspoons **bourbon** and beat until soft peaks form. Layer the peaches and cream in 4 dessert glasses; top with toasted **pecans.**

TIP

Before whipping cream, chill the beaters and the bowl in the freezer for about 15 minutes.

BLUEBERRY FOOLS

Cook 1½ cups **blueberries** with ¼ cup **sugar** and a pinch of **salt** until soft, about 5 minutes. Stir in ½ teaspoon **lemon zest** and 1½ teaspoons **lemon juice.** Remove from the heat. Add ½ cup **blueberries;** cool. Beat 1⅓ cups **cream** until soft peaks form, then beat in ½ teaspoon **vanilla** and 1 tablespoon sugar. Fold in all but ⅓ cup of the blueberry sauce. Divide among 4 to 6 glasses; top with the remaining sauce.

HAZELNUT PLUMS

Brush 4 halved pitted **plums** with melted **butter,** sprinkle with **cinnamon** and grill until soft, 6 minutes. Divide among 4 bowls; top with **hazelnut gelato** and chopped **hazelnuts.**

HOT PLUMS AND BERRIES

Mix 4 tablespoons melted **butter,** 2 tablespoons sliced **crystallized ginger,** 3 tablespoons **sugar** and 4 halved pitted **plums.** Place on a sheet of foil with 1 cup **raspberries.** Fold up the packet and grill until tender, 15 minutes. Divide among 4 bowls.

BERRY-CHOCOLATE FOOLS Toss 1 quart quartered **strawberries** with 2 tablespoons **granulated sugar** in a bowl. Beat 1 cup **cream** with 2 tablespoons **confectioners' sugar** until soft peaks form. Melt 2 ounces chopped **semisweet chocolate** in the microwave and cool slightly; swirl into the whipped cream. Layer the cream and berries in 4 glasses.

»

GLAZED GRILLED PINEAPPLE

Mix 4 tablespoons melted **butter,**
¼ cup **light brown sugar,**
¼ teaspoon each **curry powder,
cinnamon** and **vanilla,** a pinch
of **salt** and a splash of **dark rum**
in a bowl. Slice a **pineapple** in
half lengthwise, then cut each half
into 3 long wedges; cut out the
core. Place 2 wedges on a sheet
of foil; brush with the spiced
butter and fold to seal. Repeat to
make 2 more packets. Grill until
the pineapple is soft and golden
on the bottom, 15 to 20 minutes.
Cut off the peel and divide
among bowls.

WATERMELON SALAD

Bring ¼ cup each **sugar** and
water to a simmer in a saucepan
over medium heat. Remove from
the heat, add 3 **mint sprigs**
and steep 10 minutes. Discard
the mint; add the zest and juice
of 1 **lemon** and a pinch of **salt.**
Combine 2 cups **blueberries**
and 3 cups cubed **watermelon**
in a large bowl. Add the mint
syrup and toss to combine. Let
stand 15 minutes. Divide among
4 bowls. Top with chopped mint.

TIP

Instead
of grilling
fruit, use a
blowtorch to
caramelize
it, then
serve it with
ice cream.

AMBROSIA SALAD

Whisk ½ cup **coconut milk**
with **orange zest** and **vanilla.**
Toss with 1 cup each sliced
grapes, tangerines and **apples;**
chill. Divide among 4 bowls; top
with **coconut** and **walnuts.**

CITRUS SALAD

Cut the peel and white pith
off 4 **red grapefruits** and
4 **navel oranges** with a paring
knife. Cut along both sides of
each membrane to release the
segments. Squeeze the juice from
the membranes into a small bowl.
Arrange the segments in 4 bowls
and top with the citrus juice.
Chill until ready to serve. Drizzle
with **Campari.**

YOGURT WITH DRIED FRUIT

Line a sieve with a large coffee
filter and set it over a bowl. Place
4 cups **plain whole-milk yogurt**
in the filter and chill 12 hours
(you'll get about 2 cups thick
yogurt). Divide the strained yogurt
among 4 bowls; drizzle with
honey and top with **mixed dried
fruit** and chopped **walnuts.**
Serve with **almond cookies.**

VANILLA POACHED PEARS Peel, halve and core 4 **pears.** Put in a shallow dish with
1 cup **white wine,** ⅔ cup **sugar,** 2 strips **grapefruit zest** and 1 split **vanilla bean.** Cover
with plastic wrap and microwave until soft, about 10 minutes. Serve the pears in the vanilla
syrup with **whipped cream,** if desired.

BEER-PRETZEL CARAMELS
Boil half of a 12-ounce bottle of **brown ale** in a saucepan until reduced to 2 teaspoons, about 10 minutes. In another pan, cook the remaining ale, 1¼ cups **brown sugar,** ¼ cup **corn syrup,** 1 cup **cream** and 2 tablespoons **butter** until a candy thermometer registers 235°, 10 to 12 minutes. Remove from the heat; stir in the beer syrup and 1½ cups crushed **pretzels.** Spread in a buttered 8-inch-square pan; chill 1 hour. Cut into pieces.

PLUM-BERRY BLINTZES
Toss 1 chopped **plum** with ¼ cup **sugar,** 1 teaspoon **cornstarch** and ¼ teaspoon each **cinnamon** and **salt;** microwave 3 minutes. Stir and set aside. Puree ¾ cup **cottage cheese** in a blender with 1 **egg,** 2 tablespoons sugar and ½ teaspoon **vanilla.** Spoon onto the center of 4 prepared 9-inch **crêpes;** fold in the sides and roll up. Cook seam-side down in a nonstick skillet with **butter** until golden on both sides. Stir ⅓ cup **raspberries** into the plum sauce. Serve the blintzes with the sauce.

TRY THIS

Send guests home with a treat: Buy takeout boxes at a paper or party store and pack up some cupcakes or cookies.

BANANA-SPLIT WAFFLES
Prepare 4 **toaster waffles;** let cool slightly. Top each with **vanilla ice cream,** chopped **peanuts,** sliced **bananas, whipped cream, chocolate sauce** and a **maraschino cherry.**

CHEESE AND CHOCOLATE
Spread **robiola** or other soft, creamy cheese on toasted slices of **baguette;** top with **Nutella** or other chocolate spread and sprinkle with **sea salt.**

PEANUT WHOOPIE PIES
Fold ¾ cup **marshmallow cream** into ¾ cup **crunchy peanut butter** until marbled. Sandwich some of the mixture between 2 **soft chocolate cookies;** repeat to make 3 more.

PINEAPPLE S'MORES
Cut **pound cake** into small squares; spread with **dulce de leche.** Thread a square of cake, a chunk of **pineapple,** a **marshmallow** and another square of cake onto each of 4 skewers; toast over a grill or campfire until browned.

MUFFIN CUPCAKES Beat 8 ounces softened **cream cheese** and 6 tablespoons softened **butter** with 1 cup **confectioners' sugar,** 1 teaspoon **lemon zest** and ½ teaspoon **vanilla** until fluffy. Spread the frosting on 8 prepared **muffins** (such as zucchini, banana or carrot). Top with sliced **crystallized ginger.**

CHOCOLATE APRICOTS

Microwave 2 ounces finely chopped **dark chocolate** on medium power until melted. Dip **dried apricots** halfway in the chocolate, place on a parchment-lined plate and press an **almond** on each. Freeze until set, about 2 minutes.

STUFFED CRÊPES

Mix ¾ cup **ricotta** with 2 tablespoons **sugar.** Spread 8 prepared 12-inch **crêpes** with the sweetened ricotta and fold into quarters. Top with sliced **strawberries** and drizzle with warm **chocolate sauce.**

YOGURTWICHES

Place a scoop of **frozen yogurt** between **graham crackers.** Roll the edges in **chocolate chips;** freeze.

BERRY CROISSANT PANINI

Spread the inside of 4 split **croissants** with **marshmallow cream.** Fill with **bittersweet chocolate chunks** and sliced **strawberries.** Cook in a panini press.

COCONUT FRUIT SALAD

Segment 1 **grapefruit** and 2 **oranges;** reserve the juices. Toss the segments with
1 cup **pineapple,** ¼ cup **mint,** 1 tablespoon **agave nectar** and 1 teaspoon grated
peeled **ginger.** In another bowl, beat 1 cup **cottage cheese** with the citrus juice.
Divide among 4 bowls; top with the fruit, toasted **coconut** and more mint.

Perfect

S'MORES

Preheat a grill to medium high. Top a honey graham-cracker square with a ½-to-1-ounce square of semisweet chocolate. Place on the edge of the grill, away from the flame, to melt the chocolate. Meanwhile, skewer a jumbo marshmallow and hold it over the heat, turning, until soft and toasted. Put the marshmallow on top of the chocolate, cover with another graham cracker and gently press together as you slide out the skewer.

S'more S'mores Try these over-the-top combinations.

Caramel Apple S'more
cinnamon grahams
toasted marshmallow
apple slices
chocolate-covered caramel

Mint–Chocolate Chip S'more
chocolate grahams
toasted marshmallow
mini chocolate chips
peppermint patty

Cinnamon Toast S'more
cinnamon grahams
toasted marshmallow
butterscotch chips
white chocolate

Elvis S'more
honey grahams
toasted marshmallow
banana slices
peanut butter

361

METRIC CHARTS

Conversions by Ingredient

A standard cup measure of a dry or solid ingredient will vary in weight depending on the type of ingredient. A standard cup of liquid is the same volume for any type of liquid. Use this chart to convert standard cup measures to grams (weight) or milliliters (volume).

STANDARD CUP	FINE POWDER (e.g., flour)	GRAIN (e.g., rice)	GRANULAR (e.g., sugar)	LIQUID SOLIDS (e.g., butter)	LIQUID (e.g., milk)
1	140 g	150 g	190 g	200 g	240 ml
¾	105 g	113 g	143 g	150 g	180 ml
⅔	93 g	100 g	125 g	133 g	160 ml
½	70 g	75 g	95 g	100 g	120 ml
⅓	47 g	50 g	63 g	67 g	80 ml
¼	35 g	38 g	48 g	50 g	60 ml
⅛	18 g	19 g	24 g	25 g	30 ml

Liquid Ingredients

TEASPOON	TABLESPOON	PINT	QUART	CUP	OUNCE	MILLILITER
¼ tsp.						1 ml
½ tsp.						2 ml
1 tsp.						5 ml
3 tsp.	1 tbsp.				½ fl oz	15 ml
	2 tbsp.			⅛ cup	1 fl oz	30 ml
	4 tbsp.			¼ cup	2 fl oz	60 ml
	5⅓ tbsp.			⅓ cup	3 fl oz	80 ml
	8 tbsp.			½ cup	4 fl oz	120 ml
	10⅔ tbsp.			⅔ cup	5 fl oz	160 ml
	12 tbsp.			¾ cup	6 fl oz	180 ml
	16 tbsp.			1 cup	8 fl oz	240 ml
		1 pt		2 cups	16 fl oz	480 ml
			1 qt	4 cups	32 fl oz	960 ml
					33 fl oz	1,000 ml

Cooking/Oven Temperatures

	FARENHEIT	CELSIUS	GAS MARK
Freeze Water	32° F.	0° C	
Room Temperature	68° F.	20° C	
Boil Water	212° F.	100° C	
Bake	325° F.	160° C	3
	350° F.	180° C	4
	375° F.	190° C	5
	400° F.	200° C	6
	425° F.	220° C	7
	450° F.	230° C	8
Broil			Grill

Dry Ingredients

OUNCES	POUNDS	GRAMS
1 oz	¹⁄₁₆ lb.	30 g
4 oz	¼ lb.	120 g
8 oz	½ lb.	240 g
12 oz	¾ lb.	360 g
16 oz	1 lb.	480 g

Length

INCHES	FEET	YARDS	CENTIMETERS	METERS
1 in.			2.5 cm	
6 in.	½ ft		15 cm	
12 in.	1 ft		30 cm	
36 in.	3 ft	1 yd	90 cm	
40 in.			100 cm	1 m

Index

Photography Credits

PHOTOGRAPHERS

Antonis Achilleos: pages 14-18, 25-29, 89, 136, 139, 143, 154, 215, 224, 228, 236, 237, 255-277, 282, 283, 342, 346, 349, 350, 353, 357, 358, 359

Sang An: pages 21, 30-40, 220, 223, 231-235, 252, 288, 291, 296, 298, 312, 319

Roland Bello: page 7

Levi Brown: pages 28, 298, 360-361

Stephanie Foley: page 66

Steve Giralt: pages vi, 12, 97, 120, 160

Karl Juengel/Studio D: pages 28, 54-61, 72, 73, 88, 178, 181, 185, 197, 299, 326-341, 358

Jonathan Kantor: pages 72, 74-75, 284-285, 298, 299, 318, 320-321

Kang Kim: pages 107, 121, 211, 216-217, 251

Yunhee Kim: pages 78-89, 90-94, 98-104, 108-119, 156, 176, 177, 311, 322-325, 362

Charles Masters: pages 29, 122, 124-125, 182, 185, 212, 303, 318

Andrew McCaul: pages 11, 13, 304, 307

Marko Metzinger/Studio D: page 12

Marcus Nilsson: pages 186-197, 209, 358

Kana Okada: pages 159, 167-172, 198-206, 210, 238-250, 278-283

Con Poulos: pages v, 62, 69, 70, 128, 131, 132, 135, 140, 142, 143, 227, 292, 308, 315, 316, 345, 354

Lara Robby/Studio D: pages 40, 41

Tina Rupp: pages viii, 2, 4, 8, 144-155, 163, 164, 174, 175, 176, 177, 295

Kate Sears: page 282

Jonny Valiant: pages 42-53, 65

Anna Williams: pages x, 22, 300

FOOD STYLISTS

Stephana Bottom: pages 11, 13, 28, 72, 73, 88, 89, 90-94, 97, 98-104, 107, 132, 159, 163, 164, 167-172, 174, 175, 176, 177, 178, 181, 185, 197, 251, 299, 322-342, 346, 350, 353, 357, 358

John Bjostad: page 12

Anne Disrude: pages v, x, 12, 30-40, 66, 69, 78-89, 108-119, 120, 156, 176, 177, 198-206, 210, 227, 238-250, 278-283, 308, 311, 362

Victoria Granof: pages 72, 74-75, 284-285, 318

Jamie Kimm: pages vi, 7, 14-18, 25-29, 42-53, 62, 65, 70, 122, 124-125, 128, 131, 135, 136, 139, 140, 142, 143, 154, 160, 182, 185, 186-197, 209, 212, 215, 224, 228, 236, 237, 255-277, 282, 283, 292, 303, 315, 316, 318, 345, 349, 354, 358, 359

Jee Levin: pages 21, 220, 223, 231-235, 252, 288, 291, 296, 298, 312, 319

Paul Lowe: pages 304, 307

Brett Kurzweil: pages 28, 121, 298, 299, 360-361

Vivian Lui: pages 29, 54-61, 211, 216-217

Cyd Raftus McDowell: pages viii, 2, 4, 8, 144-155, 295

Lori Powell: page 282

Maggie Ruggiero: pages 22, 300

PROP STYLISTS

Tiziana Agnello: pages 21, 220, 223, 231-235, 252, 288, 291, 296, 298, 312, 319

Angharad Bailey: pages 186-194

Lynsey Fryers: pages 66, 90-94, 98, 100, 103, 104, 108-119

Robyn Glaser: pages 7, 42-53, 209

Meghan Guthrie: pages 28, 251

Marcus Hay: pages 30-38, 70, 227, 303

Paul Lowe: pages 304, 307

Marina Malchin: pages v, 14-18, 25-29, 62, 65, 69, 78-89, 97, 128-156, 160, 211, 215, 216-217, 224, 228, 236, 237, 255-277, 282, 283, 292, 308, 315, 316, 318, 342-359, 362

Pam Morris: page 300

Philip Shubin: pages 318, 320-321

Leslie Siegel: pages viii, 2, 4, 8, 11, 159, 167-172

Pamela Duncan Silver: pages x, 22, 122, 163, 164, 174, 198-206, 212, 238-250, 278-283, 311

Loren Simons: pages 121, 322

Deborah Williams: page 295

Subscribe to Food Network Magazine and save 62% off the newsstand price!

Save 10% at FoodNetworkStore.com!

EACH ISSUE has more than 100 amazing recipes, a pull-out recipe booklet, cooking secrets from Food Network Kitchens, tips from your favorite Food Network stars and much more.

GET 1 YEAR for just $15. Order a subscription online at cookbook.foodnetworkmag.com for your special introductory rate.

FOODNETWORKSTORE.COM is the place to shop for products from your favorite Food Network stars. You'll find our chefs' own products, plus other favorite brands of cookware, bakeware, cutlery, cook's tools, DVDs and more. Take 10% off your entire order*! Use coupon code C99246 during checkout.